W0254457

FEMINIST HISTORY FOR EVERY DAY OF THE YEAR

By the same author

The Joubert Family Chronicles

The Burning Chambers
The City of Tears
The Ghost Ship

The Languedoc Trilogy

Labyrinth
Sepulchre
Citadel

Other Fiction & Short Stories

The Cave
The Winter Ghosts
The Mistletoe Bride & Other Haunting Tales
The Taxidermist's Daughter
The Black Mountain (Quick Reads)

Non-Fiction

Becoming a Mother
The House: Behind the Scenes at the Royal Opera House,
Covent Garden
Chichester Festival Theatre at Fifty
An Extra Pair of Hands
Warrior Queens & Quiet Revolutionaries: How Women
(Also) Built the World

Plays

Syrinx
Endpapers
Dodger
The Taxidermist's Daughter (adaptation)
The Queen of Jerusalem

MACMILLAN

KATE MOSSE

FEMINIST HISTORY FOR EVERY DAY OF THE YEAR

First published 2025 by Macmillan, an imprint of Pan Macmillan
The Smithson, 6 Briset Street, London EC1M 5NR
EU representative: Macmillan Publishers Ireland Ltd, 1st Floor,
The Liffey Trust Centre, 117–126 Sheriff Street Upper, Dublin 1 D01 YC43
Associated companies throughout the world

ISBN 978-1-5290-6622-7

1 3 5 7 9 8 6 4 2

A CIP catalogue record for this book is available from the British Library.

Printed and bound in the UK using 100% Renewable Electricity by CPI Group (UK) Ltd

Visit **www.panmacmillan.com** to read more about all our books and buy them.

*As always, for my beloved Greg, Martha,
Felix, Ollie, Finn & Lily*

*and for my wonderful niece Ellen Huxley
(my Lionesses partner-in-crime)*

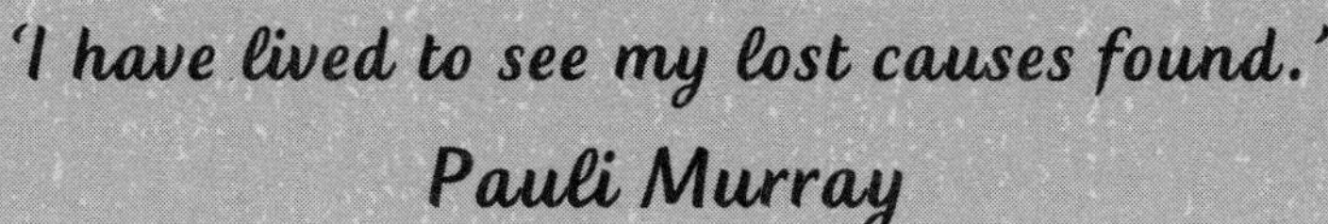

'I have lived to see my lost causes found.'
Pauli Murray

'I myself have never been able to find out precisely what feminism is: I only know that people call me a feminist whenever I express sentiments that differentiate me from a doormat . . .'
Rebecca West

'Women belong in all places where decisions are being made. It shouldn't be that women are the exception.'
Ruth Bader Ginsburg

Contents

Introduction

When you take a look in the mirror, what do you see? I don't mean the colour of your hair or eyes or skin, nor how tall you are or your clothes size. Beyond those things, what do you see? An astronaut or a doctor? A biologist or architect? An environmental activist or a headliner at Glastonbury? Perhaps a tech wizard or a Paralympian, a teacher or a police officer?

There should be no barriers to what a girl or woman can achieve, no obstacles put in her way. There should be no barriers for trans or non-binary people either, nor for boys or men. For anybody. And even though there are no individual entries for men or boys in this book – since it was inspired by the idea of putting missing women and girls back into history – there is a chapter celebrating amazing male feminist allies and how feminism is as much about an attitude, a state of mind, as gender. For things to be fairer, better, we've all got to be in this together.

But the simple truth is that, for most of history, society has tried to put limits on what women and girls are allowed to do. And it's not just the distant past. Did you know that women in Switzerland couldn't vote or stand for election until 1971? Or that until 1975 women in the UK couldn't open a bank account in their own name? Or that girls in Afghanistan in 2025 are not allowed to go to school after the age of eleven?

When people try to take away our freedoms, we have to speak up.

Pretoria Women's March of 1956

This book is a celebration of some of the trailblazers who refused to accept the limitations put on them, who campaigned and marched, battled and challenged the status quo to change the world for the better. There are stories of resilience and hope, loss and triumph, sexism and liberation, joy and brilliance. You'll meet hundreds of inspirational women, girls and non-binary people who deserve to be household names, some from the distant or recent past, others who are making history today.

They could be you. They *are* you.

This book will take you through time and space, to every corner of the world and to the stars above. From Ancient Egypt to modern-day Britain and everything in between. At its heart is the idea that everyone – wherever they come from, whatever they look like, tall or short, whatever the colour of their skin, whatever their gender or sexuality, whatever their nationality, whenever they lived – should be free to be who they want to be.

That's what feminism means – fairness.

Because I'm a writer – and passionately believe in the importance of women and girls telling their own stories – there are lots of writers in this book. If you were making your own list of trailblazers, you might choose some of the same women, or maybe come up with a completely different line-up. That doesn't matter. Since 190,000 BCE some 117 billion people have been born on Earth, and 8.2 billion are alive today. That's a lot of women jostling to be heard. *Feminist History for Every Day of the Year* is just the beginning of a conversation to put back into the history books all the women and girls whose achievements have gone unrecorded or overlooked. By saying their names loudly and proudly, we can tell the whole story of *all* the people who made history.

Together.

A couple of things to bear in mind before you start reading.

First, quite a lot of our feminist heroines are the first to do something. But these 'firsts' only count if they are the beginning of changing opportunities for other women and girls, too. After the first, there must be a second, a tenth, a hundredth, until it is no longer unusual to see a woman in a

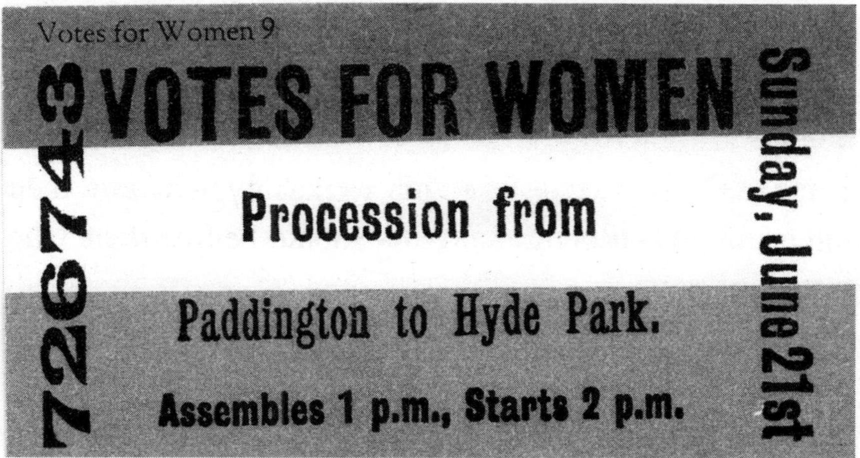

Ticket to WSPU procession on Sunday 21 June 1908

position once only occupied by a man.

Second, you can read this book any way you want. You might begin at the beginning on 1 January, or sneak a peek at your birthday, or find another date that is special to you. You could look up women you already know in the index or start with those who you've never heard of. You might be drawn to particular periods of history or parts of the world, and there's a useful glossary of abbreviations and organizations listed at the back. Again, that doesn't matter. This is your book. Being interested in history is like being a detective: following clues. You never know what you might find or what might spark your interest. Each of the entries is just a brief snapshot of the lives of an amazing woman or girl, intended to start you on your own journey of discovery. Look them up, research, find out more.

Third, although this book is a celebration of women who've done extraordinary things, we mustn't fall into the trap of only paying attention to those we like. Pirate commanders and military leaders, women of faith and women of science, climate campaigners or politicians – you don't have to agree with every single thing someone says or does to acknowledge their achievements and admire them. Some of the women in this book were complicit in dreadful things, but it's still important that we don't scrub them from history. Knowing everything is how we learn and make things fairer.

Finally, without knowing our feminist past we don't know how far we've come and who we are today. Rights are never given. They are fought for and can be taken away again. They need to be protected. History matters. Women listening to other women matters, women standing shoulder to shoulder matters.

Sisterhood works.

Now go back to the mirror. Look at yourself again and tell yourself again that you have the right to be anyone you want, to use your talent and your passion, to lead a life unlimited.

These are complicated and challenging times, but they are also beautiful and full of wonder. Spend time in the company of these extraordinary women and girls, be inspired by them, argue with them, laugh with them, remember them. Then, roll up your sleeves and take the world by storm.

Kate Mosse
June 2025

JANUARY

January

1 January ⇒ **Mary Shelley**

The Gothic masterpiece *Frankenstein; or, The Modern Prometheus* was published anonymously – as most books written by women were at this time – on New Year's Day 1818.

Shelley had the idea for the novel two years earlier when she was only eighteen. She'd already suffered a great deal of trauma in her life – her mother had died shortly after giving birth to her, she had fallen in love, eloped and later married the poet Percy Bysshe Shelley, her first child had died and they were frequently in debt and homeless.

In 1816, they were staying with their four-month-old baby and friends at Lake Geneva in Switzerland. It was a summer of black skies and endless rain. Trapped indoors, the friends challenged one another to come up with a ghost story to pass the dark evenings. One night, as thunder and lightning echoed off the lake, Shelley had a vision: 'I saw the hideous phantasm of a man stretched out, and then, on the working of some powerful engine, show signs of life.'

The monster was born, the invention of scientist Dr Frankenstein.

Often described as the first science fiction novel (though this was actually Margaret Cavendish's 1666 novel *The Blazing World*), *Frankenstein* was a runaway bestseller. Though critics condemned it as too sensationalist and gruesome – one even questioned the author's sanity – readers loved it.

It was not until a second edition, printed in Paris in 1821, that Mary Shelley's name appeared on the title page.

2 January ⇒ Florence Bridgwood

The child star Florence Bridgwood was born in Ontario on 2 January 1886. Her mother was a music hall performer who had emigrated from Ireland to Canada during the Great Famine. Bridgwood made her stage debut at the age of three – singing, dancing, reciting poems – and, by the time she was six, she was known as 'Baby Flo, the Child Wonder'.

When her mother's theatre troupe split up, Bridgwood went to America. During her long career, she appeared in almost 300 films and, at the height of her fame, she was known as the 'Biograph Girl', one of the leading ladies in silent movies produced by the film company – Biograph – she worked for. She is considered by many as the world's first movie star.

3 January ➳ Velu Nachiyar

Meet the first of our warrior queens: courageous women who took up arms to protect their land or those they loved.

Born in the southern Indian state of Tamil Nadu on 3 January 1730, Velu Nachiyar was trained in martial arts, horse riding and archery, and spoke several languages, including Urdu, French and English. At the age of sixteen, she was married to the king of Sivaganga. When he was killed in battle, Nachiyar escaped with their daughter, raised an army of 5,000 soldiers and fought against the British East India Company in 1780, who were trying to seize her lands. Victorious, she established her own women's army and ruled until her death on Christmas Day 1796.

4 January ➤➤ Ellie Simmonds

When British Paralympian Ellie Simmonds was appointed MBE in the New Year Honours List 2009, at the age of just fourteen, the newspapers made much of the fact that she was the youngest MBE ever.

In her swimming career, Simmonds broke every record going and won a cabinet's worth of gold, silver and bronze medals at the Paralympic Games, the World and the European championships. She's now an ambassador for the Scout Association, a Girlguiding leader and a patron of the Dwarf Sports Association UK (DSAuk).

5 January ➤➤ K. V. Switzer

The American long-distance runner Kathrine Switzer was born on 5 January 1947.

On a cold morning in 1967, K. V. was standing on the start line of the 71st Boston Marathon. She and her coach had studied the rules and nowhere did it say that women were not allowed to compete, so she signed the form with her initials – as she always did – and posted it in. This made her the first woman to run the race wearing an official bib – number 261.

It was not until the race had started that the director realized there was a woman running alongside the men. He tried to drag Switzer off the road and pull the bib from her back. The attempt was caught on camera and broadcast around the world. Switzer remembers a man at the roadside

Runner Kathrine Switzer attacked by race official Jock Semple while running in the 1967 Boston Marathon

yelling: 'Go home to your husband and make him dinner,' but also a woman shouting: 'Come on, honey, do it for all of us.'

As a result, the American Amateur Athletic Union (AAU) banned women from competing in races against men, but female (and some male) athletes and coaches campaigned until the ban was finally lifted. In 1972, Boston established a women's race. Switzer won the 1974 New York City Marathon in three hours, seven minutes and twenty-nine seconds – she fell short of her goal to run the marathon in under three hours, but got her personal best in the Boston Marathon the year after with 2:51:37, where she came second.

In 2017, fifty years after her first run – and wearing the same bib number, 261 – she ran Boston again, this time with more than 13,000 other women racing alongside her.

It just goes to show how one woman with determination can change the world.

6 January ➻ Roza Robota

On this day in 1945, the Polish-Jewish resistance fighter Roza Robota was executed at Auschwitz.

Robota grew up in Ciechanów in Poland. When the Nazis took control, she was forced into a ghetto, an area of the city where Jewish families were forced to live against their will in terrible conditions and kept apart from the rest of the population. During the Second World War, more than a thousand ghettos were established by the Nazis to segregate and imprison European Jewish people.

In 1942, Robota was deported from Ciechanów to a concentration camp. The rest of her family were murdered in the gas chambers, but she was assigned to one of the Sonderkommando units in Auschwitz II – Birkenau, where prisoners were forced to work for the Nazi regime. Put to work in the munitions factory, Robota and three other women smuggled gunpowder to the underground resistance in the camp, who were planning a revolt.

By 7 October 1944, everything was ready. They succeeded in blowing up one of the gas chambers and putting the other out of action. Hundreds of SS officers were injured and some killed. Robota managed to escape, but was quickly caught. Although she was tortured, she did not reveal the names of the men who had organized the revolt.

On Saturday, 6 January 1945, in the cold and the mist, the four women were hanged. It was the last public execution at Auschwitz. Two weeks later, the camp was evacuated. Three weeks after their deaths, the camp was liberated. Now 27 January each year is commemorated as Holocaust Memorial Day (HMD).

Roza Robota

7 January »→ Caster Semenya

Caster Semenya, one of the most successful female South African middle-distance runners of all time, was born on 7 January 1991.

She has won two Olympic gold medals, three World Championship golds and two from the Commonwealth Games, but despite this, Semenya has had to fight just as hard off the track as on it for her achievements to be accepted and honoured.

Semenya was born female and was raised as a girl, but because she has elevated testosterone levels she has some physical characteristics that differ from those associated with a specific gender. Some call this 'intersex', but in her autobiography Semenya rejects that term and simply describes herself as a 'different sort of woman'.

Just before competing in the 2009 World Championships, Semenya was forced to undergo tests to prove she was a woman. She won the 800 metres all the same – and World Athletics allowed her to keep her title – but after that, she was forced to take medication to reduce her naturally high testosterone levels, medication that made her ill. These matters are complicated, but victimizing a woman born differently is not the way to make things fairer. When the permitted testosterone levels were lowered again in 2018, Semenya challenged the rules in the European Court of Human Rights. Five years later, in July 2023, the Court ruled in her favour.

8 January ➻ Elizabeth Hooton

Elizabeth Hooton was a 17th-century preacher from Nottingham. She was the first female Quaker minister. The Society of Friends – known as the Quakers – was founded in England in 1652, based on principles of simplicity, peace, integrity, community, equality and stewardship. Good principles, you'd have thought, except that the ruling Protestants of the time – known as Puritans – did not allow any other forms of worship, so they persecuted the Quakers. Hooton was one of a group of maybe sixty travelling preachers in the north of England known as the 'Valiant Sixty' for their courage in speaking out against the official Church of England.

Imprisoned and tortured for her beliefs, Hooton travelled to the West Indies, Boston and Massachusetts, where Quaker communities were also under attack. Despite hardship, Hooton never stopped proclaiming what she believed in. She died in Jamaica on 8 January 1672.

9 January ➤➤ Simone de Beauvoir

The French philosopher, novelist, travel writer, political thinker and feminist activist Simone de Beauvoir was born in Paris on 9 January 1908. One of the towering figures of 20th-century literature, she is best known for her groundbreaking 1949 book *The Second Sex*, one of the building blocks of Western feminism.

With her famous phrase

de Beauvoir was the first to try to explain what we now call sex–gender distinction: that's to say the difference between biological sex and the concept of gender, which is socially constructed. She opposed marriage – though she was in a relationship with French writer Jean-Paul Sartre for most of her life – and believed in sexual freedom for women as well as men. In 1954, she was the third woman to be awarded the Prix Goncourt, the most important literary award in France.

Parisian to her bones, she died there in 1986.

10 January ➤ Ella Baker

On 10 January 1957, the Black civil rights leader Martin Luther King invited sixty Black ministers and community leaders to Ebenezer Church in Atlanta, Georgia, to debate how to make American society fairer for Black Americans. Out of that meeting came the Southern Christian Leadership Conference (SCLC), a group that became very important in the fight for racial equality.

Ella Baker was one of those advising him that day. A civil rights and human rights activist, she was the first staff member hired by the SCLC and is one of the unsung heroines of the civil rights movement.

Baker was a teacher and journalist who encouraged grassroots activism, believing that women and men should advocate for themselves and change their communities from within. She spoke out against sexism in the civil rights movement and worked for the NAACP (the National Association for the Advancement of Colored People), as well as helping to found the SNCC (Student Nonviolent Coordinating Committee).

Baker died in 1986 and was inducted into the American Women's Hall of Fame in 1994. In 2009, she was remembered by the issue of an American postage stamp with her picture on it.

11 January ➻ Nora Heysen

Born on 11 January 1911 in a small town in the Adelaide Hills in southern Australia, Nora Heysen is one of Australia's most celebrated painters. She was the first woman to win the prestigious Archibald Prize in 1938 for portraiture. Portraiture is one of the oldest forms of painting, going back at least five thousand years to Ancient Egypt – before the invention of photography, a portrait (sculpted, drawn or painted) was the only way of showing what someone looked like.

But despite Heysen's success and skill, an article published in *The Australian Women's Weekly* the following year focused on her domestic abilities rather than her artistic achievements. The headline read: 'Girl Painter Who Won Art Prize is Also Good Cook'.

In October 1943, Heysen was the first woman to be appointed as an official Australian war artist and given the rank of captain. Her job was to show the women's war effort in her paintings. Although there were limitations to where she was allowed to go, and what she was allowed to paint, she produced more than 170 works of art in three years.

12 January »→ Marie Colvin

The award-winning and fearless American war reporter Marie Colvin was born in New York on 12 January 1956.

Colvin began her career as a journalist with United Press International (UPI) a year after graduating from university in 1978 with a degree in anthropology. Six years later, she was put in charge of the Paris bureau for UPI, then moved to *The Sunday Times* as their foreign correspondent in 1985.

With her distinctive black eye patch (from an injury she got in 2001 covering the Sri Lankan Civil War), Colvin was one of the most prominent war correspondents of her generation. She was fearless and principled, reporting from Libya, Chechnya, Serbia, Sierra Leone, Zimbabwe and East Timor.

But in the end, her luck ran out. While covering the siege of Homs during the Syrian Civil War in February 2012, Colvin was assassinated in an attack organized by Syrian government forces. The people of Homs, at great risk to themselves, came out into the street to mourn her death.

13 January ➳ Maria Sibylla Merian

Meet the German bug lady!

The 17th-century scientist Maria Sibylla Merian changed how people thought about insects. A trailblazing entomologist, naturalist, scientific illustrator and botanical artist, Merian was one of the first scientists, male or female, to breed, study and illustrate insects in order to discover how their life cycles worked.

Born in Frankfurt in 1647, she had to sell her paintings in order to raise money to fund a scientific expedition to the West and East Indies. She was the first European woman to travel independently on such a scientific voyage.

From 1699, she spent two years travelling around the Dutch colony of Suriname, sketching local animals and plants, and recording indigenous names and local uses. The resulting book – *Metamorphosis of the Insects of Suriname* – is still considered a masterpiece today. She and her daughters produced 200 copies, some with colour illustrations.

Attempts were made to discredit her work but, as time passed, her findings have been confirmed. A number of butterflies have been named after her, as well as the orchid bee, a bird-eating spider, an Argentinian tegu lizard, a toad and a snail.

Merian died in Amsterdam on 13 January 1717.

14 January ➤➤ Queen Margrethe II of Denmark

On 14 January 1972, Margrethe Alexandrine Thórhildur Ingrid became Queen Margrethe II of Denmark. She was the first queen in her own right since 1412, as opposed to being the wife of the king, and the first Danish monarch since 1513 not named either Frederik or Christian. A popular ruler – who had worked as a costume designer and illustrator before becoming queen – exactly fifty-two years to the day after her coronation she abdicated in favour of her eldest son who was called . . . yes, you got it – Frederik!

15 January �»➤ Anne Locke

Anne Locke, who was born around 1533, was an English poet and translator, and the author of the first sonnet cycle to be written in English by a woman or a man. A sonnet cycle is a group of poems, often written to a particular theme, that are intended to be read as a series.

A devout Protestant, Locke was exiled during the reign of Mary I of England, who was Catholic. She returned to England when Elizabeth I was crowned queen in 1559 and became one of the most admired translators and religious commentators of her time. Her sonnet cycle *A Meditation of a Penitent Sinner* was published in book form and registered on 15 January 1560. Registering was like an early form of copyright, meaning no other publisher could reproduce a copy of it. Because Locke only signed her work with her initials A. L., she was only recently revealed as the author.

16 January ➻ Dian Fossey

In the 20th and 21st centuries, the conflict between environmental sustainability, land rights, deforestation, corporate greed and poaching has made conservation a very dangerous business.

Dian Fossey, who was born on 16 January 1932, was an American primatologist and conservationist. She spent nearly twenty years studying the mountain gorillas of Rwanda, identifying and cataloguing their behaviour. She also witnessed the violence of poaching first hand. She founded the Digit Fund to help fight the poachers, she destroyed traps and encouraged the local authorities to enforce anti-poaching laws.

Fossey was found murdered in her cabin in the Virginia Mountains in December 1985. Forty years later, still no one has been charged for her murder.

17 January ➻ **Michelle Obama**

On 17 January 1964, a little girl with big dreams was born.

Michelle Obama is an American lawyer and motivational speaker. In 2009, she became the first Black-American 'First Lady'. The term First Lady – often written as FLOTUS – is a title given to the wife of the President of the United States.

Alongside her successful legal career, Obama found time to campaign for her husband in his 2008 and 2012 presidential bids. Once she was in the White House, the official residence of the President of the United States in Washington, DC, she worked on initiatives to end poverty, to promote healthy eating and to support women's and girls' rights.

Obama's memoir *Becoming* (written with the help of a ghostwriter) sold more than 1.4 million copies in the US in its first week alone and topped the charts all over the world.

18 January ➺ Zivia Lubetkin

Lubetkin was a Jewish-Polish hero of the Warsaw Ghetto and one of the few who made it through the horrors of the Holocaust.

Born in 1914, Lubetkin was one of 400,000 Jews forced into the ghetto in Poland's capital city in 1939 when the Nazis invaded her country. She was a member of the Zionist Youth Movement, a co-founder of the Jewish Combat Organization (ŻOB), who fought against the Nazi occupation of her country – and the only woman on their high command.

When the Nazis began another deportation of Jewish people to concentration camps on 18 January 1943, Lubetkin and other members of the Resistance fought back. They used anything they could lay their hands on – guns, bricks, hand grenades, explosives. Three months later, she took part in the largest rebellion in the ghetto – the Warsaw Ghetto Uprising. Lubetkin was one of only thirty-four fighters to survive. Some 13,000 people were killed in the uprising.

After the Second World War was over, she emigrated to Palestine. In 1949, she helped found the Ghetto Fighters' House in northern Israel, the world's first museum commemorating the Holocaust and Jewish resistance.

Lubetkin died in 1978 in Israel.

19 January → **Dolly Parton**

The American country music superstar, businesswoman, philanthropist, singer-songwriter and actress Dolly Parton was born in a tiny town in East Tennessee on 19 January 1946.

In a glittering career lasting more than sixty years – and still going strong – Parton has sold more than 100 million records worldwide, making her one of the bestselling music artists of all time. She has composed more than 3,000 songs, including classic hits such as 'I Will Always Love You', 'Jolene' and '9 to 5'. She was inducted into the Country Music Hall of Fame in 1999, she performed at Glastonbury for the first time in 2014 and, in 2022, she was inducted into the Rock and Roll Hall of Fame.

Parton has founded several charitable and philanthropic organizations too, including a theme park called Dollywood and the Dollywood Foundation, and is an LGBTQIA+ icon for her support of same-sex marriage and inclusivity. On top of that, Parton has donated over 200 million books to children via her Imagination Library and funded Covid research.

A living legend.

20 January ⇥ **Toyo Shibata**

It is never too late to reinvent yourself and start again.

The Japanese poet Toyo Shibata was born in 1911 and only turned to writing at the age of ninety-two. She self-published her first poetry anthology, *Kujikenaide*, when she was ninety-eight. It sold more than 1.5 million copies, making her one of the most successful writers in modern-day Japan. After that, a publisher decided to bring out an illustrated edition of the poems and then published her second collection, *Hyakusai*, in June 2011, when Shibata was one hundred years old.

She died on 20 January 2013.

21 January ➻ Jacinda Ardern

On 21 January 2017, millions of women took part in the 2017 Women's March, a worldwide protest in opposition to Donald Trump and his attacks on the rights of women and girls. One of those was the Aotearoa New Zealand politician Jacinda Ardern.

Six weeks later, Ardern was unanimously elected Deputy Leader of the Labour Party, then Leader. After the September 2017 election, she formed a coalition government with the support of the NZ Green Party and became prime minister. Ardern was only thirty-seven years old, which made her the world's youngest female head of government. More records followed. When she gave birth to her daughter in June 2018, she became only the second elected head of government ever to give birth while in office (the first was Pakistan's Benazir Bhutto).

Ardern introduced lots of measures to improve the lives of women, children and families, including increasing paid parental leave to twenty-six weeks and providing free period products in schools.

Having led her party to a landslide victory in the 2020 general election, Ardern stood down as prime minister in January 2023, citing 'occupational burnout' as the main reason for her decision.

22 January ➔ Mariam Issoufou

Have you ever pictured your face on the cover of a magazine?

In January 2024, readers were gripped by an article in *African Magazine* celebrating the one hundred most influential Africans of the previous year. One of the stars featured was the award-winning architect from Niger, Mariam Issoufou.

Born in Saint-Étienne in eastern France in 1979, Issoufou grew up in Niger, then trained in the United States as a software engineer, before going back to university to become an architect. What makes her work special is that she uses local building materials and building methods that are suited to the climate – and the history – of the African countries where she works rather than importing European or American methods and ideas.

Issoufou set up her own architecture and research practice in Niger's capital Niamey in 2014, with offices in Zurich and New York. So far, she has built a prize-winning library and market in Dandaji and a breathtaking earth-walled housing complex in Niamey, which was shortlisted for the Aga Khan Award for Architecture. Issoufou is currently working on a museum in Senegal and a presidential centre in Liberia.

23 January ➻ Elizabeth Blackwell

Meet the founding mother of modern medicine, Elizabeth Blackwell. On 23 January 1849, she became the first American woman to receive her medical degree at a time when there was massive opposition to the idea of female doctors.

Blackwell was born in Bristol, UK in 1821, but her family emigrated and settled in Ohio. She knew she wanted to be a physician, so gave music lessons in order to raise the money to pay for her training. Since women were not accepted to medical school, one of her teachers suggested she should disguise herself as a man in order to bluff her way in. Blackwell refused and was turned down by ten different colleges.

But in the end, her persistence paid off. She was offered a place at Geneva Medical College in rural New York, but only because the male professors assumed the male students would reject a woman joining their ranks, so allowed them to vote on her admission. As a joke, they voted 'yes'.

Once there, although Blackwell faced obstacles and discrimination – she was forced to sit on her own at lectures and often excluded from the labs – she slowly earned the respect of professors and classmates and graduated top of her class.

On New Year's Day 1859, Blackwell was the first woman in the UK to have her name entered in the General Medical Council's medical register; in 1871 she co-founded the London School of Medicine for Women; and in 1895, she published her autobiography to inspire women and girls coming after her, writing: 'My whole life is devoted unreservedly to the service of my sex.'

Blackwell died in 1910 in Hastings, East Sussex.

24 January ➤➤ **Vanessa Nakate**

Ugandan campaigner Vanessa Nakate was one of several young climate activists who were invited for a weekend of workshops and panels at the annual World Economic Forum (WEF) in Davos, Switzerland, which ran from 21 to 24 January 2020.

Born in Kampala in 1996, Nakate got involved in climate activism at school. In 2019 she led a strike outside the Ugandan parliament to protest against climate inaction and rising temperatures. She is the founder of the climate action groups Youth for Future Africa and the Rise Up Movement, and also campaigns for climate initiatives across Africa, including protecting rainforests in Congo.

But there was an unpleasant twist to the Davos story. A photograph showing Nakate with four fellow climate activists – Luisa Neubauer from Germany, Greta Thunberg and Loukina Tille from Sweden, and Isabelle Axelsson from Switzerland – was cropped so that Nakate was missing. When she tweeted Associated Press news agency asking why she – the only Black delegate – had been cut out of the picture, it unleashed a storm of comments on social media about racism within the environmental movement. Nakate said it only made her more determined to ensure that the voices of Black activists and other activists of colour were heard.

25 January ➼ Cory Aquino

Known as the 'Mother of Democracy', María Corazón 'Cory' Aquino was born on 25 January 1933. After her husband was assassinated, she became a leading figure in the People Power Revolution in the Philippines. In 1986, this revolution brought to an end the dictatorship of President Marcos, who had put the country under martial law in 1972.

Aquino was the first female president of the Philippines. She faced plenty of challenges during her time in office, including the Luzon earthquake in 1990, the eruption of Mount Pinatubo the following year and tropical storm Thelma. Several coup attempts were made against her government, but she survived to retire in 1992.

26 January ➤➤ Libby Lane

Libby Lane was consecrated Bishop of Stockport at York Minster on 26 January 2015, making her the first female bishop in the Church of England.

Discussions about whether or not women should be allowed to be priests in the Church of England had become more determined in the second half of the 20th century. Women were already serving in other Christian denominations, such as the Methodists and Episcopalians, but the Anglican church was stuck in the past.

In order to break the deadlock, in 1979 the Movement for the Ordination of Women (MOW) was founded. Finally, after years of campaigning, in 1992 the General Synod – the governing body of the Church of England – voted to allow female priests. Two years later, the first thirty-two women were ordained as priests at Bristol Cathedral.

But the fight for women to be bishops was not yet over.

Libby Lane was born in Glossop, Derbyshire. After twenty years of service to the church, in December 2014 it was announced she was to be the next Bishop of Stockport. She was consecrated the following month.

At time of writing, there are eight female bishops in the Church of England out of forty-two dioceses. The first Black woman consecrated Bishop was Rose Hudson-Wilkin, who became Bishop of Dover in 2019.

27 January ➤➤ Beatrice Tinsley

Known as 'Queen of the Cosmos', the British-born New Zealander astronomer and cosmologist Beatrice Tinsley was born on this day in 1941.

Nicknamed 'Beetle' by her family and friends, Tinsley was determined to be an astronomer from the age of fourteen. She completed her Master of Science in 1962, then moved to the United States, where she completed her PhD in record time. In July 1978, she was appointed as the first female Professor of Astronomy at Yale University.

Tinsley was a pioneer of understanding how galaxies evolve, grow and die, and was brave enough to challenge the older, established male astronomers who disagreed with her. History proved her right. She changed the way distances were measured to distant galaxies and proved that the universe is still evolving.

She died from cancer in 1981 at the age of only forty. Shortly after her death, a main-belt asteroid was named after her and in 1986, the American Astronomical Society established the Beatrice M. Tinsley Prize. It is the only major award created by an American scientific society that commemorates a female scientist.

28 January ➤ Dorothée Pullinger

Move over, Lewis Hamilton, it's time to meet champion racing driver Dorothée Pullinger, who died in Saint-Peter-Port in Guernsey on 28 January 1986.

Pullinger was a brilliant engineer and car designer. She was denied membership of the Institution of Automobile Engineers on the grounds that in their rules a 'person' meant a 'man', but she was not put off. In 1919, she co-founded the Women's Engineering Society and helped set up an engineering college for women. In 1924, at the age of thirty, driving a Galloway she had helped design, she won the Scottish Six Day car trial. It is one of the most popular and respected road races, which tests not only speed but reliability, too.

During the Second World War, Pullinger set up the

Dorothée Pullinger pictured with a Galloway car

women's industrial war work programme and ran thirteen factories. She was the only woman on a post-war government committee formed to recruit women into factories.

After the war was over, the Institution of Automobile Engineers finally accepted her as their first female member. In 2012, twenty-six years after her death, she was the first woman to be inducted into the Scottish Engineering Hall of Fame.

29 January ➻ Germaine Greer

The feminist author, cultural critic and public thinker Germaine Greer was born in Melbourne on 29 January 1939.

Outspoken and forceful, Greer went to Cambridge University in the 1960s to read for a PhD on Shakespeare – it was this that formed the basis of her landmark feminist text *The Female Eunuch*. In it, Greer criticized marriage and patriarchy, and suggested women were bullied into being quiet and submissive simply to fulfil male stereotypes of what men thought women should be. Published in 1970, its British cover is one of the most iconic book jackets of all time.

1970 was an important year in feminism – many other landmark books were being published, such as Kate Millett's *Sexual Politics*; women and girls were marching for rights to equal pay and for rights over their own bodies; and the first British Women's Liberation Conference was held at Ruskin College in Oxford.

Some of Greer's views – especially on trans rights and pornography – do not always chime with a younger modern audience. But the core message of *The Female Eunuch* – that sexist stereotypes undermine women – remains as powerful today as when the book came out.

30 January ➳ Amrita Sher-Gil

The pioneering Indian avant-garde painter Amrita Sher-Gil was born in Budapest on 30 January 1913.

Her father was a Punjabi Sikh scholar and her mother a Hungarian-Jewish opera singer. Sher-Gil began formal art lessons when she was eight, once the family had moved to India, and later studied in France and Italy. She was always outspoken, had love affairs with women as well as men – this was especially controversial within conservative and traditional Indian society – and her paintings are glorious and richly coloured, usually of strong women captured in a moment of solitude or reflection. In other words, in both her life and her work Sher-Gil challenged the conventions of the time. It was her 1932 oil painting *Young Girls* – which won a gold medal at the Paris Salon the following year – that brought her to widespread public attention.

Amrita Sher-Gil, Self-portrait (1931)

She died in December 1941, a few days before the opening of her first solo show in Lahore. Her mother accused Sher-Gil's husband of murder, but it's possible she died as the result of a botched abortion.

Many of her works, including *Young Girls*, have since been designated national art treasures by the Indian government, which means that they are not allowed to leave the country. So, if you want to see the painting in person, you'll have to pack your suitcase and jump on a plane to India.

31 January ➤➤ Melitta Bentz

Some of our most important inventions come from day-to-day accidents rather than experiments in the science lab.

Melitta Bentz was born in Dresden, Germany, on 31 January 1873. One day, while helping her son with his schoolwork, she spilled her coffee and noticed how his blotting paper soaked up the dregs. She took another piece, rolled into a funnel, balanced it inside a tin and poured hot water over the coffee grounds. The same thing happened.

The coffee filter was born . . .

On 20 June 1908, Bentz patented her filter and, at Christmas of that same year, she set up a company to sell her invention to the public. More than one hundred years later, the Melitta company is still going strong. So, the next time you need a caffeine hit, think of the busy mum helping with homework whose ingenuity made your daily coffee possible.

What's in a Name?

'*I would venture to guess that Anon, who wrote so many poems without signing them, was often a woman.*'

Virginia Woolf

The writing of history, for much of human history, was carried out by men in monasteries or universities where women were not allowed. This meant that women's achievements were often erased or simply ignored. That's why it's so important that women and girls are free to write and to express their own truths. Otherwise, from Ancient China to 20th-century Russia to modern-day Afghanistan – anywhere where women and girls are prevented from sharing their stories – half the human population will be missing from the historical record.

Did you know that the first *named* writer was a woman? She was called Enheduanna and lived more than 4,000 years ago in southern Mesopotamia (modern-day Iraq). She was a high priestess at the temple of one of the most powerful goddesses, and Enheduanna's job was to write hymns of praise. What we don't understand is why she signed her name on her work. Before her, all poems dedicated to gods and goddesses were anonymous.

The preservation of ancient documents is a problem the further back in time we go. One of the most important poets in Ancient Greece was Sappho, who lived sometime between 630 and 570 BCE. Known as 'The Tenth Muse', she wrote an eye-watering 10,000 lines of poetry, though only about 650 of those have survived. We don't know much about her life, either. She is associated with the Greek Island of Lesbos (from which we get the word 'lesbian'), and we know she was exiled to Sicily around 600 BCE, but beyond that Sappho is a mystery.

Another mystery is the identity of the most famous of all Tamil poets, Avvaiyar. In fact, Avvaiyar is not a name but a title meaning 'Respectable Good Woman' and historians are pretty sure that Avvaiyar is not one woman, but at least three. A symbol of Tamil culture and wisdom, the first Avvaiyar lived during the 3rd century BCE and wrote nearly sixty poems. The second was writing during the 10th century CE. The third is the best known for writing a devotional hymn to the Hindu god Ganesh and a collection

Painting of Sappho by Julius Johann Kronberg, 1913

Illustration of Murasaki Shikibu

of inspirational sayings about how to live, one of which was included in NASA's Cosmic Questions exhibition: 'What you have learned is a mere handful; What you haven't learned is the size of the world.'

The invention of paper – in China around 200 BCE – revolutionized things and made it possible for more women to write and their words to endure. Before that people wrote on clay tiles or on papyrus, but these things were expensive so only the very wealthy could afford them. Murasaki Shikibu was born into an important family in present-day Kyoto, Japan, around 973 CE. She learned to write Chinese, the official language of the Japanese court and government at that time, by eavesdropping on her brother's lessons. Shikibu published *The Diary of Lady Murasaki* and then became a literary sensation with her epic *The Tale of Genji*, which tells the story of an emperor's son, his love affairs and the politics of court life. Coming in at more than 1,000 pages, and written in Japanese, it's considered to be the world's first novel.

But what can women and girls do if they live under regimes that forbid women to write? Some will struggle to be heard at all or face imprisonment. PEN International, an organization that champions freedom of expression, reports that at least 375 writers from 33 countries were imprisoned in 2024: China locked up more writers than any other country, followed by Iran, Saudi Arabia, Vietnam and Israel.

It's one reason why so many women – then as now – might decide to publish anonymously, or under a pen name. But there are plenty of other reasons, too. Some choose names that could be female, male or unisex to disguise their identities. Others take male names because they think that will attract more readers or get their work taken seriously. There are some writers who want to keep their private and public selves separate, or prefer different writing names for different kinds of writing.

In England in 1850, three years after *Jane Eyre*, *Wuthering Heights* and *Agnes Grey* had been published anonymously, Charlotte Brontë – the eldest of the three Brontë sisters – explained why she, Emily and Anne had originally decided to disguise themselves as Currer, Ellis and Acton Bell: 'We did not like to declare ourselves women, because – without at that time suspecting that our mode of writing and thinking was not what is called "feminine" – we had a vague impression that authoresses are liable to be looked on with prejudice.'

During the 19th century, the novel became one of the most popular forms of writing in England, Europe and North America. This book begins on 1 January with Mary Shelley's *Frankenstein*, published anonymously in 1818. Jane Austen did not use a pseudonym, but the first editions of her novels only had 'By a Lady' printed on the title page. Mary Ann Evans, author of *Middlemarch* and *The Mill on the Floss*, published as George Eliot. In Scotland, popular romance novelist and journalist Annie Shepherd Swan wrote as David Lyall. In France, the brilliant thinker and social disrupter Amantine Dupin wrote under the name George Sand, attacking the institution of marriage, and causing a scandal in the 1830s by walking around Paris in men's clothing and smoking cigars! And in Spain, campaigner Rosario de Acuña also published plays, essays and poetry under the male pen name Remigio Andrés Delafón.

Over a hundred years later, in America, Ann Petry published *The Street* in 1946 under the pseudonym Arnold Petri. The powerful story of a young Black single mother struggling against discrimination and harassment in New York during the Second World War, it was the first novel by an African American woman to sell more than a million copies.

One of the biggest-selling writers today is children's author and philanthropist J. K. Rowling, whose publisher suggested she used her initials to encourage more boys to read her books (in fact, the 'K' is a nod to her grandmother, rather than being her own initial). The Chinese-American superstar Rebecca Kuang also publishes as R. F. Kuang. And global bestselling Italian novelist Elena Ferrante has worked hard to keep her identity hidden. Others – me included – like to see our real names on the front cover of our books. There is no right or wrong decision. Every writer should have the right to decide what is best for them.

Whatever name appears on the book jacket, writing is about skill, talent, determination and hard work. No one should be prevented from doing that because of their gender. As Maya Angelou said: 'There is no greater agony than bearing an untold story inside you.'

Books foster empathy, imagination and understanding. They make sense of our deepest, most complicated emotions and encourage us to see the world through different eyes. Fiction and non-fiction, plays and poetry, journalism and comic books, every form of writing can be life-changing.

What about you? What might you write?

FEBRUARY

February

1 February ➻ Beulah Henry

When you look around your bedroom, do you ever wonder about the tiny seeds of inspiration that led to the things we take for granted? From alarm clocks to phones, sliding drawers to your duvet cover, everything was invented by someone.

Often called 'Lady Edison' – after Thomas Edison, the inventor of the light bulb – Beulah Henry was born in North Carolina in 1887. She is one of the most prolific American inventors, registering forty-nine patents, and she worked on more than 110 inventions, most of which were intended to make day-to-day life easier.

Her first invention, patented in 1912, was a vacuum-sealed ice-cream freezer. She also invented an umbrella with interchangeable covers (to match a person's outfit) and the 'Kiddie Clock' to help children learn to tell the time.

Henry died on 1 February 1973 and was inducted into the American National Inventors Hall of Fame in 2006.

2 February →→ **Ani Pachen**

In 1958, the Tibetan Buddhist nun Ani Pachen led a force of around 600 fighters against the Chinese invasion of her homeland of Tibet and the genocide of her people. The following year, Pachen took part in the Tibetan Uprising in the capital city of Lhasa.

On or around 2 February 1960, Pachen was captured by Chinese forces. For the next twenty years, she was held in some of the harshest prisons in China. For nine months of her imprisonment, she was kept in chains in solitary confinement, but she never lost her Buddhist faith.

Pachen was finally released in a thawing of relations between China and Tibet in 1981, physically broken but still strong in spirit. Knowing she might be arrested at any time, she fled on foot through the Himalayas to Nepal. She died in exile in India in 2000, a warrior nun to the last.

3 February »» Amal Clooney

British-Lebanese human rights lawyer Amal Clooney was born in Beirut, Lebanon, on 3 February 1978.

Clooney could live a very different kind of a life – she is married to one of Hollywood's most famous movie stars, after all – but instead she works incredibly hard on behalf of victims of human rights abuses, victims of mass atrocities, sexual violence and genocide. She led a task force investigating crimes committed by Russian forces in Ukraine, and represents political prisoners and jailed journalists around the world.

Clooney is also the co-founder of the Clooney Foundation for Justice, which provides free legal support to victims of human rights abuses in over forty countries.

4 February ⇒ **Constance Markievicz**

As the daughter of Lord and Lady Gore-Booth, Constance Markievicz could also have chosen to live a different life, one of comfort and privilege. Instead, she became a revolutionary and freedom fighter.

Born on 4 February 1868 in London, the Irish politician, suffragist and socialist took part in the Easter Rising in 1916, when Republicans tried to drive the British out of Ireland and establish an Irish Republic. When the uprising was defeated, she was sentenced to death. This was later changed to life imprisonment because she was a woman. In other words, being a woman saved her life!

Released by the British government in a prisoners' amnesty after the end of the First World War, in 1918, Markievicz stood as the Sinn Féin candidate for the Dublin St Patrick's parliamentary seat. She won, making her the first woman to be elected to the British parliament. She was being held in Holloway Prison at the time – for plotting against the government – and she never took up her seat. She refused to swear an oath of allegiance to the king, which all MPs have to do, and it was against her party's policy to go to Westminster. Instead, Markievicz and other Sinn Féin MPs formed the First Dáil in 1919, the government of the Revolutionary Irish Republic, making her one of the first female cabinet ministers in Europe.

When asked for campaigning advice by other women, she replied: 'Dress suitably in short skirts and strong boots, leave your jewels in the bank and buy a revolver.'

5 February » Mary Pickford

On 5 February 1919 the silent movie star and businesswoman Mary Pickford launched United Artists Corporation with her husband Douglas Fairbanks, actor Charlie Chaplin and director D. W. Griffith. It was the first major production company to be controlled by its artists rather than by the money men.

Pickford was born in Toronto, Canada, in 1892, and became one of the most powerful stars of the silent movie era. Known as 'America's Sweetheart', she was one of the first women to appear on posters under her own name. Like Dolly Parton decades later, Pickford showed the world that a brilliant and glamorous actress could also be an astute and clever businesswoman.

6 February ➳ Ellen Wilkinson

One of the great Labour politicians of the 20th century, Ellen Wilkinson died on this day in 1947 at the age of fifty-five.

Born in Manchester in 1891, Wilkinson – often described as 'Red Ellen' in the newspapers because of her socialist principles – was elected as the Labour MP for Middlesbrough East in 1924. She supported the 1926 General Strike, which was a historic walkout by British workers expressing their dissatisfaction with their working conditions and demanding fairness and change.

In 1935, Wilkinson was elected MP for Jarrow and became a national figure as one of the leaders of the 1936 Jarrow March to London, where the marchers were protesting about unemployment and widespread poverty in their town. Passionately committed to improving living and health conditions for working-class people, Wilkinson was part of Winston Churchill's wartime coalition government. When the Second World War was over, she became Minister of Education after Labour's landslide victory in the 1945 General Election.

But years of poor health and overwork took its toll. During the freezing winter of 1947, Wilkinson died from an overdose of medication for a chest infection. Though there was gossip that she had intended to kill herself, the coroner declared her death to be accidental, not deliberate.

7 February ➤ Ann Radcliffe

In the 1790s, readers all over Europe were going wild for Gothic fiction. It's a kind of writing, like *Frankenstein*, that is full of mystery, often set in castles or monasteries with hidden passages, fierce storms and landscapes, violence, supernatural elements and hints of horror.

In Britain, the queen of Gothic Fiction was Ann Radcliffe. Her romance *The Mysteries of Udolpho* was published in 1794. Telling the story of young heiress Emily St Aubert, who is forced to live with her aunt and evil stepfather in an isolated castle before being reunited with her true love, the novel was a classic of the Gothic genre and became a mega bestseller. Its success allowed her to travel, a journey she wrote about in her travelogue *A Journey Made in the Summer of 1794*. Three years later, Radcliffe published *The Italian*, the last of her five novels published in her lifetime. The money she earned made her the highest-paid professional writer of the 1790s.

She died on 7 February 1823.

8 February ➻ **Empress Matilda**

Empress Matilda, who was born on or around 8 February 1102, was the daughter of Henry I of England.

Women in medieval Europe had few rights, but nobly born women could wield significant power as daughters, sisters and wives. Like most girls in royal families, Matilda was married young, first to the Count of Anjou in France and then to Henry V, the Holy Roman Emperor (based in modern-day Germany). Marriages were not about love or companionship, but rather political alliances.

Matilda was one of the claimants to the English throne in the period of civil war between 1138 and 1153 known as the Anarchy. Henry I had named Matilda as his heir, but her cousin, Stephen, claimed the old king had changed his mind on his deathbed. The powerful English barons backed Stephen – who was both English and a man – over someone they saw as 'foreign' through her marriages, and a woman.

After nineteen years of fighting, setbacks, imprisonment and escapes, Stephen was victorious. But it was agreed that Matilda's son would inherit the throne when Stephen died, so her family legacy was preserved in the end.

9 February ➺ Zhang Ziyi

Zhang Ziyi is an internationally acclaimed Chinese actress, dancer and director. Born on 9 February 1979 in Beijing, she's best known for her performances in *Crouching Tiger, Hidden Dragon* and *Memoirs of a Geisha*. Zhang also won twelve different best actress awards for her role in *The Grandmaster*, making her the most awarded Chinese actress for a single film in history.

10 February ➳ Adella Hunt Logan

African American educator and suffragist Adella Hunt Logan was born in Georgia on 10 February 1863.

In 1895, the National American Woman Suffrage Association (NAWSA) convention was held in Atlanta, Georgia, looking for support from southern states for their campaign to secure voting rights for women. Yet the notorious Jim Crow laws meant that African American women and men were not allowed in. The Fifteenth Amendment – which later became known as the Jim Crow laws – had come into effect in 1870. The law allowed individual states to segregate white people from Black – in schools, places of work, churches, public transportation – and made Black people and people of colour second-class citizens in their own country.

All the same, Logan managed to get into the convention and was welcomed. Later she became a member of NAWSA. She campaigned all of her life for equality between men and women, and between races. But it was hard, dealing with abuse and constant setbacks and, after a period of mental ill health, she took her own life on 10 December 1915.

11 February ➸ Khawar Mumtaz

Khawar Mumtaz is a Pakistani women's rights activist, author and university professor. She was born in Karachi in June 1945 and, from her earliest days, was determined to challenge laws and customs that discriminated against women.

When the military dictator Zia-ul-Haq seized power in 1978, he introduced a series of repressive laws against women, effectively making women and girls second-class citizens. In response, Mumtaz and others founded the Women's Action Forum (WAF).

On 11 February 1983, Mumtaz was making her final preparations for a huge Women's March to be held in Lahore the following day. As the sun rose, Mumtaz, members of WAF and the Punjab Women Lawyers Association set off to march to the Lahore High Court. They were tear-gassed and baton-charged by police, many women were injured and more than fifty protesters were arrested. But their courage was reported by the world's media and made it clear that women would not accept being treated differently from men in their own country.

In memory of that day, 12 February has been honoured as National Women's Day in Pakistan since 2012.

12 February ▶▶ Caresse Crosby

When you are next getting ready for a party, or to go to college or for a run, give a thought to socialite and publisher Caresse Crosby.

Crosby was born in 1892 in New York City into a wealthy family. When preparing to go to a debutante ball one evening in 1910, she put on her restrictive corset under one of her favourite dresses as usual. The whalebone cover stuck out, and it was uncomfortable. She'd had enough. Crosby took off the corset and, instead, sewed a simple bra from two handkerchiefs and pink ribbon.

Seeing how freely she moved, friends – then strangers – asked her to do the same for them. Though there had been several similar designs before, Crosby's was the first patent to be granted on 12 February 1910. The bra, as we know it, was born.

13 February ➟ Sarojini Naidu

One of India's leading feminist campaigners, Sarojini Naidu was born on 13 February 1879 in Hyderabad.

A political activist and poet, she played a key role in achieving Indian independence. She was the first Governor of the United Provinces after independence from Britain in 1947 and the first woman to be president of the Indian National Congress.

Naidu was a celebrated poet, too. Known as the 'Nightingale of India', a nickname given to her by Mahatma Gandhi, she also wrote for children, and her collected speeches were published in 1918.

As one of India's most inspirational feminists, her birthday is celebrated as National Women's Day in India.

14 February ➤ The First Valentine's Letter, 1477

Valentine's Day is a much older tradition than you might think. Although the Feast Day of Saint Valentine was established in 496 CE, the saint only became associated with lovers in the 14th century, when the writer Geoffrey Chaucer linked the date with lovers in his poem *The Parlement of Foules* (*The Parliament of Fowls*). Written sometime around 1380, he imagined different kinds of birds gathering together on this date to choose a mate.

By the 15th century, the idea of 14 February being a special day for lovers had taken root. In February 1477, in a village called Topcroft in Norfolk, Margery Brews dictated a letter to her suitor John Paston III. She describes him as her 'right well-beloved valentine', expresses her love, and includes a few lines of poetry. Her words form the oldest known Valentine's letter in English.

Nearly seven hundred years later, the tradition of sending love letters on Valentine's Day is still going strong, although in 2025 it's just as likely to be a text or a voice note . . .

15 February » Susan B. Anthony

The leading American women's rights activist Susan B. Anthony was born on 15 February 1802 in Massachusetts.

Anthony was a Quaker, so believed in the 'equality of all people before God'. Even when she was a child she campaigned for equal treatment and education for boys and girls, and for an end to slavery. When she was working as a teacher in New York in 1848 and discovered that male teachers received a monthly salary of $10 while female teachers received only $2.50 for doing exactly the same job, she spoke up. This is what is known as the gender pay gap and it's still something that exists in 2025.

In 1851, Anthony met Elizabeth Cady Stanton. It was a friendship that would last the rest of their lives. Together, they founded the American Equal Rights Association to fight not only for equal rights for women, but also for African Americans. With the science journalist Matilda Joslyn Gage, they wrote what would become the six-volume *History of Women's Suffrage.*

Anthony didn't live long enough to see the results of her campaigning – she died in 1906, fourteen years before the Nineteenth Amendment, which gave American women the right to vote, was passed. It is known as the Susan B. Anthony Amendment in her honour.

16 February ➤➤ Muriel Matters

In her fight for women's rights, the Australian-born suffragette Muriel Matters came up with a unique way of promoting the cause. In 1909, she pulled off one of the most brilliant PR coups of the suffrage campaign.

Matters had come from Adelaide to London four years earlier and was in charge of the 'Votes for Women' caravan that toured south-east England. Her aim was to take the message of women's equality beyond the streets of London, Manchester, Edinburgh and Belfast to smaller towns and rural communities.

But Muriel didn't want to speak only to those already

interested in women's suffrage. She wanted everyone to sit up and take notice.

So, on 16 February 1909, she hired an eighty-foot airship, intending to shower Parliament Square with pamphlets as the king processed to the Palace of Westminster for the State Opening of Parliament. Decorated in the suffragette colours of purple and green, with 'Votes for Women' on one side and 'Women's Freedom League' on the other, the airship bravely took to the air. But the weather was terrible and she never made it out of Hendon Aerodrome.

All the same, photographs of Matters in a tiny wicker basket beneath the balloon, holding her hat firmly to her head and distributing her leaflets, made newspaper headlines all over the world. No one ever forgot Muriel Matters.

17 February ➡ **Wu Zetian**

Born in 624 CE, Wu Zhao – usually known as Wu Zetian – was the first and only female emperor of China.

She was a woman of extraordinary political ability, who ruled as the 'Holy and Divine Emperor' of the Second Zhou Dynasty for fifteen years. She was also ruthless – she poisoned the crown prince, exiled her rivals, established her eldest son on the throne when her husband died, then got rid of him six weeks later in favour of his younger brother.

Once in power, Wu Zetian established a formidable network of spies and expanded her empire by invading Korea in 688 CE. She was finally overthrown in 704, when she was eighty years old.

18 February ➻ Audre Lorde

One of the most brilliant voices and writers of the feminist movement in America, Audre Lorde was born in Harlem on 18 February 1934.

Describing herself 'Black, lesbian, mother, warrior, poet', Lorde was a champion of intersectionality and of using righteous anger to drive positive change. Her essay 'The Master's Tools Will Not Dismantle the Master's House', published in 1984, is a rallying cry analysing her experiences as a Black feminist. Forty years later, the essay is just as important and powerful as it was then.

19 February ➤ Doria Shafik

On 19 February 1951, the Egyptian poet, editor and feminist Doria Shafik stormed the Egyptian parliament with a delegation of 1,500 women to demand equal rights. A key campaigning feminist voice – once described in a newspaper as the 'only man in Egypt', that's to say (in rather sexist terms) the only person seen as capable of getting things done – Shafik was instrumental in women being granted the right to vote in 1956 and to be allowed to run for political office.

In 2016, Google celebrated her birthday – 14 December 1908 – with a Doodle.

Doria Shafik

20 February ➳ Mary Barbour

Mary Barbour was born in a village in the west central lowlands of Scotland on 20 February 1875.

A politician and political activist, she is the heroine of the Glasgow Rent Strike of 1915, where tenants fought against landlords raising rents too high. Barbour was one of the founders of the Women's Peace Crusade and the first female bailie in Glasgow – a bailie in Scotland is the equivalent of a magistrate or alderman in England. Dedicating herself to improving the lives of women and children, Barbour was one of five women elected as councillors to Glasgow Town Council in 1920.

Mary Barbour statue in Govan Cross, Glasgow, by Sculptor Andrew Brown

After she died in 1958, her reputation faded. But in 2013, the 'Remember Mary Barbour Association' was founded to campaign for a statue. Showing Barbour hatted and booted, with her right hand raised, the artwork was unveiled at Govan Cross in 2018.

Such is the power of campaigning . . .

21 February ➡ Nina Simone

One of the greatest American jazz singer-songwriters and pianists, Nina Simone, was born in North Carolina on 21 February 1933.

Simone wanted to be a concert pianist and, with the help of supporters in her hometown, she enrolled in the Juilliard School of Music in New York. She then applied for a scholarship to the Curtis Institute of Music in Philadelphia but, despite doing a fantastic audition, she was refused a place because of her colour. (In 2003, days before her death, the Institute awarded her an honorary degree as a form of apology.)

Her work was not initially political, but after the bombing of a church in Alabama in September 1963 – where four children were killed – Simone wrote the extraordinary 'Mississippi Goddam' in protest at the continued murder and oppression of African Americans. Although many radio stations in the South banned the song, it became an anthem for the civil rights movement.

Simone left America after the assassination of her friend, civil rights leader Martin Luther King, in April 1968. For the next thirty years, she continued to tour and perform in Africa, Europe and the Caribbean, and in 1991 published her autobiography, *I Put a Spell on You.*

She died in the south of France in 2003.

22 February →→ Sophie Scholl

Many of those who stood firm against the Nazis were young people whose courage and conviction were inspirational.

One of these was Sophie Scholl. After Nazi Germany invaded Poland on 1 September 1939, and her older brothers were sent to fight, Scholl began to speak out against the Nazi party. She enrolled as a student at the University of Munich to study biology and philosophy. There, with her brother Hans and three friends, they formed an organization called the White Rose. From June 1942, they published five pamphlets attacking Nazi policies and propaganda, distributing them to students and young people throughout the city.

One day, Scholl's luck ran out. A janitor, who was a supporter of the Nazi Party, saw her delivering the leaflets and reported her. Her brother was caught with the draft of a sixth pamphlet in his bag. Convicted of high treason, Scholl was executed by guillotine on 22 February 1943 at the age of only twenty-one.

Friends managed to smuggle the last pamphlet to the British and, five months later, the Royal Air Force dropped millions of copies over Germany with the heading: 'The Manifesto of the Students of Munich'.

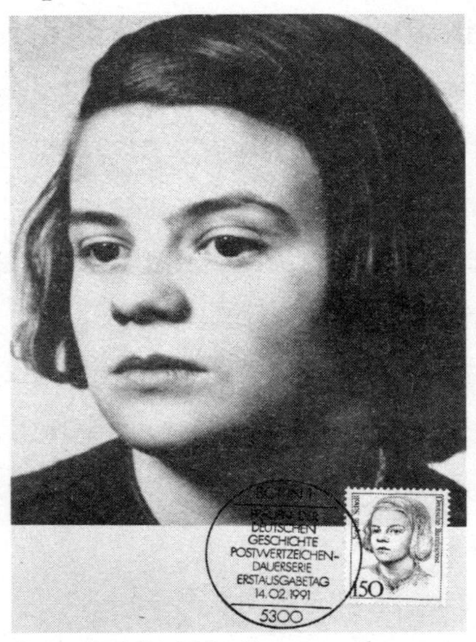

A stamp printed in Germany shows Sophie Scholl, circa 1991 – part of the 'Women in German History' series

23 February ➤➤ Edith Morley

England's first female professor, Edith Morley, was born in London in 1875. From her earliest days, the education pioneer, activist and scholar hated the restrictions put upon middle-class girls (such as always having to wear gloves and a veil) and she insisted on being sent away to school like her brothers for a good education, rather than being sent to a local school with large classes of mixed-age children and few opportunities to shine.

Morley achieved a First Class Honours degree as an external student at Oxford University, despite being barred from lectures and the libraries. She wasn't awarded her degree – at the time, women in the UK were not allowed to receive degrees – but she started her academic career nonetheless.

In 1903, Morley began work as an assistant lecturer in English at University College in Reading. Four years later, when the college wanted to be reclassified as a university, it gave professorships to all heads of departments . . . except for Morley, who was the only woman. She objected, fought her case and won. In 1908, she was finally appointed a professor, making her the first female professor in England.

Fifty years after her death, in February 2017, it was agreed that a building at the University of Reading should be renamed in her honour to coincide with the annual Edith Morley Lecture.

24 February ➤➤ **Boudica**

Of all the warrior queens, here is one of the most fearless and legendary. The one and only Boudica was queen of the Iceni, a tribe in the east of England in the 1st century CE.

At this time, much of what is now Great Britain was under Roman occupation. When Boudica's lands were illegally seized by the governor, she protested. She was not given a fair hearing and she and her young daughters were publicly raped. This outrage united the Iceni with a neighbouring tribe, and in around 60 CE Boudica led the combined forces against the Roman invaders.

Her army destroyed modern-day Colchester, then marched on St Albans and London, where she was finally defeated. History is not sure what happened next. Boudica may have

Boudica statue on Westminster Bridge in London

fallen in battle, though it's possible she died by suicide rather than let herself fall into her enemy's hands.

A statue – 'Boadicea and Her Daughters' – commemorating the brave and warlike Queen Boudica (in Victorian times she was known as Boadicea) was commissioned in the 1850s and finally installed on Westminster Bridge in 1902. Boudica is driving her chariot with two horses, a scythe blade on each wheel, a spear in her right hand and her left raised in triumph, with her two daughters crouched behind her.

On 24 February 1958, the statue was designated as a Grade II listed monument – in the UK, there are three grades of listed buildings and monuments intended to preserve and protect buildings of exceptional or special interest.

25 February ➺ Eliza Haywood

Eliza Haywood was an English writer, actress and publisher. In her long writing career, she produced more than seventy works – fiction, drama, translations, poetry and periodicals (a form of early magazine) – and is seen as one of the founders of the novel in English.

Much of her life is shrouded in confusion and she went to great lengths to keep her personal life private. The only thing we know for certain is that she died on 25 February 1756. Mysterious to the last, Haywood was buried in an unmarked grave in St Margaret's Church, Westminster.

26 February ➺ Sue Dauser

Sue Dauser was the first woman given the rank of captain in the US Navy, only months after President Franklin D. Roosevelt signed a law paving the way for women to enter the Navy as officers and enlisted personnel.

Born in California in 1888, Dauser attended the California Hospital School of Nursing, then became a navy nurse in 1917. After the First World War was over, she was put in charge of nursing at the US Naval Hospital in San Diego, California, and during the 1920s she served on board several ships and overseas postings in Guam and the Philippines.

At the outbreak of the Second World War, she was appointed superintendent of the Navy Nurse Corps. In December 1942, she was given the temporary rank of captain, the first woman to receive this rank in the history of the US Navy. On 26 February 1944, this was changed to a full commission.

27 February ⇢ **Nan Shepherd**

The Scottish writer, poet and hillwalker Anna 'Nan' Shepherd died on 27 February 1981.

Born near Aberdeen in 1893, Shepherd's love for the landscape around her shines through all of her writing. She published three novels, many poems and pieces of travel writing, but it is for her memoir *The Living Mountain* that she is lauded. Inspired by her experiences walking in the Cairngorms, it is a mixture of ecology, spirituality and personal reflection. A classic of nature writing, Shepherd wrote the book in the 1940s, though it wasn't published until 1977. *The Guardian* described it as 'the finest book ever written on nature and landscape in Britain'.

28 February ➤➤ Rosalind Franklin

Have you heard of the 'Matilda Effect'? It's a phrase coined by the American science historian Margaret W. Rossiter in 1993 to explain the high number of female scientists whose work was stolen or misattributed to the male scientists whom they worked alongside.

The British chemist Rosalind Franklin is one of the most notorious victims of the 'Matilda Effect'. Often known as the 'Dark Lady of DNA' or the 'wronged heroine of DNA', Franklin was born in London in July 1920. She was a chemist and X-ray crystallographer, and her work was central to the understanding of the molecular structures of DNA. A crystallographer studies the atomic and molecular structure of materials to understand how their properties are related.

First, a male colleague by the name of Wilkins shared Franklin's findings with fellow biologists without her permission. Then, on 28 February 1953, two other male colleagues named Watson and Crick announced they had discovered the structure of DNA without acknowledging Franklin's role. Crick and Wilkins were jointly awarded a Nobel Prize in Chemistry in 1962, four years after Franklin's death.

In the last decades, however, Franklin's crucial role has been acknowledged, as well as the sexism of the science community of the time who undervalued her work. There is an asteroid named after her and a university named for her in America, the first honouring a female scientist.

29 February ➳ Hattie McDaniel

On 29 February 1940, the comedienne, singer-songwriter and actress Hattie McDaniel became the first African American actress to win an Academy Award (an 'Oscar') for her portrayal of Mammy in the film *Gone with the Wind.*

McDaniel had to put up with racism and racial segregation throughout her career. She wasn't allowed to attend the premiere of *Gone with the Wind* in Atlanta, because it was being held in a whites-only cinema, and at the Oscars ceremony in Los Angeles, she was forced to sit at a segregated table at the side of the room. Times were different, but surely her co-stars should have refused to go unless every cast member was treated equally?

In 1952, McDaniel died of breast cancer. Even then, her final wish to be buried in Hollywood Cemetery was denied because the graveyard was reserved for whites only.

Stamp of Hattie McDaniel – part of the US's Black Heritage commemorative series

In recent years, her talent and contribution to American cinema have been acknowledged. She has two stars on the Hollywood Walk of Fame, was inducted into the Black Filmmakers Hall of Fame in 1975 and, in 2006, McDaniel became the first Black Oscar winner honoured with a US postage stamp.

She Roars, She Scores!

On 31 July 2022, a crowd of 87,192 people watched the Lionesses – the English women's national football team – win the European Championship Final against Germany by two goals to one, under the leadership of manager Sarina Wiegman. More than 17.5 million more watched on television and big screens all over the UK and the global audience was more than 50 million. The lads had been trying to 'bring football home' since 1966 – the last time a senior England team won a major tournament – and the anthem 'Three Lions' (aka 'Football's Coming Home'), first released for the men's Euros in 1996, had even been rewritten by David Baddiel, Frank Skinner and the Lightning Seeds to celebrate the Lionesses' journey to the final. But it wasn't until Chloe Kelly scored the clinching goal in extra time that it really sank in.

No more years of hurt. The girls had done it!

Something else important was happening, too. Broadcasters, journalists, commentators were realizing that – in contrast to what had always been said – everybody loved watching twenty-two skilled, professional female footballers play. In other words, it was no different from watching twenty-two skilled, professional male footballers play . . .

It reminded me of when I was growing up in the 1960s and 1970s and asked a teacher why there was no women's football on the television. She said it was because broadcasters said no one was interested. I didn't discover for years that this was fake news – in fact, it had been the very popularity of the women's game that had led to its downfall.

The villain of the piece was the English Football Association (FA) itself. During the First World War, when the men were away in the trenches fighting, there were plenty of women's football teams. Many of them were attached to the munitions factories, where women worked to produce the weapons and explosives their fathers, husbands, sons, brothers, uncles and friends would use in combat. There was no women's league, so the matches were all played for charity and to raise money for injured soldiers.

You might think that when the men came back in 1918, interest in the women's game would have fallen away. But although crowds went back to watching the male footballers, they carried on watching the women's game, too. On Boxing Day 1920, a crowd of more than 53,000 fans squeezed into Liverpool's Goodison Park (with another 14,000 or so

Dick, Kerr Ladies Team, 1923

waiting outside) to watch Dick, Kerr Ladies (DKL) take on St Helen's Ladies. The DKL team included the superstar striker Lily Parr, and their captain Alice Kell, who scored a hat-trick. The final score was 4–0 to DKL and the match raised a record amount of money for a charity devoted to Discharged and Demobilized Sailors and Soldiers. The Lord Mayor of Liverpool presented DKL with a medal in recognition.

Enter the FA, who didn't like the lack of control they had over the women's game and were jealous of the attention they thought it took away from the men's game. So they decided to kill women's football stone dead.

First, they claimed that football was 'quite unsuitable for females' and that it could damage a woman's fertility – arguments about what is or what is not ladylike have been used throughout history to stop women and girls doing things. They're not based on science or biology, but rather on prejudice.

Next, the FA forbade any top division football clubs – like Everton and Manchester United – from letting the ladies play on their pitches. If they did, the clubs would be fined. This meant that the women's matches were relegated to muddy and uneven fields where there was nowhere for the fans to watch in comfort.

The ban was passed on 5 December 1921 and stayed in place for fifty years.

But in 1971, a new generation of brilliant female footballers decided that they would change things for themselves. They formed leagues, persuaded broadcasters to screen the matches, and eventually the FA lifted the ban.

Since then, superstars such as Megan Rapinoe of the USA or Brazil's Marta Vieira da Silva have become familiar names and faces. The most capped English footballer of all time is Fara Williams and, in 2023, England goalkeeper Mary Earps won BBC Sports Personality of the Year.

There is still a massive gender pay gap in football and a way to go to achieve equality between women and men in sport. But the Lionesses and the other Home Nations teams are inspiring a new generation of players and fans, there are more girls playing football for fun and in school and leagues than ever before, and attendances at women's matches are up too.

And it's not just football. Women's hockey, women's rowing, athletics, rugby, cricket, boxing, tennis, golf, athletics – there is no sport that a talented woman or girl should be prevented from playing.

What about you? What sport makes you feel excited? How might

Fara Williams in 2014

you challenge yourself and stay healthy in the process?

Don't let anyone tell you what is ladylike or not. If you are doing it, and enjoy it, then it means that sport is right for you. 'Ladies' come in all shapes and sizes, after all . . .

MARCH

March

1 March ⇢ Catherine de' Medici

One of the most influential women in 16th-century Europe was Catherine de' Medici. She played a key role in the Wars of Religion in France between Huguenots – the French Protestants – and Catholics, which began on 1 March 1562.

Born into the wealthy Italian de' Medici family in Florence in 1519, Catherine became queen of France on her marriage to Henry II. She was also an adviser to three of her sons, after her husband died in a jousting accident. A regnant, or regent, is someone, usually a relative, who rules in place of a child who is not yet old enough to take the throne in his (or sometimes her) own right.

Her reputation is complicated and she is usually presented as devious, scheming and ruthless. But history tells us that strong women are often presented in negative ways – in other words, for speaking their minds and for displaying characteristics that, in men, are seen as admirable. She had to put up with a great deal in her life – Henry humiliated her publicly with his mistress for years, she outlived eight of her ten children, and she had to watch as her throne finally passed out of her family despite all of her best efforts.

Having said that, there is no doubt de' Medici did everything to promote her own best interests. She was accused of poisoning her rivals and was implicated in plots such as the St Bartholomew's Day Massacre in Paris in August 1572, when some 10,000 Huguenots were slaughtered in the course of one night.

Was she a saint? No. But was she worse than any other male leader of the time? Probably not. As always, we must go behind the clickbait headlines in search of the real woman behind the crown.

2 March ▸▸ **Rita Levi-Montalcini**

A pioneer in the treatment of cerebral palsy, Levi-Montalcini was born in Turin, Italy, in 1909 to Italian-Jewish parents. She had to fight to be allowed to train as a doctor at all – her sex and her faith were against her – but she was brilliant. Her training was cut short by the Italian dictator Benito Mussolini's introduction of anti-Semitic laws banning Jewish people from academic and professional careers. Refusing to be beaten, Levi-Montalcini set up a makeshift laboratory in her bedroom and kept working in secret.

During the Second World War, she managed to escape to America. In 1945, she was invited to Washington University in St Louis to repeat some of her groundbreaking bedroom experiments. She succeeded and was offered a research position there, a post she held for the next thirty years.

In March 1963, she became the first woman to win the Max Weinstein Award for her life-changing and groundbreaking research. In 1986, she was jointly awarded a Nobel Prize in Physiology. And in 2009, Levi-Montalcini became the first Nobel laureate to live to the age of one hundred.

Photographs of her show a tiny and elegant woman, with a cloud of white hair, a mischievous smile and, sometimes with a glass of champagne in her hand, still taking the world by storm in her second century.

Rita Levi-Montalcini

3 March »→ Empress Regnant Genshō

On 3 March 724 CE, the Empress Regnant Genshō of Japan abdicated the throne after nine years as ruler in favour of her nephew.

Born in 680 CE, she was the fifth of eight women to take on the role of Empress Regnant. The first was Suiko, who ruled from 593–628 CE. Genshō is also the only empress in the history of Japan who inherited her title from another empress regnant rather than from a man.

Genshō lived for another twenty-five years after stepping down, choosing not to marry or to have children. Her grave is in Nara, an early capital city of Japan, and she also is venerated at a Shinto shrine in the same city.

4 March ➼ Ding Ling

The brilliant Chinese writer and feminist political prisoner Ding Ling – whose real name was Jiang Bingzhi – spent much of her life being victimized by the communist authorities for her work.

In 1942, Ding wrote an article called 'Thoughts on March 8' for International Women's Day. Printed in a Communist Party newspaper, it was about the position of women in Chinese society and criticized the double standards of how female and male party members were treated. The reaction was immediate. Accused of being too 'Rightist', that's to say not communist enough, Ding was forced to apologize and undergo a public self-confession – rather like the kind of thing we might see on Twitter/X these days.

In 1948, Ding wrote a novel about peasant life that the authorities approved of. In 1951, *The Sun Shines over Sanggan River* won the Stalin Prize for Literature, but it made no difference. Accused of being pro-Western, Ding was denounced and purged from the party six years later – in political terms, purging is removing or even executing people considered undesirable by those in power – and her work was banned. Imprisoned and sentenced to manual hard labour, she was not 'rehabilitated' – that's to say, allowed back from exile to take her place in Chinese society – for nearly twenty years.

Despite all this, Ding never lost her faith in the power of literature to bring people together. She died on 4 March 1986.

5 March ➡ Anna Akhmatova

Another woman who suffered horribly at the hands of her communist government was the Soviet poet Anna Akhmatova, who died on 5 March 1966.

Akhmatova is one of the most significant Russian poets of the twentieth century, and her masterpiece, *Requiem*, is a beautiful tribute to the suffering of the Russian people during 'The Great Terror'. Also known as 'The Great Purge', this was a two-year period in the 1930s when the Soviet leader, Joseph Stalin, and his secret police carried out a campaign of murder, exile to prison labour camps – known as gulags – assassination, starvation and violence against their enemies and political rivals. As many as 1.2 million Soviet citizens were killed.

Requiem was created over decades. Akhmatova wrote and rewrote on scraps of paper, holding the words in her head until she could record them without fear of them being used against her, and carrying the precious manuscript with her wherever she went. Much of her other work was destroyed by the Soviet authorities.

Requiem did not appear in book form in Russian until 1963 and the complete poem was not published in the USSR (the Soviet Union) until 1987, more than twenty years after her death.

6 March ➵ **Pauline Boty**

Imagine how tough it would feel to be the only girl in a group of boys, wanting to be taken seriously as an artist but instead always being judged on your looks.

That's what it was like for the British artist Pauline Boty, who was born on 6 March 1938. Because she was glamorous and blonde, she was often described as the 'Wimbledon Bardot' at art school in the 1950s – after the film star Brigitte Bardot – as a way to undermine her talent.

But Boty was one of the founders of the British pop art movement in the 1960s and her first solo show in 1963 established her as an important British artist. Her work was joyous, brightly coloured and liberating, challenging the everyday sexism of the world around her, and it made her a feminist hero.

Like Amrita Sher-Gil, Boty burned bright and died young at the age of only twenty-eight. Her paintings were stored in a barn and her role in the development of British pop art was forgotten.

So, seek out her paintings, visit the National Portrait Gallery in London and see her work hanging on the wall. Help put Boty's work into the history books where it belongs.

7 March ➡ Yasmina Benslimane

In March 2017, the Moroccan activist Yasmina Benslimane founded Politics4Her, an intersectional feminist youth-led digital platform and global movement advocating for the inclusive participation of young women and girls in politics, civil society and decision-making processes.

Born in Rabat in 1994, Benslimane is a human rights defender, climate justice activist and campaigner against gender-based violence. A dynamic mentor for young feminists and committed to encouraging women and girls from global majority countries to get involved in politics, she's appeared in the BBC's 100 Most Inspiring and Influential Women, in the *Forbes* '30 Under 30' list in August 2023, the *New African Magazine's* Top 100 Under 40 Most Influential People of African Descent, and won many awards . . . and she has only just turned thirty!

8 March →→ International Women's Day

How could we have anything else for 8 March?

Now, IWD is big business – some would say it's become too commercialized – and celebrated all over the world. But it wasn't always like this. It developed out of the labour movement, and global suffrage and civil rights movements in the early 20th century. It wasn't until 1975 that the United Nations (UN) adopted 8 March as International Women's Day.

It started in New York in 1908, when about 15,000 women marched through the streets demanding shorter working hours, better pay and the right to vote. It was the German socialist activist and labour leader Clara Zetkin who first suggested an annual IWD and proposed the idea to an International Conference of Working Women in 1910. The one hundred women there, representing some seventeen countries, voted unanimously in favour. The following year, on 19 March 1911, the first IWD was held in Austria, Denmark, Germany and Switzerland. More than one million people took part in events, marches and protests.

In the years that followed, IWD was celebrated in additional countries and on varying dates. On 8 March 1917, Russian textile workers in Petrograd (now St Petersburg) staged a strike to protest against food shortages and poor living conditions. As we've seen, other countries such as India and Pakistan celebrate on other days.

But whenever, and however, you mark IWD, remember that you are following in the footsteps of millions of women wanting to create a fairer and equal world for women and girls.

9 March ⇉ Mary Elmes

When Mary Elmes was a child, she witnessed the sinking of the British passenger ship the *Lusitania* by German forces off the coast of Cork in 1915. She never forgot what she saw – people drowning, the ship blown to pieces – and it made her determined to help people in need.

Elmes became a humanitarian aid worker, going wherever she could be useful. She drove an ambulance in the Spanish Civil War in 1938. When General Franco's fascist forces advanced, she fled north over the Pyrenees into south-west France with the opposing Republican soldiers and set up makeshift refugee camps.

During the Second World War, after France surrendered to the Nazis in 1940, those camps were repurposed for Jewish people being deported to Nazi concentration camps in Poland and Czechoslovakia. Elmes began her campaign of 'spiriting away' children who would otherwise be lost. At great danger to herself, she smuggled them out hidden beneath potato sacks on the back seats of cars, in farm trucks, even inside wicker farm baskets. In all, she saved more than 650 Jewish children from almost certain death.

Elmes is the only Irish woman to be named as Righteous Among the Nations, a title given by Yad Vashem, Israel's Holocaust remembrance organization, to non-Jews who risked their lives during the Second World War to help Jewish people.

10 March ▸▸ Harriet Tubman

When you hear the phrase the 'underground railroad', what do you imagine? An old-fashioned stream train like the Hogwarts Express? Ancient tunnels beneath London with ghostly tube trains? Or perhaps you know the story of the incredible Harriet Tubman, who died on 10 March 1913.

Born into slavery in the early 1820s in Maryland, Tubman's childhood was hard and filled with beatings, overwork and a violent assault that had consequences for all of her life. In 1849, Tubman decided to escape and head for the northern states of the USA, where slavery was illegal. She went via the Underground Railroad, an activist movement made up of secret routes along rivers, canals, ferries, roads and hiking trails. All along the route, there were safe houses and people who offered shelter and help to enslaved people trying to get to freedom.

Once she was free, Tubman became a guide on the Underground Railroad and helped as many as seventy enslaved people to escape, including members of her own family. None of the 'passengers' she helped were ever caught. She was so successful that the authorities offered a reward of $40,000 – a huge fortune then and equivalent to about $1.6 million today – for anyone who could capture her. In 1861, when the American Civil War started between the Confederate States of the South (pro-slavery) and the Union States of the North (anti-slavery), Tubman put her huge knowledge at the service of the Union.

When she died in March 1913, she was buried with full military honours. A hundred years after her death, President Obama announced the creation of the Harriet Tubman Underground Railroad National Monument in Maryland.

11 March ⇒ Elizabeth Mallet

Meet the first 'First Lady of Fleet Street'.

Elizabeth Mallet was an entrepreneur, journalist, bookseller and printer who lived just off Fleet Street in London. During the 1670s and 1680s, she and her husband printed and distributed speeches made by condemned prisoners at Tyburn before their execution – Tyburn was where most criminals and convicted traitors at that time, as well as religious martyrs, were hanged.

When her husband died, Mallet took charge. Disguising her female identity and working from home, *The Daily Courant* hit the streets for the first time on 11 March 1702. It was a single sheet and carried a digest of foreign, rather than domestic, news. She wrote under a gender-neutral name – E. Mallet – and promised to provide only the facts rather than editorial comment. Soon, other proprietors realized that there was an appetite for daily news and a whole new industry was born, thanks to the first 'First Lady of Fleet Street'.

12 March ➤➤ Angela Berners-Wilson

We've already met Libby Lane, the first woman to be consecrated Bishop in the Church of England.

Nearly twenty years before that, the first woman to become an Anglican priest was Angela Berners-Wilson. She was ordained in Bristol Cathedral on 12 March 1994, one of thirty-two female deacons ordained that day. A plaque was put up in Bristol Cathedral to commemorate the historic occasion.

Twenty-eight years later, a new plaque was put up in its place. Why? Well, because the original plaque only named the men who had carried out the ceremony, not any of the women who were ordained . . .

13 March → Alicia Garza, Patrisse Cullors and Opal Tometi

On 13 March 2020, an African American medical worker called Breonna Taylor was shot by officers from Louisville Metro Police Department (LMPD), who had forced themselves into her home. Her death, and the cover-up that followed it, brought widespread public attention to the #BlackLivesMatter campaign that had been growing stronger for several years.

The hashtag #BLM was created in 2013 by three pioneering activists – Alicia Garza, Patrisse Cullors and Opal Tometi – in response to the acquittal of Trayvon Martin's murderer. Martin, an unarmed seventeen-year-old African American boy, had been shot in Florida in February 2012.

Two months after the murder of Breonna Taylor, the killing of George Floyd in Minneapolis took the #BLM campaign beyond America to the rest of the world. Floyd's arrest – including footage of a white officer kneeling on his neck for eight minutes and forty-six seconds – was viewed by millions on social media and led to protests all over the USA and across the world in support of the Black Lives Matter movement. Hundreds of millions of people posted black squares on their social media platforms and marches were organized in cities and towns across the world.

14 March ⇒ **Simone Biles**

In July 2024, millions of fans tuned in to watch the four-foot-eight dynamo Simone Biles win her eighth Olympic gold medal at the Paris games. Her incredible technique, her bravery and her silver goat pendant – to show that she's the 'Greatest Of All Time' – have made the African American gymnast a superstar in the world of sport.

Biles was born on 14 March 1997. She is the most decorated gymnast in history, with a total of forty-one Olympic and World Championship medals. She is also a role model for young women everywhere. When she had to withdraw from the 2020 Olympics with an attack of the 'twisties', a condition that made it impossible for her to carry out some of the most complex gymnastics moves, Biles was attacked by the media. She robustly defended her decision and won even more fans for prioritizing her own mental health.

Biles has also talked openly about her ADHD diagnosis and mental health challenges, and being a survivor of sexual abuse. With a celebrity co-writer, she published a memoir, *Courage to Soar: A Body in Motion, A Life in Balance*, which hit number one on the *New York Times* YA bestseller list in January 2017. In July 2022, she became the youngest ever recipient of the Presidential Medal of Freedom, which is America's highest honour presented to those who have made outstanding contributions to American society, world peace and prosperity.

Inspirational.

15 March ➺ The First Women's Boat Race, 1927

Opportunities for women in sport are getting better all the time, but this hasn't happened by chance. It's been down to determined women (and male allies) who have protested, fought and campaigned to be allowed to fulfil their potential. The world of rowing is no exception.

On 15 March 1927, the very first women's boat race between the University of Oxford and the University of Cambridge took place on the River Isis in Oxford. It was far from straightforward. *The Times* reported that 'large and hostile crowds gathered on the towpath', and for some reason the two crews were forbidden from racing next to

each other – one reason given was that the women might not be able to cope if they hit one another with their oars, though I suspect it might also have been because it was seen as a novelty event rather than a sporting one. The winners were also judged for style – the elegance of their rowing strokes, decency and competence – as well as for speed. Oxford were declared the winners.

The first side-by-side races began in 1936. The Women's Boat Race became an annual event in the 1960s. Now, nearly one hundred years after that first competition, the women's head-to-head takes place on the same day and in the same location as the men's race. More than that, some of the most recognizable names in women's sports are superstars of canoe, scull and kayak. The current Chair of UK Sport is Scottish rower Katherine Grainger (in illustration), who, with gold and silver Olympic medals, and six world titles, is the most decorated female rower in British history.

16 March → Caroline Herschel

From a queen of the water to a queen of the stars.

The German astronomer Caroline Herschel was born in Hanover on 16 March 1750. She caught typhus when she was ten years old, which led to her losing the sight in one eye and only growing to just over four feet tall. She lived a confined life with almost no formal education until she was twenty-two.

But after her father's death, her brother William invited her to join him in Bath in England, where he taught music and staged concerts. The intention was that Caroline would have a career as a singer. However, the Herschel siblings were more interested in astronomy and soon, after William's discovery of the planet Uranus, they moved to Windsor and Caroline's career in astronomy began.

And what an amazing career it was! She discovered eight comets and has many 'firsts' to her name: she was the first woman in England to receive a salary as a scientist; the first to publish scientific findings in the *Philosophical Transactions of the Royal Society*; the first to be awarded a Gold Medal of the Royal Astronomical Society, in 1828; and the first woman to be named an honorary member of the society, alongside Mary Somerville, in 1835.

Grief-stricken after her brother's death, Herschel returned to Hanover and died there in 1848. The American poet Adrienne Rich's 1968 poem 'Planetarium' celebrates her life and scientific achievements, and Herschel has a place setting at Judy Chicago's 1979 feminist art installation *The Dinner Party* (see 20 July).

Photo of 'The Dinner Party' by Judy Chicago

17 March ➤➤ **Golda Meir**

On 17 March 1969, Golda Meir was elected as the first female prime minister of Israel.

Born in Kyiv, Ukraine, in 1898, Meir was an Israeli teacher, a supporter of the kibbutz movement – a form of communal living in Israel where people work and live together, often on farms – a stateswoman and a politician. She was the fourth prime minister of Israel, having previously served as Minister of Labour and as Foreign Minister. Her tenure was controversial – not least because of her leadership during the Yom Kippur War and inflammatory statements about Palestinians – and she has been criticized for not using her power to tackle inequalities between women and men in society. Although this is a fair criticism in Meir's case, it's important to note that women – and also Black people and other people of colour – are often judged more harshly than men for not prioritizing their own communities. Expectations are always higher and, perhaps, impossible to meet.

Meir died in Jerusalem in 1978.

18 March ➤ **Helena Kennedy**

On 18 March 2024, the International Bar Association (IBA) announced that Helena Kennedy had been appointed Lady of the Most Ancient and Most Noble Order of the Thistle by King Charles III a few days earlier. The Order of the Thistle is the highest honour in Scotland and is a rare personal gift that can only be bestowed by the monarch. It recognizes individuals who have held public office and/or have made a significant contribution to national life.

With a career spanning more than half a century, Kennedy is one of most distinguished, campaigning and groundbreaking barristers in the world. Born in Glasgow in May 1950, she has acted in many prominent trials, including that of the serial child murderer Myra Hindley after her attempted escape from prison, the Brighton bombing and the Guildford Four appeal. An expert in civil liberties, constitutional issues and human rights law, she gives a voice to those with less power in society and has made an immense contribution to the treatment of women under the law, particularly in areas of domestic violence. A member of the House of Lords since 1997, in 2021 she led the evacuation and resettlement of more than one hundred female judges, lawyers and their families from Afghanistan after the Taliban regained control of the country.

A woman of courage, integrity, stamina and purpose, Kennedy is a shining light for every woman and girl who dreams of making a difference in the world.

19 March ➺ **Fay Weldon**

People often talk about a generation gap, but women of different ages talking to one another – about subjects on which they agree, and disagree – is essential.

In the course of her fifty-five-year writing career, the novelist, playwright, screenwriter, feminist and advertising guru Fay Weldon did just that. She never stopped supporting younger women whom she taught or mentored. A trailblazing writer, her feminist novels such as *The Fat Woman's Joke* and *The Cloning of Joanna May* changed the sorts of heroines readers expected from fiction.

Around about this date in 1983, Weldon's new bestseller *The Life and Loves of a She-Devil* was hitting the shelves. She described the heroine as an 'overweight, plain woman' who takes revenge on her ex-husband and his beautiful young lover. The novel was an immediate hit and, in 1986, a television mini-series starring Julie T. Wallace and Patricia Hodge was one of the most watched shows of the year. A film with Hollywood A-listers Roseanne Barr and Meryl Streep followed three years later.

Weldon also wrote for radio and television, West End musicals and plays. In 2006, in her seventies, she was appointed Professor of Creative Writing at Brunel University in West London. In 2012, a few months shy of her eightieth birthday, she became Professor of Creative Writing at Bath Spa University.

Fun, sassy and exuberant, when so many women and girls

silence themselves by fearing to offend, Weldon was a breath of fresh air. She died in January 2023, at the age of ninety-one, still living life to the full.

20 March ›› Tcheng Yu-hsiu

We don't think of judges as being the most rebellious of people, but Tcheng Yu-hsiu was determined to write her own story.

Born in central China on 20 March 1891, Tcheng was the first female lawyer and first female judge in Chinese history. Having studied in Tokyo and Paris, she became president of the University of Shanghai School of Law in 1931. She advocated for women having choices in marriage and was a skilled orator. All the same, when her autobiography *My Revolutionary Years* was published in 1943 (under her married name), despite her own extraordinary accomplishments it was promoted as having been written by the wife of the Chinese ambassador to Washington rather than her being celebrated as an author in her own right.

21 March ⇒ **Frene Ginwala**

On 21 March 1960, a crowd of as many as 5,000 people gathered outside the police station in the township of Sharpeville, South Africa, in what was then Transvaal Province. They were there to protest against the racist apartheid Pass Laws, part of the apartheid system of racial segregation and discrimination that was in place in South Africa from 1948 to 1994.

Known in slang as the *dompas* – an Afrikaans phrase meaning 'stupid pass' – it was a kind of internal passport, and every Black person over the age of sixteen had to carry one at all times. It restricted where Black people could live, travel and work, who they could marry, and they could be thrown in jail for refusing to show it.

At 1.30 p.m., without warning, the police fired into the crowd, killing and injuring hundreds. For fifty years, the police records claimed that sixty-nine people were killed and 180 injured, twenty-nine children among them. But recent research has shown that the casualties were far higher than that.

The Sharpeville Massacre made headlines all over the world and marked a turning point in attitudes to apartheid. Now, 21 March is a public holiday in South Africa commemorating the massacre and celebrating human rights.

The courageous Indian South African journalist and politician Frene Ginwala, who was born in Johannesburg in 1932, helped establish underground escape routes for members of the ANC (African National Congress) in the period following the massacre and the declaration of the state of emergency. The ANC is a political party that began life as a liberation movement opposing apartheid and formed the first democratically elected government after the end of formal apartheid in 1994.

Ginwala was an architect of South African democracy and a woman who campaigned tirelessly for equal rights for all in the country. She later became the first speaker of the National Assembly of South Africa in 1994.

22 March ➡ Caroline Norton and Blue Plaques

When British women married in the 19th century they had no right to keep their own property or inheritance, no right to their own earnings and no right to have access to their children. Married women were, essentially, the property of their husband and had no independent existence in the eyes of the law.

Born on 22 March 1808 in London, Norton was a novelist, a wealthy socialite, a playwright, pamphleteer and poet. Despite her advantages, she was married to an emotionally abusive and jealous man. He ill-treated her to such an extent that she left him in 1836. In retaliation, he accused her of adultery – known as 'criminal conversation' – and took her to court. The case was thrown out, but Norton was left nearly bankrupt and separated from her three sons.

Most women would have admitted defeat – in Victorian England, the law was administered by men, for the benefit of men. That's just how it was. But Norton refused to accept the injustice and began a campaign to change the law. Thanks to her, and others, three key pieces of legislation affecting women's lives were passed, including the Married Women's Property Act in 1870. This ruled that women should be able to keep and control their own property in certain circumstances, and allowed a woman's earnings to be considered her own property, not her husband's.

In 2021, more than 140 years after her death in 1877, her

biographer Antonia Fraser unveiled a blue plaque at Norton's former house in London's Mayfair. We'll come across several blue plaques in the months that follow. They are put up on buildings in London – and all over England – to mark places of historical or cultural importance. In Scotland and Wales, local authorities run similar schemes. In Wales, on IWD 2017, a group of volunteers launched the Purple Plaques scheme with the aim of celebrating women's contribution to Welsh life.

Blue plaques honour those who've made a significant contribution in their field – politicians, scientists, artists, anybody of note. The scheme has been running since 1866 but, to start with, very few women were commemorated. By the early years of the 20th century, there were still only five women with plaques, including George Eliot and Welsh actress Sarah Siddons. In recent years, things have started – slowly – to change. English Heritage took over the scheme in 1986 and, in 2016, launched a campaign to have more women nominated. Now, about 15 per cent of plaques in London are to women. There is still a grave imbalance for Black people and people of Asian heritage – fewer than 5 per cent of plaques in London commemorate Black or Asian people.

But the good news is that now anyone can nominate someone for a blue plaque. So why don't you campaign for a blue plaque for someone you admire? Go to the English Heritage website to find out how to do it, though bear in mind the person has to have been dead for more than twenty years, there must be a building on the spot or nearby where they lived or worked, and no imaginary characters are allowed!

23 March ➤➤ Pauli Murray

Most people know the story of Rosa Parks and the Alabama Bus Boycott in 1955, which was a turning point in the overturning of the Jim Crow laws in America. But have you heard of an earlier 'freedom rider', the activist, law professor and award-winning author Pauli Murray?

Murray was born in Baltimore in 1910. On 23 March 1940, Murray was arrested in Virginia for refusing to move out of the whites-only section of the bus and charged with 'disorderly conduct'. Her reaction was to enrol in law school to better understand the system she was fighting to change.

Denied opportunities because of her race and because she was a woman (though she often passed as a young man), Murray fought her way to the top. In 1946, she became the first Black deputy attorney general licensed by the Californian bar and, twenty years later, she was the first African American to receive a doctorate in juridical science from Yale University. As a professor at Brandeis in Massachusetts, Murray was responsible for introducing the first African American studies and the first women's studies courses. It was she who coined the phrase 'Jane Crow', making the comparison between gender discrimination and race discrimination, and how Black women suffer from both.

When she was in her sixties, Murray went from being an icon of progressive activism to following a different path. She enrolled in theological college and, in 1977, became the first African American woman ordained an Episcopal minister.

Why is Pauli Murray not better known?

Well, it might be because of her gender identity. Language we use today to describe people who are non-binary or trans was not in use then, but Murray wrote about her 'in-betweenness'. Forty years after her death, we cannot know what she might have thought about current debates. But we can celebrate her extraordinary achievements and the myriad ways in which she fought to make the world a fairer place.

Pauli Murray

24 March ➤➤ Harriet Martineau

In March 1855, the great social thinker, political theorist and education reformer Harriet Martineau sat down to begin writing her autobiography.

Of French Huguenot descent, Martineau was born in Norwich in 1802. A translator and writer, she was one of Queen Victoria's favourite authors and was even invited to her coronation. Passionately committed to the importance of education for girls as well as boys, Martineau devoted her time to campaigning for the abolition of the slave trade. She gave lectures and published papers and pamphlets in Britain and America. Her memoir took a back seat.

She died in Cumbria in 1876. Her autobiography was published posthumously the following year.

25 March ➻ Gloria Steinem

Happy birthday to one of the queens of the second-wave American feminist movement and founder of *Ms* magazine, Gloria Steinem. So called 'second-wave feminism' was rooted in the 1960s and 1970s and focused primarily on social equality for women and girls, especially in the areas of reproductive rights and workplace rights. First-wave feminism is the period at the end of the 19th and early 20th centuries focused on suffrage; third-wave feminism is the period of new campaigning in the late 1990s focused particularly on body image and inclusivity within feminist movements; fourth-wave feminism began in the 2010s and prioritizes intersectionality and gender equality.

Born on 25 March 1934, Steinem is a journalist who talked openly and fearlessly about a woman's rights over her own body in terms of contraception and pregnancy, and about the sexism inherent in society that treated women as second-class citizens.

In 1963, Steinem went undercover as a Playboy Bunny at the New York Playboy Club in order to write about the lives of the women working in the club and how they were treated and exploited. Steinem was one of the key figures in the campaign to get the ERA (the Equal Rights Amendment) ratified in the 1970s. The ERA was first brought before Congress in 1923 and is still not passed in all US states . . .

In July 1971, Steinem was one of more than 300 women who founded the National Women's Political Caucus

(NWPC), alongside other feminist trailblazers Bella Abzug, Betty Friedan, Shirley Chisholm and Myrlie Evers-Williams.

After six decades as a feminist activist and campaigner, Steinem might have felt she had earned the right to hang up her marching boots. But, no. She keeps speaking out and speaking up, even though she is now in her nineties.

Age is just a number . . .

26 March ➡ Hilary Pearson and Susan Shaw

On 26 March 1973 Hilary Pearson (then Hilary Root) and Susan Shaw were the first women members admitted to the trading floor of the London Stock Exchange. It meant that they could buy and sell shares on behalf of their clients or companies.

The fact that the law had changed to allow women on the trading floor did not indicate a shift in some men's attitudes. Shaw and Pearson were subject to lots of verbal abuse, and barriers were put in their way, but it was an important moment in the City (London's financial district).

As of 2020, still only 20 per cent of traders at the Stock Exchange in London were women.

27 March ⇒ Hrotsvitha

In many countries throughout the world (though not the UK), 27 March is World Theatre Day. So, when better to celebrate the German playwright, author and poet Hrotsvitha?

Born around 935 CE in Lower Saxony (north-western Germany), she entered the Gandersheim Convent as abbess. Hrotsvitha was the first playwright in the modern era to write dramatic pieces, often inspired by her own life and that of other women. Though she wrote in Latin, she is thought to be the first named female writer from Germanic lands, the first female historian and the first German female poet.

A legend in her own lifetime, she died towards the end of the 10th century and her writings were lost. Nearly five hundred years later in 1493, her manuscripts were discovered in a monastery. They were published in the original Latin in 1501, and translated into English in the 1600s.

Like several of the feminist heroines in this book, Hrotsvitha has her own place setting at the table in Judy Chicago's art installation, *The Dinner Party* (see 20 July).

28 March ➽ Hilda Clark

Anyone who has seen the film *The Sound of Music* will know about the Anschluss, the invasion (though they called it an annexation) of Austria by Nazi Germany on 12 March 1938.

Around about that same time, the British doctor, tuberculosis expert and Quaker humanitarian aid worker from Somerset, Hilda Clark, arrived in Vienna with the intention of helping Jewish people to escape from Nazi persecution.

Hilda Clark wearing the Quaker star armband, circa 1915

Clark's humanitarian work began during the First World War, when she founded a maternity hospital in France with fellow Quaker and nurse Edith Pye. There is a wonderful photograph of Clark from that time standing beside a car, wearing a trench coat and her Quaker armband on her left sleeve.

She returned to England in 1939, but continued her humanitarian work in London and Kent until her Parkinson's disease became too severe. Parkinson's is a progressive brain disorder that causes nerve cells to die, leading to shaking, stiffness and balance problems.

As her symptoms worsened, Clark returned home to Somerset and died there in 1955. When Pye died ten years later, she was buried beneath the same headstone.

29 March ➤➤ Odaline de la Martinez

One of the great concert halls of the world is the Royal Albert Hall in London, which opened its doors on 29 March 1871. It is home to the Promenade Concerts – the Proms – which were set up by Henry Wood in 1895 as a way of making classical music more accessible.

But Proms audiences would have to wait for over ninety years before they saw a woman conductor on the podium. Not until July 1984 did the trailblazing Cuban-American conductor and composer Odaline de la Martinez raise her baton and make music history.

30 March ➳ Anne Lister and Ann Walker

The Netherlands was the first country to legalize same-sex marriage in 2005. As of 2025, thirty-eight countries have legalized same-sex marriage in some capacity. The first same-sex marriages took place in the UK on 29 March 2014.

But although this was a landmark, in fact there had been other documented same-sex couples going through some form of marriage ceremony much earlier in history.

One of the most celebrated is the lesbian marriage of the British diarist and landowner Anne Lister to Ann Walker. They made their vows on 10 February 1834, exchanged rings a week later and on 30 March 1834 – Easter Day – they took communion together in Holy Trinity Church in York to seal their union. The building now displays a commemorative rainbow plaque to mark this historic – and joyous – moment.

In the end, history catches up . . .

31 March ⇒ Toni Morrison

On 31 March 1988, the African American novelist Toni Morrison won the Pulitzer Prize – the USA's most prestigious literary award – for *Beloved.* Based on the true story of an enslaved woman in the years after the American Civil War, the novel was in the US bestseller lists for twenty-five weeks.

Born in Ohio in 1931, Morrison was one of the giants of contemporary American literature and someone who put on the page the complications, the tragedies and the evils of slavery in America.

She began working in publishing as an editor – she was the first female Black editor at Random House in New York in the late 1960s – but soon began to concentrate on her own writing career. Her brilliant debut novel *The Bluest Eye* was published in 1970, her critically acclaimed *Song of Solomon* won the National Book Critics Circle Award in 1978 and, after winning the Pulitzer in 1988, Morrison was awarded the Nobel Prize in Literature in 1993, making her the first ever Black woman laureate.

Morrison was a rare writer, one who is admired and lauded by her peers and by institutions – but also beloved by readers. She died in New York City in 2019, but her words live on.

This is Planet Earth

'In every out-thrust headland, in every curving beach, in every grain of sand, there is the story of the earth.'
Rachel Carson, *Silent Spring*

Anybody who follows the news knows that climate change is one of the biggest threats facing our planet.

At time of writing, 2024 was officially the hottest year in history, one of the most terrifying on record in terms of extreme weather and destruction of habitat. There was extreme heat in Europe in the summer months, where wildfires ravaged the ancient woodlands of Greece and Portugal; there was an inferno in the Amazon; devastating flooding in Nepal; and millions of people were affected by floods and mudslides in Chad, Niger, Nigeria and the Democratic Republic of the Congo. In October in the USA, a tropical storm named Hurricane Helene swept through ten states including Florida, North and South Carolina and Tennessee, destroying entire communities, killing hundreds, leaving hundreds of thousands displaced, and millions without power or shelter. It was followed two weeks later by Hurricane Milton. In December, Cyclone Chido became the worst cyclone to hit the French territory of Mayotte in the Indian Ocean in ninety years. Hundreds were killed and many thousands of people were left without water, electricity or shelter. Between the time of writing and you holding this book in your hand there will have been many more extreme weather happenings. During the first seven months of 2025, there were several violent weather events – including the devastating fires in Los Angeles and lethal floods in Texas– and it's likely things will get worse, not least of all because of the empowerment of climate deniers thanks to the election of Donald Trump for a second term as the President of the USA and the consequent rolling back of policies designed to tackle climate change.

High winds and destruction of natural habitat make the conditions for wildfires more likely. The reason for the sharp rise in the intensification of tropical cyclones is because greenhouse gases heat the ocean. Cyclones tap into that energy supplied by hotter seas. An early estimate is that global heating caused 50 per cent more rainfall during Hurricane Helene.

There is incontrovertible evidence that the polar ice caps are melting. According to NASA, Antarctica is losing ice mass at an average rate of about 150 billion tons per year, and Greenland is losing about 270 billion tons per year, again adding to the threat of rising sea levels.

What can any of us do?

Well, we mustn't give up. We've already met Vanessa Nakate and Dian Fossey, and there are more activists to come – courageous young people are following in the footsteps of pioneering environmental and climate change activists before them, who've fought against the greed of oil prospectors, poachers and deforesting plantation owners, as well as some national governments, to protect our planet. If we do not keep going, there will be no future for life on Earth at all. This is captured best by the saying attributed to the Cree nation: 'When the last tree has been cut down, the last fish caught, the last river poisoned, only then will we realize that we cannot eat money.'

Resistance matters, reversing the damage matters. But so does preservation and regeneration.

To meet one of the very first recorded female gardeners, we need to go to Aotearoa, the Māori name for New Zealand. There were once more than a thousand islands in the Pacific Ocean, and New Zealand is formed of the two of the largest. According to Māori oral history, the first Polynesians reached the southern oceans somewhere around the year 640 CE, travelling in double-hulled canoes with sails and navigating by the stars.

Six hundred years later, between 1200 and 1300 CE, the first seafarers decided to settle. Among them was Whakaotirangi. She recorded the techniques she used to plant, grow and store seeds, making it possible for her people to stay comfortably in one place, rather than move as nomads when food sources ran out.

Centuries later, in 1885, the American horticulturist Kate Sessions opened a plant nursery in San Diego. She arranged to lease thirty acres of land from the city council in exchange for planting one hundred trees a year there, plus another three hundred in the rest of the city. Known as the 'Mother of Balboa Park', Sessions single-handedly transformed a dry cityscape with almost no plant life into an urban landscape enlivened with flourishing green spaces.

As of 2025, there are more than 1,000 seed banks all over the world, special vaults designed to survive the worst apocalypse imaginable and so preserve samples of all the world's crops. One of the most well-known is the 'Doomsday vaults' in Svalbard. The largest is the Millennium Seed Bank in Sussex, managed and coordinated by the Royal Botanic Gardens, Kew. It opened in 2000 and holds seeds from almost 40,000 species around the world, including nearly all of the UK's native trees and plants.

In the 20th and 21st centuries, as well as global youth-led movements such as Fridays for Future, there has been a huge increase in direct action groups and non-violent civil disobedience campaigns.

In the 1980s, a large environmental peace movement emerged in East and West Europe, opposed to American plans to station nuclear missiles in Europe. One of the most famous actions began in September 1981 at the US military base at Greenham Common in Berkshire, when a group of Welsh women – Women for Life on Earth – set up camp. The camp was only for women and it grew and grew, and days of mass action such as 'Embrace the Base' saw women and girls from all over the country coming to join the protest. I was one of them. The last missiles left Greenham in 1991, but the camp remained in place until September 2000 when it was agreed to build a memorial on the site.

On the night of 10 July 1985, French secret agents blew up the Greenpeace ship *Rainbow Warrior* in the Pacific.

Greenpeace was protesting against nuclear testing in the Pacific Ocean and the destruction of the natural environment. The onboard photographer was killed.

The consequences of this state-sponsored attack were not what the French government had intended. As details of the plot emerged, waves of outrage rippled across the globe and brought the debate about nuclear weapons testing to widespread public attention. In the end, it culminated in the Comprehensive Test Ban Treaty of 1996.

Two of the newest environmental activist organizations are Extinction Rebellion and Just Stop Oil. Extinction Rebellion was founded in 2018 to challenge the UK's reliance on oil and other fossil fuels. They are campaigning for the British government to declare a climate emergency, to legally commit to reducing carbon emissions to net zero – their initial target date was 2025, which will not be met – and for a citizens' assembly to oversee the changes. Just Stop Oil started four years later, in February 2022, and

Just Stop Oil supporters protesting in Whitehall, London, in 2023

began protesting at oil refineries that April. Although their campaign of civil disobedience was intentionally disruptive – they felt it was the only way to make the press and politicians pay attention – and some of their methods divisive, there's no doubt they brought the crisis of human-created climate change to widespread public attention. The organization disbanded in May 2025.

Finally, the UK General Election of 2024 put pollution and sewage dumping in the spotlight. The Liberal Democrats made it a key part of their campaign to highlight the ways in which privatized water companies were illegally dumping tons of raw and untreated sewage into the seas and rivers of the British Isles. The Lib Dems won a record number of seats in the election, proving that protecting the environment can be a vote winner. In Scotland, the Green Party was part of an unofficial ruling coalition from 2021 to 2024.

So, although the scale of environmental damage can feel overwhelming, laws can be rewritten, and public opinion can be changed. When we are united, we are strong. Campaign lawfully and legally. Don't attack works of art or priceless manuscripts – fighting destruction with destruction makes no sense, and there are better ways. Write to your MP, join conservation organizations, make your voice heard.

Together, we can protect our wonderful and beautiful planet.

APRIL
THE WORKERS UNITED WILL NEVER BE DEFEATED
WOMEN'S SUFFRAGE

April

1 April ⇝ Eleanor of Aquitaine

One of the best-known medieval queens, Eleanor of Aquitaine was a patron of the arts, a leader of armies, and a skilled diplomat and strategist. She was Queen Consort of France from 1127 to 1154, then Queen Consort of England from 1154 to 1189. Eleanor faced setbacks and personal attacks on her character, but emerged triumphant despite being forced to live in a kind of semi-exile for sixteen years by her estranged husband. When he died in 1189, Eleanor became Queen Regent for her son, Richard I of England – Richard the Lionheart – while he was away on Crusade.

She died at the age of eighty-two on 1 April 1204 at Fontevraud Abbey in the Loire Valley, France, where her tomb can be found.

2 April ➻ Jayaben Desai

In 1976, Jayaben Desai led a walkout of workers at the Grunswick film processing plant in north-west London. They were protesting against poor working conditions and the lack of respect shown to immigrant workers, many of them Asian women.

Desai was born on 2 April 1933, in Gujarat in India. In 1956 she moved to Tanzania, where she married a factory owner, then came to Britain in the 1960s. As an immigrant, Desai was obliged to take up low-paid employment, working first as a sewing machinist, then processing film in the Grunswick factory.

Her courage in standing against unfair employment practices triggered the support of other workers for the Grunswick strikers. For the next two years, Mrs Desai (as she was always known) led the pickets in their battle. Although their protest was not ultimately successful, she remains a powerful role model.

3 April ➺ **Hikaru Saeki**

Hikaru Saeki was the first female admiral of the Japan Maritime Self-Defence Force (JMSDF) and the first woman across the entire Japan Self-Defence Force (JSDF) to reach a 'star rank' – the handful of ranks at the very top of military organizational structures.

Saeki was born on 3 April 1943. She went to medical school, then worked as a nurse before enrolling in the JMSDF as a physician. She swiftly rose up through the ranks. In 1997, Saeki was put in charge of a JSDF hospital, and two years later was appointed Director of the JSDF hospital in Nagasaki. In March 2001 she was promoted to the rank of *kaisho-ho*, equivalent to rear admiral in the Royal Navy, and one of the highest ranks in the armed forces, before retiring in 2003.

4 April ➳ **Bettina von Arnim**

The German author Bettina von Arnim was born in Frankfurt on 4 April 1785.

As well as writing and publishing, von Arnim was a composer and a singer, an artist, a patron of the arts and a social activist. She held salons (gatherings, rather like a book club or musical society, where like-minded people get together to exchange ideas and chat) attended by many of the leading artists of the day, including Goethe and Beethoven, and she was admired by composers such as Fanny and Felix Mendelssohn, and Clara and Robert Schumann. Von Arnim also used her social influence to advocate for the Jewish community, who were being victimized and oppressed in Prussia at the time.

5 April ➻ Women's Peace Petition, 1923

On 5 April 2023, a hundred-year-old Peace Petition signed by almost 400,000 Welsh women was returned to Wales, marking the centenary of a women-led, Welsh anti-war campaign.

In 1923, five years after the horrors of the First World War had shattered Europe, four Welsh women led an anti-war movement to convince America to join the League of Nations to help prevent a second global conflict. Gladys Thomas, Mary Ellis, Annie Hughes-Griffiths and Elined Prys gathered nearly 400,000 signatures (only women were

Gladys Thomas, Mary Ellis, Annie Hughes-Griffiths and Elined Prys hold the women's peace petition outside the White House in 1924

invited to sign). The petition was said to be nearly seven miles long! The four friends then presented the petition to the women of America in an attempt to unite the women of both nations in a shared fight for a world without war. Presented in 1924, the petition had been preserved and exhibited by the National Museum of American History in Washington, DC ever since.

Now back in Wales, work is underway cataloguing and digitizing the petition at the National Library of Wales. Why not go online and see if any of your ancestors signed the Women's Peace Petition?

6 April ➻ Helen Waddell

The 20th-century Ulster-Scots writer Helen Waddell is one of the reasons I became a historical novelist.

I first learned about Waddell in an English lesson at school. We were studying a (very boring) poem by Alexander Pope inspired by the love affair between the medieval scholar, mystic and nun Héloïse d'Argenteuil and her former tutor, Peter Abelard. Captivated by their story, my teacher told me that a writer called Helen Waddell had written a novel – *Peter Abelard* – about their doomed affair. It was published in April 1933 and brought medieval France vividly to life. It was the first historical novel I read and made me realize how the women of the past could be inspiration for the stories of the present.

7 April ➤➤ Mary Wortley Montagu

Mary Wortley Montagu was born in 1689. A traveller and gifted travel writer, she was a society lady who recorded her experiences while living in Turkey and the Ottoman Empire with her husband, who was the British ambassador.

Wortley Montagu was also a pioneer of inoculation. In the 18th century, smallpox killed more children than any other disease. In Europe alone, an estimated 400,000 people died from smallpox each year and more than 90 per cent of those were children under the age of ten. Smallpox was also responsible for one-third of all adult blindness.

Mary herself was a smallpox survivor, with a scarred face from the disease. She realized that inoculation – giving a dose of live smallpox infection to help build resistance – was common folk practice in Turkey. While she was there, she successfully inoculated her son.

Back in England, there was a major smallpox outbreak in April 1721, so she inoculated her three-year-old daughter. She faced great criticism for it; the male doctors were sceptical and described her as 'ignorant.' But her daughter survived and there's no doubt that Wortley Montagu's work helped prepare the way for Edward Jenner's smallpox vaccine in 1796.

8 April ➤➤ Rachel Luzzatto Morpurgo

We're often told that women in the past accepted the limitations put on their lives simply because of their sex, but this isn't necessarily true.

The Jewish-Italian poet Rachel Luzzatto Morpurgo was born on 8 April 1790 in Trieste. She was the first Jewish woman to publish poetry under her own name in Hebrew in 1,000 years. This went against tradition and she was attacked by male critics, who did not believe a woman capable of writing in Hebrew at all.

In her writing, Morpurgo captured the confinement of women's everyday lives, and the inequalities and injustices they suffered. She signed some of her poems as: 'Wife of Jacob Morpurgo, stillborn.'

Heartbreaking.

9 April ➤➤ Hind al-Husseini

On 9 April 1948, Zionist paramilitaries attacked the hilltop village of Deir Yassin near Jerusalem, murdering hundreds of Palestinian men, women and children. The massacre was carried out despite the village having agreed to a non-aggression pact, which should have protected them.

At this time, a mass expulsion of Palestinians from their villages and towns was taking place in order to clear the way for the creation of the state of Israel, which came into being on 14 May 1948. This is known by Palestinians as the *Nakba* – 'the catastrophe'. Some 700,000 Palestinians would leave or be forcibly driven from their homes.

As news of the Deir Yassin massacre spread, thousands of people in neighbouring villages fled to avoid suffering the same fate. A few days later, the Palestinian civil rights activist Hind al-Husseini came upon fifty-five orphaned survivors who had been abandoned in Jerusalem. She converted her grandfather's house into an orphanage, then transformed it into a school to provide education for them and other displaced Palestinian children. Passionately committed to girls' education and opportunities, Hind al-Husseini established a college for women in 1982.

She died in Jerusalem in 1994.

APRIL

10 April ➻ Queen Anne

The last monarch of the Stuart dynasty, Queen Anne, was the youngest daughter of James II. Until the 2018 film *The Favourite*, starring Olivia Coleman, Anne was little remembered. But she was an important and powerful ruler, and during her reign from 1702 to 1714, Britain changed beyond measure. Anne set in place systems and traditions that still form the basis of modern British society today.

One of the key acts of her reign was the Statute of Anne (also known as the Copyright Act). Passed on 10 April 1710, it was the first copyright law passed anywhere in the world and was intended to encourage learning and support the book trade. Most of all, it protected authors and publishers by making it illegal for others to simply reproduce books and pass them off as their own. The statute put down, in black and white, that the author owned the copyright of their own work. Thanks to generative AI and unscrupulous tech companies, in 2025 these rights are under threat.

Authors everywhere salute you, Queen Anne.

11 April ➻ Mo Mowlam

On 11 April 1998, Easter Saturday, the newspapers were full of coverage of the signing of the Belfast Agreement on the previous day.

Usually known as the Good Friday Agreement, this historic document had been ratified twenty-four hours earlier by the British and Irish governments. It brought to an end many decades of fighting and laid out the framework of how Northern Ireland should be governed.

One of the four signatories to the agreement was the popular Labour politician Mo Mowlam. As Northern Ireland Secretary, she played an essential role in getting those on all sides of the conflict to the negotiating table. Her no-nonsense approach – when she was hot in meetings, she would remove her wig and put it on the table (she was undergoing treatment for a brain tumour, so had lost her hair) – was essential in breaking the deadlock.

Having kept the severity of her cancer diagnosis secret, Mowlam died on 19 August 2005 at the age of fifty-five. Her funeral was conducted by the Reverend Richard Coles, previously with the 1980s band The Communards, later a Church of England priest and now a bestselling crime writer . . .

Mo Mowlam, doing things her own way to the last.

12 April ➻ Joyce Banda

Joyce Banda was born in Malawi on 12 April 1950. She was her country's first female vice president, Malawi's first female president, the second female president in Africa (after Liberia's Ellen Johnson Sirleaf) and the second female head of state in the Commonwealth after Queen Elizabeth II.

Throughout her career, Banda prioritized improving maternal health and reproductive rights, specifically through her support of safe motherhood initiatives. She also introduced pioneering schemes to fight hunger and poverty. In truth, her work in office simply continued her life's work. Before going into politics, Banda had been an educator, women's rights activist and businesswoman. She'd run a garment-manufacturing business, a bakery, and set up the National Association of Business Women of Malawi and the Joyce Banda Foundation, an organization dedicated to rural development and improving the lives of women and children.

13 April ➤➤ Annie Jump Cannon

Known as the 'Harvard Computers', an all-female group of data scientists were brought together at Harvard University in Massachusetts in the late 19th century by the astronomer and physicist Edward Pickering. Their job was to map and define every star in the visible universe.

Born in 1886, Annie Jump Cannon was one the stars of the programme and one of the founding mothers of modern American astronomy. She lost almost all of her hearing when she was young, but her mother inspired in her a love of the night sky. She joined Pickering at Harvard in 1896 and became known as the 'census taker of the stars'. She published her first catalogue in 1901, and was made Curator of Astronomical Photographs at Harvard in 1911. On the eve of the First World War, Cannon was finally admitted as an Honorary Member of the Royal Astronomical Society.

In 1919, after Pickering died, Cannon took over as the director of the project. She manually classified more stars in her lifetime than anyone else, around 350,000. The system she devised to map the stars – known as the Harvard spectral classification system – is still studied by astronomers today.

She died on 13 April 1941.

14 April ➤➤ Amalie Noether

Born in Germany in 1882, Amalie Noether – always known as Emmy – was a leading German-Jewish mathematician and possibly the best-known female mathematician of her day, particularly in the field of algebra. She developed theories of rings and fields, and discovered the connection between symmetry and conservation laws. This became known as Noether's theorem.

Although her students were devoted to her – and she often allowed others to take the credit for her own work – Noether had to fight to be recognized alongside her male counterparts at the university and to be paid properly.

In 1933, when the Nazis sacked all Jewish professors from university teaching positions, Noether managed to get to America and take up a position at Bryn Mawr College in Pennsylvania. She died there suddenly on 14 April 1935, from complications following an operation to remove a tumour.

15 April ➤➤ Emma Watson

The English actress and activist Emma Watson, born on 15 April 1990, has always managed to combine her working life with her educational and campaigning life. Famous for playing Hermione Grainger in the *Harry Potter* films, and for roles in independent movies including *My Week with Marilyn* and *The Bling Ring*, after she graduated from university in 2014, Watson was appointed a UN Women Goodwill Ambassador. She helped launch the UN Women HeForShe campaign, which advocates for gender equality. Four years later, she helped launch Time's Up UK and was appointed to a G7 advisory body for women's rights. She is also an advocate for sustainable fashion.

16 April ➻ **Aphra Behn**

Theatres were closed in England during the Civil War, a conflict fought from 1642 to 1651 between Parliamentarians, who were Protestants (or Puritans) led by Oliver Cromwell, and Royalists loyal to King Charles I. After the Parliamentarian victory, between 1651 and 1660 (known as the Interregnum, from the Latin for 'between kings'), the theatres remained closed, as the Puritans considered them immoral. Only when Charles II came to the throne were they allowed to open again.

The era that followed is called the Restoration, and playwrights worked round the clock to come up with new work to satisfy the public's appetite for comedy and drama. One of the hardest working – and most glamorous – of all playwrights was the English author and poet Aphra Behn.

Behn was one of the first British women to make her living as a writer. Much of her younger life remains a mystery: she may have been born in Kent, or not; she may have spent time in Suriname, or not; she may have been a Catholic and worked as a spy for Charles II during the Interregnum, or maybe that was another fiction.

But, in the end, does it matter? What we do know is that Behn was a versatile and colourful writer who wrote frankly about desire and sexuality, about her life as a woman, about politics. She was clever and witty, publishing poetry, novels and drama. Her fantastic Restoration comedy drama *The Rover*, which premiered in 1677, features a group of English lads and lasses on the loose in Naples during the Carnival. And her novel *Oroonoko*, published in 1688, tackles themes of racism and misogyny in a way that would not be out of step with modern attitudes.

Behn died on 16 April 1689. For years afterwards, her reputation was attacked and her work dismissed. But, in the 20th century, and partly because of the admiration of writer Virginia Woolf, a new generation of scholars began to seek out Behn's work once more.

A trailblazer.

17 April →→ Emily Williamson

Emily Williamson was born in Didsbury, Greater Manchester, on 17 April 1855.

Appalled by the senseless slaughter of exotic birds for their plumage to decorate ladies' hats, fans and coats, Emily Williamson asked her friends to sign a pledge to not wear feathers. In 1889, she founded the all-female Plumage League, partly because the all-male British Ornithologists' Union refused to do anything to stop this awful trade. Two years later, her group merged with the Croydon-based Fur, Fin and Feather Folk, founded by Belfast-born humanitarian Eliza Phillips, evangelical Christian Etta Lemon and others to form the Society for the Protection of Birds. This later would become the organization we know as the RSPB. After years of campaigning, in 1921 the Plumage Act was passed and the names of the three women disappeared from

Emily Williamson sculpture created by Eve Shepherd MRSS SPS

the history books. But more than a hundred years later, after a local campaign, a statue of Williamson was commissioned to stand in Fletcher Moss Botanical Garden in Didsbury. She is holding a copy of the Act in her hand and her skirt is inspired by the different species of birds she and her friends helped to save.

The statue was unveiled on 17 April 2023, the anniversary of her birth.

18 April ➤➤ **Adrienne Rich**

On 18 April 1974, the American lesbian-feminist poet, essayist and thinker Adrienne Rich won the National Book Award for Poetry. Also shortlisted were Alice Walker and Audre Lorde.

Before the ceremony, the three friends agreed that whoever won would accept on behalf of all three of them. When Rich took to the stage, she did just that.

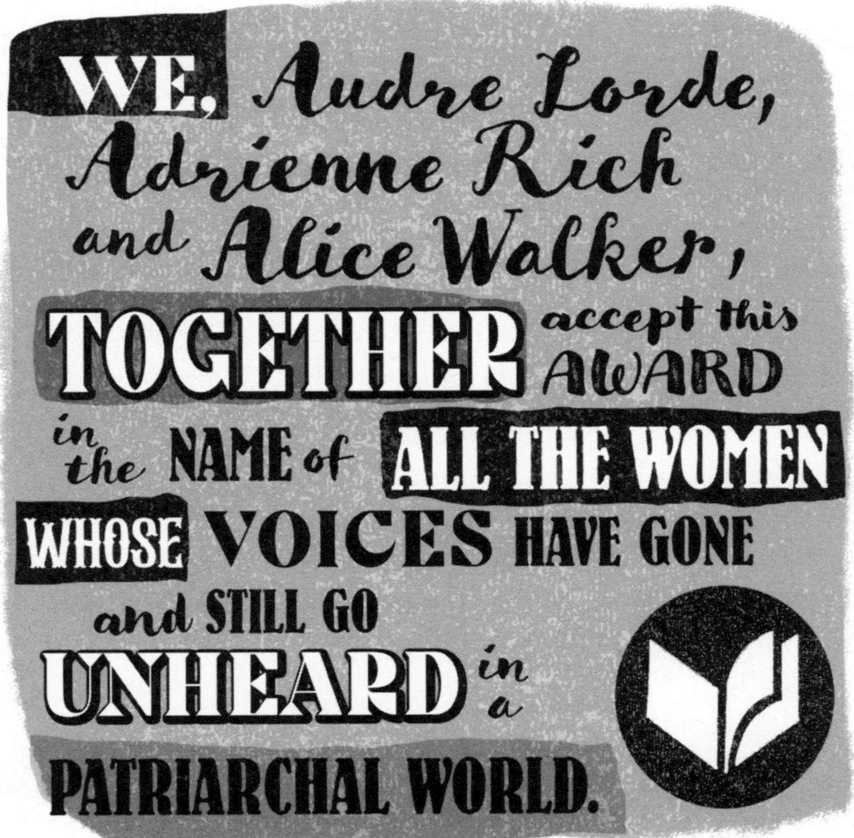

Adrienne Rich

19 April ⇥ Stella Rimington

Forget about Judi Dench in the James Bond films – brilliant as Dame Judi was – and meet the real-life M!

In 1992, Stella Rimington became the first female head of MI5 and one of the most powerful women ever in British security. She began her working life as an archivist at the County Record Office in Worcester in 1959. When her husband was offered a posting at the British High Commission in India in 1965, she went with him to New Delhi and was approached there to join MI5. She worked in all three branches of the Security Service and oversaw the PR campaign to improve the openness of the Service and increase public accountability.

In April 1996, she retired from the Security Service. Rimington went on to publish her memoirs – *Open Secret* – and a series of crime novels starring a female intelligence officer. As creative writing tutors sometimes advise students, write what you know . . .

20 April ⇥ **Nanny of the Maroons**

On 20 April 1740, a treaty was signed in Jamaica between the British colonial government and the Windward Maroons, bringing to an end a long-running conflict.

For years, resistance to British rule had been led by the legendary Queen Nanny, one of the most spectacular and revered women in Jamaican history. Little is recorded about her early life, but Nanny was born in Ghana around 1686 and we know that she and other previously enslaved people – the Maroons – sought refuge in the Blue Mountains in Jamaica, where they established a settlement they called

Nanny Town. Under Nanny's leadership, they ran a guerrilla war against the occupying British forces.

Nanny Town was destroyed in 1734 after six years of conflict. It's not clear whether Nanny herself went into exile or was killed in the fighting, but someone else signed a peace treaty and oversaw the building of another settlement that became known as New Nanny Town (now Moore Town).

Whatever happened to Nanny, her legacy is secure. In 1974 the Bank of Jamaica issued a 500 Jamaican Dollars banknote with her image on it, and in 1975 she was declared a National Hero by the Jamaican government, the only woman and only Maroon to have been commemorated in this way.

21 April ⇥ Elizabeth Peratrovich

Elizabeth Peratrovich of the Tlingit nation was born in 1911. She was Grand President of the Alaska Native Sisterhood and was instrumental in the passing of Alaska's anti-discrimination act of 1945, the first legislation of its kind.

Throughout her life, Peratrovich fought tirelessly for the rights of First Nation Americans to be treated equally and fairly. Her personal papers, detailing her campaigns, were given posthumously to the Smithsonian National Museum of the American Indian in 1958.

In 1988, thirty years after her death, 21 April was renamed as Elizabeth Peratrovich Day in Alaska for 'her courageous, unceasing efforts to eliminate discrimination and bring about equal rights'.

22 April ➵ Ethel Smyth

Born in 1858, the British composer and suffragette Ethel Smyth was a celebrity in her day.

Smyth was a conductor in times when public opinion had it that women couldn't conduct. She was also a composer of opera and symphonies when music critics insisted women were only capable of writing small works for the piano and chamber orchestras – a review of her first performed work was dismissed as being 'devoid of feminine charm and therefore unworthy of a woman'. Smyth took no notice. She was famous for speaking her mind and for her distinctive fashion sense – she'd walk around London in specially tailored masculine tweed suits, small 'mannish' hats, and bright ties in the WSPU (Women's Social and Political Union) colours of purple, white and green.

Smyth was a close friend – probably a lover – of the suffragette leader Emmeline Pankhurst and wrote 'The March of the Women' for the WSPU. When Smyth was arrested and taken to Holloway Prison for taking part in a suffragette march in London in 1912, she conducted a rousing chorus of women marching around the prison yard singing the anthem with her toothbrush!

Smyth never stopped fighting for the right to be herself. She was a keen golfer, and when she died in 1944, she left instructions to her friends that they were to scatter her ashes near her home, on Woking Golf Course, which had not allowed her to be a member because she was a woman. A legend in her lifetime, and beyond.

23 April ➤➤ Margaret Fell

Margaret Fell is often called the 'Mother of Quakerism'.

Because everyone in England had to belong to the Church of England in the 17th century, Quakers were persecuted for their beliefs. Fell was arrested in Westmoreland and imprisoned with her six daughters in Lancaster Castle for preaching and organizing prayer meetings. She published a pamphlet in 1666 called *Women's Speaking Justified*. It was Fell's success as a preacher that led to Samuel Johnson's regrettable comment: 'Sir, a woman's preaching is like a dog's walking on its hind legs. It is not done well; but you are surprised to find it done at all.'

Fell died on 23 April 1702.

24 April ➤➤ Millicent Garrett Fawcett

If you find yourself in Parliament Square in London, say hello to Millicent Garrett Fawcett, suffragist leader and social campaigner. Her statue, created by the British artist Gillian Wearing, was the first ever statue of a woman erected in Parliament Square.

Fawcett is holding a banner with her inspiring slogan from her 1920 speech: 'Courage Calls to Courage Everywhere.' Around the plinth are the names of fifty-nine women and four men who supported women's suffrage, just a handful of those who were involved in the campaign to achieve voting equality for women and men. The statue was unveiled on 24 April 2018, after a long campaign led by feminist writer and campaigner Caroline Criado Perez.

Millicent Garrett Fawcett statue in London

25 April ⇥ **Khutulun**

On 25 April 1926, the Teatro alla Scala in Milan was filled with elegant ladies and gentlemen waiting for the conductor to raise his baton for the world premiere of Puccini's new opera *Turandot*. Puccini himself was not there to see it, having died the previous year, leaving another composer to write the final act.

But how many in that glittering audience were aware that the leading character, Princess Turandot, was based on a real-life 13th-century wrestling champion and Mongolian princess? Wrestling? Yes, because wrestling was the national

sport for both men and women in Mongolia at the time and, by all accounts, Khutulun was the one to beat.

Khutulun was the great-great-granddaughter of the notorious warrior Genghis Khan. By 1260 his Mongol Empire was starting to crumble, and Khutulun's father was one of those vying to take over. He relied on his beloved daughter to consolidate his power, but he needed her to marry. She agreed, provided the man could beat her in a wrestling competition: if he lost, then he had to present her with a hundred horses (some stories say a thousand). Whether or not this is true, we don't know . . . only Khutulun is said to have owned a bigger herd of horses than anyone else in Mongolia.

26 April ➤➤ **Petronella van Heerden**

Petronella van Heerden, who was born in Bethlehem, South Africa, on 26 April 1887, was a pioneering gynaecologist and the first Afrikaner woman to qualify as a doctor in South Africa. She wrote her PhD on endometriosis – a devastating condition that causes extreme pain and can prevent women from becoming pregnant. Awarded in Amsterdam in 1922, it was the first doctoral medical thesis written in Afrikaans.

Van Heerden settled in Cape Town, served on the Committee of the Cape National Party, and published two memoirs, as well as many articles on feminism, gender inequality and sexual identity.

27 April ➤➤ Mary Wollstonecraft

We began our feminist historical adventures on 1 January with Mary Shelley. Let's now meet her mother, the brilliant writer and thinker Mary Wollstonecraft.

Wollstonecraft's *A Vindication of the Rights of Woman* was published on 27 April 1792. It is one of the most important feminist essays ever written in English, and lays out principles of equality and fairness that would form the basis of women's rights campaigns for the next two hundred years and more. Wollstonecraft made it clear that what she cared about was equality and fairness.

Mary Wollstonecraft

28 April ➤➤ **Prudencia Ayala**

The Salvadoran writer, feminist and social campaigner Prudencia Ayala was born on 28 April 1885. From 1913 onwards, she began to publish opinion pieces in the newspapers, speaking out against anti-imperialism, the US invasion of Nicaragua, and in favour of women's rights. In 1919, she was jailed for her writing, and was later arrested in Guatemala accused of being an enemy agent.

Ayala was the first woman to run for president in El Salvador, indeed in all of Latin America. In 2017, an avenue in the capital San Salvador was renamed in her honour, one of only two streets in the city named after a woman.

29 April ➤➤ The Ford Machinists' Strike, 1968

In June 1968, after management had downgraded their jobs, female machinists at the Ford car plant in Dagenham, East London, went on strike to draw attention to the unfairness of the gender pay gap. Led by Rose Boland, Eileen Pullen, Vera Sime, Gwen Davis, Violet Dawson and Sheila Douglas, and supported by other unions and some Labour politicians, the women were on strike for three weeks.

It was a landmark moment.

In April 1970, the Labour government introduced a bill that would lead to the passing of the Equal Pay Act on 29 May 1970. Finally, here was the acknowledgement that women should be paid the same as the men working alongside them for doing the same work.

Fifty-five years later, although it is narrowing, there is still a gender pay gap in most countries. In the UK in 2024, the pay gap was 14.3 per cent, which essentially means that women effectively have to work for 52 days for free compared with their male colleagues. The gap remains stubbornly wider for Black women and other women of colour, and for older women. In 2010, a film, *Made in Dagenham*, was made of the strike, starring Sally Hawkins. In 2014 a stage musical version premiered, with Gemma Arterton in the lead role.

30 April ➻ **Maria Ogilvie Gordon**

Let's bring April to a close with one of the most brilliant of Scottish scientists, the palaeontologist and geologist Maria Ogilvie Gordon. Born in Aberdeenshire on 30 April 1864, Gordon originally studied music before realizing her heart lay in science. Her studies took her to Munich and, in 1891, she was invited to accompany an eminent geologist on a field trip to the Dolomite Mountains in Italy.

Gordon spent her summers climbing and hiking, collecting and studying fossils. In 1893, she published an article in the quarterly journal of the Geological Society detailing some 354 species of molluscs and corals. She was also the first woman to receive a PhD from the University of Munich. In a terrible blow, the original manuscript of her findings was lost, so she had to rewrite the whole thing from scratch! It was finally published in 1927.

Gordon died in June 1939. Her body was brought home to Scotland and laid to rest in Allenvale Cemetery in Aberdeen.

Bonnets, Bikinis and Bloomers

Some people love fashion – working out that special look, the outfit that makes you feel 'you'. It is one of the ways we present who we are to the world. A particular dress or coat, pair of trousers or shoes, a hairstyle – all these can help you feel great. Others, of course, find fashion dull and see clothes as merely functional.

But what if you didn't have the choice? Clothing can be political and the list of what garments and colours women are allowed – or not allowed – to wear is a slice of political history in itself. At the same time, throughout history, women have chosen to defy custom.

In Ancient Egypt, the female Pharaoh Sobekneferu is shown in portraits wearing both male and female clothes, as is Pharaoh Hatshepsut in the 15th century BCE. In the Roman Republic in 215 BCE, the Lex Opia was a law limiting how much gold women could wear and controlling the colours of their tunics.

In the medieval Catholic Church, bans were issued on silk gowns, fur trims and elaborate hairstyles. In England in the 16th century, laws imposed a strict code of dress that made it clear what class or status a person was at a glance.

The French poet Louise Labé was an accomplished archer and horsewoman. She fought at the siege of Perpignan in 1542 and is reported to have gone into battle in men's clothing. Obviously trousers would be more practical – and safer – than long skirts on a battlefield. And it was French female revolutionaries in the 1770s who first demanded freedom of dress and the right to wear pantaloons, not least because women's clothing was banned from having pockets (an issue that still drives some of us mad today).

Several of the most legendary 18th-century female pirates – such as Anne Bonny and Mary Read in the Caribbean – dressed as men. Sometimes, the notorious Zheng Yi Sao, pirate queen of the South China Seas at the end of that century, did the same.

Imagine being in Paris on 7 November 1800, when the prefecture of police issued an order prohibiting women from wearing 'men's' clothing in public. They claimed that wearing trousers was dangerous to women – and to others (suggesting it would affect a woman's fertility and blur the distinctions between women and men) – and decreed any woman who did would have to have a permit. The writer George Sand – whom we met earlier – ignored the ban and refused to apply for a permit. She was attacked in the French press for it, but her fame protected her against censure. Although this restriction was ignored in the 20th century, the actual law remained on the statute books until 2013!

In 1863, the Californian city of San Francisco also passed laws making it illegal for women to wear trousers in public. The White House didn't allow women to wear trousers to work until 1973, and Congress didn't allow it until the mid-1990s. Though there was never a legal ban in the UK, many schools and private clubs did not permit women or girls to wear trousers until well into the 20th century – if they admitted women at all.

Restrictions are often brought in as a response to women wanting to make their own choices. Other times, it is about women being forced to adhere to male ideas of beauty. The terrible practice of foot binding, which began in China during the 10th century, happened because smaller feet were considered more attractive. To achieve this 'look', the bones in a girl's foot were broken (often repeatedly) and then tightly bound. It was painful and led to permanent disability, and hugely restricted women's mobility. The practice was officially banned in China in 1911, but continued in isolated rural areas until the 1930s.

An illustration of Amelia Bloomer in *The Illustrated London News*, 1851

In European countries in the 19th century, the bustle and the corset – which tightly pulled in a woman's waist – led to problems with breathing. Bustles made it hard for women to run or move freely. This led to what was known as the 'free fashion' movement. One of the heroines of the movement was American women's rights campaigner and journalist, Amelia Bloomer. She advocated the rejection of heavy skirts and the wearing of 'Turkish pantaloons' instead, a kind of trouser that became known as 'bloomers' in her honour.

Today, in certain countries

such as Iran and Afghanistan, women's clothing is severely controlled by the state. Women have been imprisoned and killed in Iran for not wearing the hijab (or headscarf) correctly and there are plans to open a 'treatment clinic' for women who defy the mandatory hijab laws. Since 2024 in Afghanistan, women and girls are not allowed to appear in public with any part of their bodies or faces showing.

There is a pattern here, of course.

It is not really about what anyone should or should not wear, but power. In the light of this, we should try not to judge other women and girls for their choices. Enjoy fashion if you want, or take no notice of it if it's not something that interests you. Wear clumpy platform soles or high heels, whatever makes you feel good. Cover up or wear a bikini on the beach. Short hair or long, make-up or not, to shave or not to shave your legs or underarms, bright colours or dark, piercings, tattoos and bright nails, or everything left 'natural'. What matters is that your choices are for yourself.

Remember the words of the indomitable Amelia Bloomer: 'The costume of women should be suited to her wants and necessities. It should conduce at once to her health, comfort and usefulness; and, while it should not fail also to conduce to her personal adornment, it should make that end of secondary importance.'

It's up to you, but use your freedoms wisely.

MAY

May

1 May ➤➤ **Christine Granville**

We've met the real-life 'M', so now welcome the fearless and glamorous spy who could be the inspiration for any future female James Bond.

The Polish-British agent of Jewish descent, Christine Granville, became a spy behind enemy lines in the Second World War. Born Krystyna Skarbek into an aristocratic family in Poland on 1 May 1908, Granville could ski, shoot, run, hide and often worked undercover in Nazi-occupied countries. She was Prime Minister Winston Churchill's favourite spy and was described by journalist Alistair Horne as 'the bravest of the brave'.

Granville survived the war, but was murdered by an obsessive stalker in London in 1952.

2 May ➤➤ **Elizabeth Alkin**

Here's another female spy, this time from the 17th century.

Known as 'Parliamentarian Joan', because she worked for Cromwell's side in the English Civil War, Elizabeth Alkin was employed as a spy in 1645 after her husband had been hanged. Much of what we know about her activities – both her work as an agent, but also as a news-seller and publisher, later as a nurse in the Anglo-Dutch War in 1653 – comes from records of payments she received.

Like too many women, Alkin vanishes from history. The last record we have of her is on 2 May 1655, when she petitioned for financial relief because she had fallen upon hard times. It is likely she died soon afterwards.

3 May ➤➤ Anne Frank

On 3 May 1960, the Achterhuis – a museum dedicated to the life of Anne Frank – opened in Amsterdam.

Anne Frank is one of the most famous teenagers who has ever lived. The story of how she and her family hid for more than two years in a secret, cramped attic in Amsterdam to escape the Nazi occupation of the Netherlands is known all over the world.

In August 1944, the Frank family was betrayed – history is not quite sure by whom – and soldiers raided their attic home. They were arrested and sent to Auschwitz concentration camp. Anne was transferred to Bergen-Belsen camp and died there in March 1945, just weeks before the end of the Second World War. She was only fifteen.

The reason we know so much about Anne is because she wrote a diary and that diary survived. Her father, Otto, who was the only member of the Frank family not to die in the camps, edited *The Diary of a Young Girl*. He cut out anything he didn't like or approve of – the kind of things that any ordinary teenage girl might write in her private journal about boys she liked, her first kiss, or her honest thoughts about the world. Anne's edited diary was published under

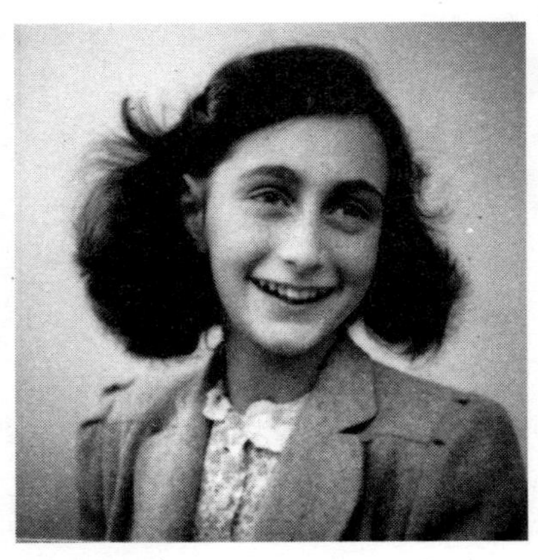

Anne Frank

the title *Het Achterhuis* (*The Secret Annex*) in 1947. The first English translation came out in 1952 and a fuller version of the diary, as Anne wrote it, was published later.

4 May ➤➤ **Nettie Stevens**

The American geneticist Nettie Stevens was born in Vermont in 1861. She had to raise money to fund her studies, so worked as a teacher until she was in her thirties and could afford to go to Stanford University and begin her research in earnest.

Stevens was the biologist and geneticist who discovered sex chromosomes – the chromosomes that carry the genes that determine the sex of an individual and later became known as the X and Y chromosomes, building on the earlier work of Gregor Mendel in the late 19th century.

At first, her findings about sex determination were challenged and disbelieved, but over time her work was acknowledged as crucial.

Stevens died on 4 May 1912 in Baltimore.

5 May ➤➤ Nellie Bly

Meet the intrepid journalist, explorer and inventor, Nellie Bly.

A woman of great energy and enthusiasm, in 1889 Bly was commissioned by *The World* newspaper in New York to recreate the fictional voyage around the world undertaken by the lead character in Jules Verne's 1873 novel *Around the World in Eighty Days.*

She beat the imaginary character by eight days! The paper dedicated the whole front page of its 26 January 1890 edition to her triumph with the headline: 'Nellie Makes the News'. A cartoon showed Bly in her tweed travelling clothes surrounded by male travellers from history.

Bly was born on this day in 1864 and died in 1922, but the memory of her extraordinary around-the-world adventure lives on.

Nellie Bly in *The World* newspaper in 1890

6 May ⇒ **Chiaki Mukai**

Chiaki Mukai, the first Japanese woman to go into space, was born on 6 May 1952.

Growing up, Mukai was inspired by the stories of Yuri Gagarin, the first man in space, and Valentina Tereshkova, the first woman in space. Because Japan didn't have a space programme at the time, Mukai trained as a doctor instead. But she never gave up on her dreams.

Her chance came in 1985, when the National Space Development Agency of Japan chose her to be an astronaut. Mukai went to the United States and worked as a visiting scientist at NASA. In July 1994, she became the first Japanese woman in space, flying on the space shuttle *Columbia*, then went back into space in October 1998 on *Discovery*.

7 May ➤➤ Olympe de Gouges

The rather devil-may-care words below – that would turn out to be a premonition – were written by the French playwright, feminist and abolitionist, Olympe de Gouges, who was born on 7 May 1748.

In 1791 – a year before Mary Wollstonecraft published her groundbreaking *A Vindication of the Rights of Woman* – de Gouges wrote *Declaration of the Rights of Woman and of the Female Citizen*. This was the time of the French Revolution and she was outraged that women were left out of the new republic's Bill of Rights.

A vehement critic of the double standards that allowed women to be judged differently from men, de Gouges came under attack from all sides of the political spectrum – the British prime minister called her a 'hyena in petticoats'. Outspoken and courageous, she was charged with treason and sent to the guillotine in 1793.

Olympe de Gouges

8 May ➵ **Truganini**

The woman often described as the last surviving Tasmanian Aboriginal person, Truganini, died on 8 May 1876.

Truganini was an activist, a leader and daughter of a chief. Much of her history has been distorted. Tasmania (known then as Van Diemen's Land) had been colonized by the British, and the indigenous people who refused to work for the colonizing regime, or fought against them, were hunted down, put in camps or executed. Truganini became an outlaw, but was caught and imprisoned before being forcibly resettled.

Her life is commemorated in many songs, pieces of theatre and works of literature, but one of the reasons Truganini is so well known is the shocking story of what happened to her after she died in 1876.

Two years after her death, her skeleton was dug up and placed on display. This was against Aboriginal custom and traditions. It wasn't until 1976, one hundred years after her death, that Truganini's remains were finally cremated and scattered according to her wishes.

9 May ➤➤ **Margaret Clap**

Imagine yourself in the narrow, dirty streets of Holborn in 18th-century London. Coffee shops were all the rage and had sprung up all over the city. So had taverns and inns known as molly houses, which were mostly frequented by gay men. Male homosexuality was illegal (under a 1533 law called the Buggery Act) and punishable by a fine, imprisonment or even the death penalty.

Despite this, men who simply wanted to be allowed to live their lives freely were drawn to molly houses and specialist coffee houses. The word 'molly' was slang for a gay man at the time.

Margaret Clap – known as 'Mother Clap' – ran a molly house in Field Lane between 1724 and 1726. She was famous within the underground gay community; she looked after her customers and, unlike most molly houses, hers was not a brothel where men paid for sex, but rather more like a private club where people could meet like-minded people.

In February 1726, the premises were raided and about forty people were arrested. Mother Clap herself was charged with running an immoral house, ordered to stand in the pillory – a wooden device with holes for securing the head and the hands set in a public place – in Smithfield Market, to pay a fine, and was sentenced to two years' imprisonment. Not only was the pillory uncomfortable at best, painful at worst, but the victims had to put up with being jeered at or having chamber pots emptied over their heads.

Clap died soon after. On 9 May the same year, five of the men arrested during the raid were executed at Tyburn.

10 May ➻ Cecilia Payne-Gaposchkin

Meet the woman who discovered what the universe is made of . . .

Born on 10 May 1900, Cecilia Payne was a British-born astronomer and astrophysicist. Having completed her studies at Cambridge, she moved to Harvard in the United States, where she was the first woman to become a full professor. Payne established what the universe was made of by working out that stars were composed primarily of hydrogen and helium. She published her groundbreaking doctoral thesis in 1925. It was rejected at first because it contradicted the scientific beliefs of the time, but independent observations

eventually proved she was correct.

In 1926, Payne-Gaposchkin became the youngest person to be listed in the *American Men of Science* reference guide – note the title. Against the customs of the time, she also refused to give up working when she married and had children. She knew her work mattered.

11 May ➤➤ Laskarina Bouboulina

The heroine of the Greek War of Independence in 1821 did not have the best start in life.

Although Laskarina Bouboulina was born in prison on 11 May 1771 in Constantinople (now Istanbul) – her parents were fighting against Ottoman (Turkish) occupation of their country – she grew up hearing stories of the sea and sailing.

Much of her life is well documented. Bouboulina was widowed twice, and left with seven children from two marriages, and a large fortune. She built up her own fleet of ships, including an eighteen-foot warship and, on 13 March 1821, Bouboulina raised the Greek flag and began a naval blockade against the Turkish fleet. She is thought to be the first woman to have been made an admiral.

The later years of Bouboulina's life are murkier, and she was killed in a domestic dispute rather than in battle, but her legacy as a fearless woman lives on. There is a museum dedicated to her on the island of Spetses, which has her sword and her silk headscarf on display. A superb bronze statue stands at the harbour entrance looking out over the waves she once commanded.

Oil painting of Bouboulina

Another heroine of the lab is the British Nobel-winning chemist and biochemist Dorothy Hodgkin.

Born on 12 May 1910 in Cairo, Egypt, Hodgkin's research revolutionized the lives of millions. Her first major discovery came in 1945, when she worked out the structure of penicillin using X-ray crystallography – this made it possible for the drug to be used more effectively to treat serious illness. In 1954, she published the structure of vitamin B12 – this would prove essential for the treatment of anaemia. Despite this, when she won a Nobel Prize in Chemistry in 1964 – the first British woman to do so and only the third woman overall – the headline in the *Daily Mail* on 30 October read: 'Oxford housewife wins Nobel Prize'. The *Daily Telegraph* was also more interested in how she managed to juggle family responsibilities with working than her groundbreaking scientific discoveries.

Hodgkin just kept working. In 1969, she discovered the structure of insulin, which made a huge difference in the treatment of diabetes.

Truly, the first lady of crystals.

13 May ➻ Julian of Norwich

In 1373, at the age of thirty, a woman known as Julian of Norwich lay dying. She was a spiritual adviser to many and an anchoress, that's to say a religious woman who lived in isolation in a cell rather than within the convent community.

On 8 May she was given the last rites. But as the priest held a crucifix above her head, Julian began to have a series of visions – or 'shewings', as she later described them – of Jesus and his suffering. Over the next few hours, and the following night, as she hovered between life and death, she had fifteen visions of Christ.

On 13 May, against all the odds, Julian recovered completely. She began to write down her experiences, producing two versions and working on what is now known as *The Long Text* over many years. She died sometime after 1416 and the manuscript was lost. Centuries later, it was discovered and published in book form in 1670 as *Revelations of Divine Love.* It is considered to be the earliest surviving book in English known to have been written by a woman.

14 May ➤➤ **Mary Seacole**

The story of Mary Seacole is another example of 'people power'. The nursing pioneer, healer and businesswoman Mary Seacole was a legend in her lifetime, but was lost to history until a public campaign nearly one hundred years after her death brought her back into the spotlight.

Born in 1805 in Jamaica, Seacole was the daughter of a white Scottish father and Black mother, from whom she learned many of her healing skills. Seacole nursed victims of the 1850 cholera epidemic in Kingston, and sufferers in the yellow fever outbreak three years later. She also travelled

to Cuba, Haiti and the Bahamas, before heading to London and offering her services to the British government, who were engaged in the Crimean War. The war was a conflict between an alliance of countries, including Britain, and the Russian Empire.

When the government refused her help, Seacole funded her own journey to the Crimea – what is now Ukraine – and set up her own hospital to care for wounded soldiers. She became so famous that after she returned to Britain when the war ended in 1856, the following year a four-day fundraising gala was held in her honour on the banks of the River Thames in London. Her autobiography – *Wonderful Adventures of Mrs Seacole in Many Lands* – also came out in 1857 and was a huge bestseller.

Seacole died in London on 14 May 1881. Fame failed to protect her legacy – racism and class played their part – and there was no one keeping her memory alive. Thankfully, thanks to the Mary Seacole Trust and other campaigners, there is now a blue plaque at her former home in Soho Square. In 2004, Seacole was voted the greatest Black Briton in a poll of more than 10,000 people, and in 2016 a statue of her was erected in the grounds of St Thomas's Hospital in London.

Viva Mrs Seacole!

15 May ➤➤ Anne Boleyn

In 2017, at a small venue at the Edinburgh Fringe Festival in Scotland, six students took to the stage to tell the stories of wives of Henry VIII. The musical begins as a kind of *X-Factor* singing competition between the queens, but turns into a way of each of them reclaiming their own identity and stepping out from Henry's shadow.

Written by Toby Marlow and Lucy Moss, *SIX* was an immediate hit, a brilliant modern mash-up musical which continues to thrill audiences all over the world with its message of female empowerment and taking back control.

But spare a thought for the real queens who suffered at the hands of serial adulterer and bully-boy, Henry. The second of his six wives was the English noblewoman Anne Boleyn, the mother of the girl who would grow up to be Elizabeth I. On 15 May 1536, she was put on trial in London on charges of treason, adultery and incest. It was a sham – everyone knew that Henry wanted to be rid of her so he could marry Jane Seymour, with the hope of having a son. The specially chosen, all-male jury – with her own uncle in charge – found Anne guilty all the same and sentenced her to death.

16 May ➤➤ Junko Tabei

On 16 May 1975, the Japanese mountaineer and environmental campaigner Junko Tabei was standing at the top of the world. Literally. After a gruelling and dangerous climb, Tabei reached the summit of Mount Everest, making her the first woman to climb the planet's highest mountain.

Tabei was born in 1939 and, though she studied English and American literature at university, her passion was mountaineering. Lots of men refused to climb with her because she was a woman, so in 1969 she founded the Ladies' Mountaineering Club. It was the first of its kind in Japan. Tabei helped fund her expeditions by working as an editor for a scientific journal.

She was determined to climb Everest one day, and although she – and other female climbers – were repeatedly told they should be 'raising children instead', she continued to train. She made much of her own equipment from scratch and sewed her climbing trousers from a pair of old curtains.

Finally, in April 1975, the fifteen women were ready. Tabei was accompanied on the first part of the climb by journalists and a camera crew. But disaster struck. On 4 May, an avalanche hit their camp. Tabei and four of her fellow climbers were buried under the snow. Injured and barely able to walk, Tabei refused to be beaten. A few days later, she continued her ascent. She returned home to Japan a national heroine, though she was uncomfortable with the level of fame.

Sixteen years after her historic triumph, she became the first woman to complete the Seven Summits – climbing the highest mountain on every continent.

A woman of principle, who cared about the environmental impact of climbing – particularly the devastation caused by waste left behind by climbing groups – Tabei refused to take any corporate sponsorship. Instead, she continued to work as a mountain guide, tutoring children in English and music, and published seven books to fund her climbs. Having completed a postgraduate degree in environmental studies, she led 'clean-up' climbs in the Himalayas with her husband and children. She died in 2016.

Junko Tabei climbing in 1985

17 May ➤➤ Rosalía de Castro

17 May 1863 saw the publication of *Cantares Gallegos* by the Galician poet and novelist Rosalía de Castro. It was the first book ever to be published in the Galician language. Galicia is an autonomous region in north-western Spain and the language is spoken by about 2.4 million people.

This might not seem a big deal. But throughout history, rulers and tyrants have tried to stamp out minority languages spoken by one particular part of the population to shore up their own power. So, this was a huge moment in Galician literature.

Rosalía de Castro was born in Santiago de Compostela in February 1837 and died in Galicia in 1885. In recognition of her huge influence in Spanish and Galician literature, there are many universities and schools named after her, not only in Spain, but also in Russia, Venezuela and Uruguay, as well as parks, plazas, streets and statues.

18 May ➺ Mary McLeod Bethune

The African American educator, civil rights activist, philanthropist and presidential adviser (to Franklin D. Roosevelt, as well as to Coolidge, Hoover and Truman) Mary McLeod Bethune was born in South Carolina in 1875. At the turn of the last century, she founded a private school for African American girls in Daytona, Florida – there's a wonderful photograph from around 1905 of her standing in line with some of her students on a dusty road: the youngest girls are in white dresses, the intermediate class are wearing white shirts and knee-length skirts; the oldest are in white shirts, long skirts, black boots and straw boater hats. In 1935, she also founded the National Council of Negro Women.

Bethune died on 18 May 1955 in Daytona Beach.

Mary McLeod Bethune with her students, circa 1905

19 May ➻ Lorraine Hansberry

The brilliant playwright Lorraine Hansberry was born in Chicago on 19 May 1930.

In 1959, Hansberry became the first African American woman to have a play – *A Raisin in the Sun* – staged on Broadway. She was also the youngest ever winner of the New York Drama Critics Circle Award and the first African American winner.

Hansberry also worked for the Black newspaper *Freedom.* She wrote about segregation and the civil rights movement, but also about feminism and sexuality. She was briefly married, though she was lesbian – her ex-husband tried to delete all references to this when he donated her unpublished scripts and notebooks to the New York Public Library after her death.

She coined the famous phrase 'young, gifted and black' when talking at a creative writing conference, and later used it as the title for an autobiographical play. It also inspired a song by the legendary Nina Simone (see 21 February).

20 May ➤➤ **Nichola de la Haye**

The 13th-century stateswoman Nichola de la Haye is often described as the 'woman who saved England'.

A diplomat, politician, a woman strong of heart and character, de la Haye inherited the position of Constable of Lincoln Castle from her father. In 1216, despite being a woman and in her sixties, she was appointed by King John as Sheriff of Lincolnshire.

On 20 May 1217, she successfully defended the castle during the Battle of Lincoln in the first Barons' War and defeated the troops of Louis of France. It was a key turning point in English history.

21 May ➤➤ **Mary Anning**

Meet queen of the fossils, Mary Anning.

The British palaeontologist and fossil hunter was born on 21 May 1799 in Lyme Regis. Though she was well known in her day, for over a hundred years after her death in 1847 Anning's achievements were forgotten and her discoveries misattributed to the collectors and dealers who bought fossils from her. But it was Anning who helped change scientific thinking about prehistoric life and the Earth's history, thanks to her excavations of the Jurassic Coast marine fossil beds in the cliffs of Dorset.

In the 20th century, fellow geologists and palaeontologists started to talk about her importance, and her reputation steadily grew. In 2010, the Royal Society included Anning in a list of ten British women who had most influenced the history of science. A glorious painting of her with her basket, fossil-hunting hammer and her little dog, Tray, at her heels, hangs in the Natural History Museum in London.

In 2018, a campaign was started by eleven-year-old Evie Squires from Dorset. Called 'Mary Anning Rocks', Evie's hope was to get support for a statue. A crowdfunding campaign raised enough to commission sculptor Denise Dutton, and Dorset Council gave permission to use a space on the promenade overlooking the cliff Black Ven in Lyme Regis.

The statue was unveiled by Evie and Professor Alice Roberts on 21 May 2022, the 223rd anniversary of Anning's birth.

22 May ⇒ Lily Parr

We've celebrated the Lionesses and the explosion of women's and girls' football at professional and grassroots level all over the world. Now let's meet the greatest English striker you might not have heard of, Lancashire lass Lily Parr.

Born in St Helen's in 1905, Parr grew up playing football with her brothers on waste ground near where they lived. When the First World War broke out, she went to work in the munitions factory and was quickly scouted for the factory's football team – Dick, Kerr Ladies. Parr was legendary for having a hearty appetite, always smoking Woodbine cigarettes and for scoring more goals in her career than pretty much any other player, male or female – a staggering tally of 967 goals between 1919 and 1951.

After the First World War was over, Parr trained as a nurse. It was while working at the Whittingham Mental Hospital in Preston that she met her life partner, Mary, who also worked there. They settled in Goosnargh, lived openly as a couple – which was unusual at the time – and remained together for the rest of their lives.

Parr died on 22 May 1978, having lived long enough to see the FA lift the ban on women's football. She was the first woman to be inducted into the National Football Museum's Hall of Fame in 2002 and, in 2019, the museum unveiled a statue to her, all five-foot-ten of her. Created by the Sussex artist Hannah Steward, it was the first statue of a female footballer in the UK.

A true footballing – and LGBTQIA+ – icon.

23 May ➤➤ **Margaret Fuller**

Born on 23 May 1810 in Massachusetts, Margaret Fuller was America's first female war correspondent – most notably writing from Rome during the first Italian War of Independence in 1847 – and the first full-time female book reviewer.

Her early years were filled with difficulty and financial hardship. But in 1840, she became editor of a quarterly magazine and began to publish reviews, poetry and critiques. Four years later, Fuller became literary critic at the *New York Tribune* and published essays about literature and art.

In 1845, she published a landmark book, *Woman in the Nineteenth Century*, which was a passionate plea both for political equality and for women's emotional, intellectual and spiritual fulfilment. The book's frank discussions of marriage and male–female relationships scandalized many, but the first edition sold out in a week. Tragically, in 1850, a ship she was travelling on was wrecked off Fire Island, in New York. Fuller, her husband and son, and the unpublished manuscript of her next book, all went down with the ship.

The Eurovision Song Contest, 1956

Terry Wogan, Graham Norton, Dana International, Lordi – these days the Eurovision Song Contest is a global institution, attracting millions of viewers from all over the world. It's a festival of kitsch, over-the-top costumes, national juries awarding nul points, crazy stage sets.

The idea for a singing competition between European nations was the brainchild of the Italian national broadcasting organization. The first contest took place in Lugano, Switzerland, on 24 May 1956 and seven countries took part – the Netherlands, Switzerland, Belgium, Germany, France, Luxembourg and Italy. (The UK should have been in the line-up, but it missed the deadline for submissions!)

The winner was the Swiss singer Lys Assia with a song called 'Refrain'. The first British winner was Sandie Shaw in 1967 with 'Puppet on a String'. The most successful winners are Celine Dion and ABBA – the latter stormed to victory in 1974 with 'Waterloo' and have never looked back . . .

25 May ➤➤ **Dorothy Porter**

Dorothy Porter was born on 25 May 1905 in Virginia.

A five-foot high dynamo, Porter was a librarian-scholar and bibliographer and the first African American woman to complete a degree in library science at Columbia University in New York. In 1930, Porter was appointed Librarian at Howard University in Washington. Over the next forty-three years, she built up a comprehensive collection of Black history and culture, as well as celebrating African American scholars and history. She also reorganized the classification system to prevent Black authors from automatically being pigeonholed under either 'colonization' or 'slavery' rather than being valued as writers in their own, and any, field.

26 May ⇒ Dorothea Lange

The American photojournalist and social justice warrior Dorothea Lange was born on 26 May 1895 in New Jersey. She wanted her photographs to change the world and documented, and recorded, real people's lives as a way of effecting social change.

Her most iconic shot was of thirty-two-year-old Florence Owens Thompson and her children, taken in March 1936 in Nipomo, California. The photograph, which became known as 'Migrant Mother', was published in the *San Francisco News* to accompany a piece about how politics was failing its most vulnerable citizens and became a symbol of the desperation and hardship suffered by ordinary people during the Great Depression. It remains one of the most powerful, and important, portraits in American photography.

Dorothea Lange's 'Migrant Mother'

27 May ⇒ **Faith Bandler**

On 27 May 1967 a referendum was held in Australia to change the constitution so that indigenous people would be treated equally under the law. It came after years of campaigning. One of the leaders of the referendum movement was Faith Bandler.

She was born in New South Wales in 1918 to a Scottish-Indian mother and South Sea Islander heritage father. He had been kidnapped from his home on Ambrym Island in 1883 – a practice known as 'blackbirding' to get workers for the sugar cane plantations – and forced into slave labour. His experiences, and the racism she encountered as an indigenous woman of mixed-race heritage, fuelled Bandler's activism.

During the Second World War, Bandler worked in the Australian Women's Land Army, but received lower pay than the white workers. After being discharged in 1945, she started to campaign for equal pay for indigenous workers. She was the co-founder of the Aboriginal Australia Fellowship with Pearl Gibbs in 1956 and became involved in the campaign to hold a countrywide referendum to remove discriminatory provisions from the Australian constitution. When the vote was held in May 1967, an overwhelming 90.77 per cent of voters ticked 'yes' on their ballot paper.

Bandler died in Sydney in 2015 at the age of ninety-six.

28 May ⇒ Irene Khan

On 28 May 1961, Amnesty International was founded to stand up against injustice and to help defend human rights for all, anywhere in the world. The first female Secretary General – who was also the first Asian woman and the first Muslim Secretary General – was Bengali Irene Khan. The Secretary General is Amnesty International's primary spokesperson and leader of its human rights work.

Born in Dhaka in 1956 (then in Pakistan, now in Bangladesh), Khan trained as a lawyer. She served as Amnesty's Secretary General from 2001 to 2009. The current Secretary General is French human rights activist Dr Agnès Callamard.

IT'S TIME FOR US
to REMEMBER
that
RIGHTS
ARE NOT handed on a
PLATTER by
GOVERNMENTS,
THEY HAVE
TO BE
WON.

Irene Khan

29 May ➤ Laverne Cox

The American actress and producer Laverne Cox was born on 29 May 1972 in Alabama. She was the first openly transgender person to be nominated for a Primetime Emmy Award in 2014 for *Orange Is the New Black* and the first transgender person to appear on the cover of *Time* magazine in June that same year. In the accompanying article 'The Transgender Tipping Point', written by journalist Katy Steinmetz, Cox talked about the importance of understanding that all trans people are not the same. She also spoke out against bullying and violence against trans people, and advocated for fairer healthcare provision. Cox was also the first transgender person to win a Daytime Emmy as a producer.

30 May ➟ Joan of Arc

Jeanne d'Arc, also known as 'La Pucelle' or the 'Maid of Orléans', is one of the most famous women in history. Born in the village of Domrémy in north-eastern France in 1412, she was still in her teens when she joined the army of the French king at Orléans in April 1429. The city had been besieged by English forces for seven months. Jeanne was a devout Catholic and claimed to have seen visions of angels, telling her to fight. The English forces were superior in every way, so when the French broke the siege just nine days after Jeanne's arrival, the legend of La Pucelle was born.

She was a freedom fighter and a true warrior queen. But in 1430, Jeanne was captured by the English and, after a show trial, she was convicted as a heretic and burned at the stake on 30 May 1431, at the age of only nineteen. One of the charges against her was that she wore men's clothing.

The story of this determined, courageous teenager has inspired writers, filmmakers, historians, theologians and artists ever since. In 2024, American singer-songwriter Chappell Roan channelled Joan of Arc while performing her latest hit single, 'Good Luck, Babe!', at the MTV Video Music Awards. The village where Jeanne was born has been renamed Domrémy-la-Pucelle in her honour, in 1920 she was named a saint, and she has stood as a symbol of France from the 15th century onwards.

31 May ➳ Chien-Shiung Wu

The Chinese-American particle and experimental physicist Chien-Shiung Wu was born on 31 May 1912.

Sometimes called the 'Chinese Marie Curie' or the 'First Lady of Physics', Madame Wu went to the United States in 1936 to study. In 1944, she began working on the Manhattan Project, which was a classified US government project to create the first atomic weapons. Wu's contributions helped determine the process for separating uranium, a crucial step in being able to create uranium in large enough quantities to make an atomic bomb.

Despite this, when the experiment often referred to as the 'Wu Experiment' won the Nobel Prize in Physics in 1956, her two male colleagues were honoured and she was not.

Wu was the first woman to serve as president of the American Physical Society and received more than fifteen major awards, as well as honorary degrees and fellowships, in her long career.

Deeds Not Words

The importance of women being allowed to vote and participate as equal citizens is a thread running through this book. The phrase 'Deeds Not Words' was coined by the suffragette Emmeline Pankhurst to explain how women had to *do* things in order to draw the British government's attention to their cause, not simply talk about change. This could be anything from gathering names for a petition, campaigning and speaking at meetings, to acts of civil disobedience, such as chaining themselves to railings outside the House of Commons or dropping pamphlets from an airship!

Of course, what women can hope to achieve in terms of equality depends greatly on the country in which they live, the time in which they are living and the nature of government or ruling family in place.

There have been many different kinds of government throughout human history. The expectations of a woman in 4th-century India, or 7th-century Persia, would be very different, say, from the expectations of someone in 16th-century England or 19th-century Australia. But the determination of women to be allowed full and equal lives is common to all societies.

Absolute monarchies – where a king, emperor, Pharaoh, or khan held sway – have been the most typical, with a ruling family holding power for generations. From Japan to China, Mongolia to medieval France, the names of those ancient rulers are well known. In Europe, this was known as the 'Divine Right of Kings' and came from the idea that the monarch was directly chosen by God to rule. Today, there few absolute monarchies left, Saudi Arabia being a rare example. In most other countries where there is still a queen or a king, the monarch is more or less a symbolic head of state. The business of running the country, fixing laws and taxes, is undertaken by an elected government. The UK, the Netherlands, Spain, Thailand and Jordan are all examples of constitutional monarchies.

There are also theocracies, where religious leaders form the government and rule the country. England in the 15th century was a mixture of an absolute monarchy and a theocracy guided by the Catholic Pope in Rome. Today's theocracies include Sudan, Iran, Yemen and Afghanistan.

In a dictatorship, ordinary citizens have no say in the running of their country. The term 'dictator' comes from the Latin word *dictare*, meaning 'to assert, order or repeat'. It originated in the Roman Republic around the 6th century BCE as the name for a magistrate who was given temporary, absolute power, to deal with an emergency, and did not originally have negative connotations. Today's dictators have often seized power in a military coup – such as in Argentina in the 1970s – and dictatorships are characterized by human rights abuses and a willingness to torture, murder or gaslight its citizens and eliminate their opponents. Recent military dictatorships include those in Brazil and Argentina, both of which ended in the 1980s, and the ongoing one in Myanmar.

In most Western countries, the drive in the 20th and 21st centuries has been towards democracy, a system where all are supposed to be equal under the law, though in 2025 that principle is coming under threat. The word itself comes from the Greek words *demos*, meaning 'people', and *kratos*, meaning 'power'. But it is worth bearing in mind that in Ancient Athens – the birthplace of democracy around the 5th century BCE – only adult, free male citizens were allowed to vote: women, enslaved people and immigrants were not.

Looking back, it is no surprise that it is in countries with some form of democracy that the women's suffrage movement took hold. Women in the UK had to wait until 1918 for some to be allowed to vote and until 1928 for all women over the age of twenty-one to be treated on the same terms as men.

It's worth reminding ourselves why women were prepared to give their lives to make it happen. The answer is simple: that everyone, whoever they are, whatever they look like, whatever their

French feminist Hubertine Auclert, holding a banner saying 'Women's Suffrage'

background, should have the right to make a contribution to the society in which they live. If women's voices are absent, then our needs and priorities run the risk of being overlooked. Governments come, and governments go, but they should rule on behalf of the whole country and all its citizens.

So, in honour of all the women who marched for women's rights, here are a few more names to add into the mix with Emmeline Pankhurst: Hubertine Auclert in France, Catherine Spence in Australia, Carrie Chapman Catt in America, Thérèse Casgrain in Canada, Marie Stritt in Germany, Clara Campoamor Rodríguez in Spain, Rosika Schwimmer in Hungary, Yevgenia Bosch in Ukraine, Rosina Sky in England, Helen Crawfurd in Scotland . . . and many others whose names have been forgotten or gone unrecorded.

Deeds not words.

JUNE

June

1 June ➻ Helen Keller

How would you navigate the world if you couldn't see nor hear? If you couldn't read or listen to music, or see your friends?

This was the situation of the American disability activist, Helen Keller, who was born in Alabama in 1880. She lost both her sight and her hearing when she was little more than a baby. At that time, people with disabilities were often put into institutions and shunned. But thanks to the determination of her parents, and the support of an incredible teacher, Anne Sullivan – who taught Keller to read by tracing words on her hand – Keller became an author, teacher and leading light in the disability rights movement. Sullivan herself was partially blind.

Keller was the first D/deaf and blind person in the United States to take a degree. She wrote fourteen books and hundreds of speeches and campaigned for women's rights and for disability rights.

She died on 1 June 1968 and her ashes were buried in the Washington National Cathedral, alongside those of her amazing teacher Anne Sullivan, who died in 1936. Keller's story of resilience and hope goes to show that disability is not about what a person cannot do, but rather what they can.

2 June ➻ Queen Elizabeth II

Can you remember where you were when you heard the late queen had died? I was at Victoria Station in London on 8 September 2022, having just met my one-day-old grandson for the first time, when the news flashed up on the screen.

Elizabeth II had been queen of Great Britain and Northern Ireland since 1952. Her reign – seventy years and 214 days – was the longest of any British monarch and the second longest in history. Her coronation took place on 2 June 1952 at Westminster Abbey in London. It was the first British coronation, and one of the first major international events, to be televised. It is also another date of personal significance to me – it was the day that my father took a chance and proposed to my mother. Luckily, she said yes . . .

Queen Elizabeth saw seismic changes in her lifetime – the Cold War and the Berlin Wall being built and being torn down; countries seeking independence; environmental catastrophes; personal tragedies and challenges; pandemics and wars. But she had a strong sense of duty and worked hard until the very last days before her death at the age of ninety-six.

After she died, nearly 250,000 people paid their respects by filing past her coffin in Westminster Hall, with another 33,000 people in Edinburgh. The state funeral was held on 19 September. The streets were lined by hundreds of thousands of people and millions of others watched the funeral on television all over the world.

It was the end of an era. And there is unlikely to be another queen by right, as opposed to by marriage, in our lifetimes . . .

3 June ➤➤ Josephine Baker

The American-born, French-by-adoption, brilliant Josephine Baker was born in St Louis, Missouri on 3 June 1906.

A trailblazer in so many different fields, she was – take a deep breath – an actress, a singer, a music hall star, a cabaret artist and a film star. Her nicknames include the 'Bronze Venus' and the 'Black Pearl'. She was the first African American woman to star in a major movie and often appeared on stage with her pet cheetah, Chiquita.

Baker was also a pilot, a lieutenant in the French Air Force, a Resistance secret agent during the Second World War and, later, a civil rights activist. She was the only woman who spoke at the 1963 March on Washington before Martin Luther King gave his famous 'I Have a Dream' speech.

She died in Paris in 1975, and in 2021 Baker became only the sixth woman – and first woman of colour – to be buried in the Panthéon, an honour awarded to those who have served France at the highest level. Others include scientist Marie Curie, Resistance fighters Geneviève de Gaulle-Anthonioz and Germaine Tillion (although their remains were not actually transferred there) and feminist icon and lawyer Simone Veil.

Quelle femme – what a woman!

4 June ➤➤ **Emily Davison**

Emily Davison is one of the best-known British suffragettes, partly because of the tragic circumstances of her death.

Born in 1872, Davison joined the WSPU in 1906 and soon became known for engaging in civil disobedience and her enthusiastic direct action – breaking windows, throwing stones, setting fire to post boxes, even hiding in the House of Commons on the night of the 1911 census.

The 1913 Derby was due to be raced at Epsom in Surrey on 4 June. The Derby is one of the most prestigious British horse races and King George V himself had a horse running. As the field thundered past, Davison ducked under the rails, ran out in front of the king's horse and was trampled. She died of her injuries four days later. At her funeral, a procession of 5,000 suffragettes accompanied her coffin and nearly 50,000 people lined the route to pay their respects.

Yet many questions remain. Davison did not discuss her plans with anyone and a return railway ticket to London was found in her handbag – does that suggest that she had only intended to disrupt the race, not sacrifice herself? We will never know.

5 June ➤➤ **Wang Zhenyi**

The Chinese queen of the stars is the 18th-century mathematician and astronomer Wang Zhenyi, who was born in 1768.

In a time when most women in China were denied an education, she taught herself astronomy, mathematics, geography and medicine. She published articles challenging accepted scientific beliefs and the idea that girls should be

denied education. She tutored boys as well as girls, and was also a poet versed in history, literature and martial arts.

When she knew she was dying in 1797, she gave her works and manuscripts to her best friend, who passed them to Wang's nephew, who eventually published them. Her ideas would become the foundation for astronomy in the 19th and 20th centuries. In June 1994, the International Astronomical Union (IAU) named a crater on Venus after her. As it happens, all craters on Venus are named after famous women, or have female names.

6 June ⇥ Christian Lamb

On 6 June 1944 – after months of planning and misinformation to mislead the Nazis as to the exact date and timing of the invasion – the D-Day landings in France were launched by Britain and its Allies. Shortly after midnight, Operation Neptune began. It was the largest invasion from the sea in the whole of human history and marked a turning point in the Second World War.

One of the few women back at Allied Command HQ in London was Christian Lamb. She was a Wren (a member of the Women's Royal Naval Service, or WRNS) and an expert in plotting routes for landing craft and ships. Her work was essential to the success of the operation, though she rarely spoke about it after the war had ended.

Lamb became a horticulturalist, though continued to be intrepid – for her 103rd birthday, after a glass of champagne, she was taken up in a Miles Magister open-air training plane! She has published five books, including a memoir *Beyond the Sea – A Wren at War* in 2021. At the eightieth anniversary commemorations of D-Day in France in 2024 – it was the first time Lamb had attended any of the D-Day celebrations – the French president Emmanuel Macron presented her with the Légion d'honneur medal, France's highest honour.

7 June ➻ Virginia Apgar

Born on 7 June 1909 in New Jersey, in 1952 the American scientist and doctor Virginia Apgar came up with a simple, but brilliant, five-point scoring method designed to focus on a newborn baby's vital signs just after being born as a way of predicting and improving child health.

Named after her, Apgar's system is still in use today all over the world.

8 June ⇒ Phan Thị Kim Phúc

You might not know Kim Phúc's name, but you will know her face. Phan Thị Kim Phúc became famous – without her permission or her intention – as the 'girl in the picture' or 'Napalm Girl' when she was photographed as a nine-year-old child in the Vietnam War on 8 June 1972, running naked down a road after a napalm attack. Napalm is a chemical weapon and Kim Phúc received third degree burns. It was the photographer himself who rushed her, and other injured children, to hospital in Saigon. She was not expected to survive.

The photograph won a Pulitzer Prize and helped turn public opinion against the war. But Kim Phúc found it distressing that her image was used as propaganda by both sides in the conflict, not only by American protesters campaigning against the war, but also by the Vietnamese communist regime. It was as if she had no control over her own image.

In 1997, Kim Phúc established the KIM Foundation International in Canada, to provide medical assistance and counselling for child victims of war. Years later, she was reunited with both the photographer who took that famous picture and the surgeons who saved her life. She is still an activist and campaigner, honoured all over the world for her efforts to promote peace.

9 June ➤➤ **Elizabeth Garrett Anderson**

The British medical pioneer, suffragist and politician Elizabeth Garrett Anderson was born on 9 June 1836. She was the first woman in Britain to qualify as a physician and surgeon and, in 1873, became the first woman to join the BMA (British Medical Association). The following year, she co-founded the London School of Medicine for Women (with Sophia Jex-Blake), the first hospital in the UK to be staffed wholly by women and the only teaching hospital in Britain to offer medical courses for women.

As if that was not enough, in 1883 Garrett Anderson became the first female dean of any medical school in Britain and was also the first female doctor of medicine in France. A political campaigner and suffragette – her sister was Millicent Garrett Fawcett – she became the first elected female mayor for the town of Aldeburgh in Suffolk in 1909. She died there in 1917.

10 June »→ Hedy Lamarr

The Austrian-born American movie star Hedy Lamarr was born in 1914. Considered one of the most beautiful women in the world, she made some thirty films between 1930 and 1958, including *Samson and Delilah*, which broke all box office records.

But Lamarr was also an engineer and the inventor of Wi-Fi. Incredible as it sounds, at the same time as taking Hollywood by storm, she was inventing a radio guidance system for Allied torpedoes. She applied for a patent for her discovery on 10 June 1941 and, although the technology was not put into use until the 1960s, it forms the basis for Bluetooth, GPS and Wi-Fi technology.

Lamarr is the only person, woman or man, to have both a star on the Hollywood Walk of Fame and to have been inducted into the American National Inventors Hall of Fame.

11 June ⇢ Julia Margaret Cameron

Julia Margaret Cameron was determined to make photography an art form. Born in Calcutta (now Kolkata) in India on 11 June 1815, she was recovering from an illness in South Africa in 1836 when she met the British astronomer John Herschel, a nephew of astronomer Caroline Herschel. He introduced her to photography.

However, Cameron's career as a photographer only began twelve years later, when one of her daughters gave her a camera. She discovered her own innovative and highly distinctive style, intentionally out-of-focus and dreamy, often including smudges, scratches and other little clues to her process.

Cameron's first exhibition was held in 1865 at the South Kensington Museum (now the Victoria and Albert Museum). Three years later, they gave her two rooms to set up a portrait studio, making her – in effect – the first-ever Artist in Residence at the V&A. Today, the museum holds more than 900 of Cameron's photographs and letters.

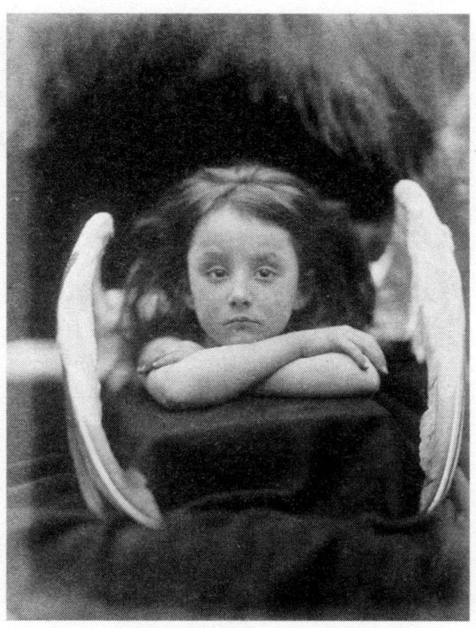

'I Wait' – a photograph of Rachel Gurney taken by Julia Margaret Cameron in 1872

12 June ➵ The Women's Prize for Fiction

On Thursday 12 June 2025, hundreds of writers, publishers, journalists, opinion-formers, artists, booksellers, judges past and present gathered in London's Bedford Square Gardens. Shortly before seven o'clock, I took to the stage as the Founder Director to host the celebrations for the thirtieth Women's Prize for Fiction.

The inspiration for the prize was an all-male Booker prize shortlist in 1991. That, of itself, is not a problem, in that the judges of any literary prize have the right to choose the books they like the most. The issue was that nobody noticed there were no women. We tried to imagine the outcry there might have been if there had been no men on the list – the press would have shouted 'foul' and claimed it was political. But the absence of women was seen as 'business as usual'. Since we knew that the majority of novels published were authored by women, the problem clearly wasn't a shortage of books to choose from. So, a group of us – writers, journalists, booksellers, literary agents, publishers – vowed to set up a prize for fiction that would ensure that, every year, a spotlight would shine on brilliant, inspiring, exceptional novels written in English by women from all over the world.

The Women's Prize for Fiction was born.

It was tough in the early years. We were criticized from all sides, accused of being sexist, women writers were attacked as second rate for failing to win the 'real prizes', but we knew the problem was not the quality of books written by women but rather a system that saw men's writing as 'literature' and women's books as less important. The simple truth is that readers – men, women, everybody – deserve to hear about the best novels being published.

The Women's Prize is now the biggest annual celebration of women's creativity in the world. Our first winner was Helen Dunmore for *A Spell of Winter*; our biggest-selling winner so far is Andrea Levy's *Small Island* and the 'winner of winners' chosen to celebrate twenty-five years of the WPF was Chimamanda Ngozi Adichie's *Half of a Yellow Sun*. The 2025 winner was *The Safekeep* by Yael van der Wouden, the first intersex woman to win the prize. As a special celebration for the thirtieth anniversary, an Outstanding Achievement Award was presented to Bernadine Evaristo in recognition of her contribution to literature and for her advocacy for other women.

In 2023, we launched a sister prize – the Women's Prize for Non-Fiction – to shine a spotlight on all the exceptional and groundbreaking writing that was often not getting the attention it deserved. The 2025 winner was palliative care doctor Rachel Clarke for *The Story of a Heart*.

13 June ➤➤ **Katharine Burr Blodgett**

The soundtrack to Katharine Burr Blodgett's life should be Johnny Nash's 'I Can See Clearly Now'. Why? Because the American physicist and chemist was the woman who invented 'invisible glass', a hugely important discovery for making spectacles, lenses, film cameras and periscopes.

Born in 1898, Burr Blodgett was the first woman awarded a doctorate from the University of Cambridge and the first female scientist at General Electric. On 13 June 1951, the first Katharine Burr Blodgett Day was celebrated in her home town of Schenectady, New York, where she lived with her partner, Gertrude Brown.

Christine de Pizan was born in Venice around 1364, then moved to Paris with her family when she was four or five when her father was appointed as a physician to the French court.

De Pizan was perhaps the first woman in France – maybe in all of Europe – to make her living solely by writing and teaching. She began working at the age of twenty-five, when her husband died leaving her with young children to support. She got caught up in costly cases in court trying to recover some of his earnings. One of the writs was issued on 14 June 1389. At that time it was unusual – almost unheard of – for a woman to take a man to court.

In her 1405 work *The Book of the City of Ladies*, de Pizan brought together famous women from history to build an imaginary city – using books as bricks to support her argument of how important a contribution women made to society. This and *The Treasure of the City of Ladies* (probably published in the same year) are also extraordinary because of their beautiful and glorious illustrations. She herself appears in some images and both books are rather like glossy magazines, giving an idea of the fashions of the time.

De Pizan also wrote *The Song of Joan of Arc* in 1429, celebrating the end of the siege of Orléans. Apart from the records of Jeanne's trial in 1431, it is the only surviving contemporary record of La Pucelle.

15 June »» Vera Atkins

Vera Rosenberg Atkins – who was born on 15 June 1908 in Romania to a German-Jewish father and a British-Jewish mother – was the intelligence officer in charge of France section (F section) for British intelligence during the Second World War.

Atkins came to the UK in 1937, when the clouds of war were already gathering, and joined the Special Operations Executive (SOE) in 1941. Her role was to recruit and deploy British agents, including some thirty-seven women. She is often seen as a controversial figure, not least because of suspicions surrounding the capture of one of her agents – 'Madeleine' – and the consequent deaths of several agents at the hands of the Nazis. But I can't help wonder if the fact she was a woman, and a Jewish woman at that, played a part in why her loyalty and competency were challenged.

Whatever the truth of the matter, after the war came to an end and the SOE was wound down, Atkins joined MI6 and went to look for her agents who had not returned. Thanks to her, plaques for the twelve female agents who died in the Nazi concentration camps were put up.

She died in 2000.

16 June ➻ **Valentina Tereshkova**

On 16 June 1963, the Soviet astronaut Valentina Tereshkova became the first woman to go into space aboard the spacecraft Vostok 6.

Born in 1937, Tereshkova was also active in Soviet politics. She directed the Soviet Women's Committee in 1968, and served as a member of the Supreme Soviet Presidium. In 2011, she was elected to the Russian parliament (the Duma) and – less wonderfully – was the person who removed the limits on how long Vladimir Putin could remain in office . . .

17 June ➤➤ Susan La Flesche Picotte

The pioneering First Nations American physician Susan La Flesche Picotte was born on the Omaha Reservation in north-east Nebraska on 17 June 1865. A reservation is an area of land set aside for First Nations tribes to live on, self-governed rather than being governed by the state or national government.

La Flesche Picotte was the first indigenous woman in the United States to take a medical degree. Having graduated top of her class, she returned home to look after a population of more than 1,300 people, many of whom were suffering significant ill-health due to poverty, displacement and discrimination. In 1913, she finally succeeded in opening a hospital in the reservation town of Walthill. She died there in 1915, having transformed her community.

18 June ➤➤ Gráinne O'Malley

The pirate queen and folk legend Gráinne O'Malley is a towering figure in 16th-century Irish history.

One of the legends is that when she asked to accompany her father on a trading trip to Spain, he refused on the grounds that her long hair would catch in the ship's ropes. As a reaction, she chopped off her hair, earning her the first of her nicknames, 'Gráinne Mhaol' – *mhaol* means 'bald', or 'cropped hair', in Irish.

When her father died, O'Malley took the helm as captain of the fleet and head of the O'Malley clan. In 1593, when her sons and half-brother were captured by the English, O'Malley sailed to England to petition Queen Elizabeth I for their release.

Surprisingly, given how she lived, she survived into her seventies and died in Rockfleet Castle on 18 June 1603.

19 June ➤➤ Regan Russell

On 19 June 2020, sixty-five-year-old Canadian animal rights activist and protester Regan Russell was run over and killed by a livestock transport truck at a demonstration outside a pig slaughterhouse in Ontario, Canada. The driver was convicted of causing death by careless driving.

Russell was a member of Toronto Pig Save, a branch of the animal rights organization Animal Save Movement, and a campaigner for living a compassionate vegan lifestyle. After her death, animal rights activists all over the world organized protests, from outside the Canadian High Commission in London to outside a food distribution centre in Mumbai, India.

20 June ➻ Margaret Maughan

Britain's first Paralympic gold medallist, at the first games in Rome in 1960, was archer, swimmer and bowling champion Margaret Maughan.

Born in Preston on 20 June 1928, Maughan was paralysed in a road accident in Malawi in 1959 and flown back to Britain to Stoke Mandeville hospital for treatment. There she took up archery, hoping it would help her keep in balance in her wheelchair, and discovered she was really good.

At about the same time, the Paralympic movement was growing. It had begun as a small gathering of Second World

War veterans in 1948, with a doctor at Stoke Mandeville hospital finding ways to help his patients. The first international games were held there four years later, when veterans from the Netherlands competed alongside British teams, and it became an annual fixture in the calendar.

The games in September 1960 in Rome are considered the first Paralympic Games. Twenty-three countries took part, sending 400 athletes – all in wheelchairs – who competed in eight sports. Maughan not only won a gold medal in archery, but she also won gold in the fifty-metres women's backstroke. Four years later, she won another gold in dartchery (the pairs archery competition) and then two silver medals in Toronto in 1976. Her final gold came in lawn bowls in the women's pairs in 1980.

In 2012, at the age of eighty-five and looking glorious in the British team's white and sky-blue tracksuit, Maughan lit the flame at the opening of the London 2012 Summer Paralympics.

21 June ➡ The Women's Sunday March, 1908

Some of the most iconic images of British suffragettes are photographs from the WPSU Women's Sunday March in London on 21 June 1908. What made it so special was not only the numbers involved – estimates say about half a million took part, men as well as women – but also that the marchers were encouraged to wear white.

The plan was that seven different groups would start at various muster points and come together in Hyde Park. Most of the leaders of the British suffrage movement were involved: Elizabeth Wolstenholme-Elmy, who was the first full-time employee of the British movement, led the marchers from Euston Road; Oldham's Annie Kenney headed the march from Paddington; Christabel Pankhurst and Bristolian Emmeline Pethick-Lawrence set off from Victoria Embankment.

Just imagine the sight in Hyde Park on that summer's day – white dresses, hats and sashes, with splashes of suffragette purple and green, banners flying beneath a blue sky.

Emmeline Pankhurst and Elizabeth Wolstenholme-Elmy at the head of the Women's March in Hyde Park, London, Sunday 21 June 1908

22 June ➤➤ **Cicely Saunders**

The founder of the modern hospice movement, Cicely Saunders, was born on 22 June 1918. She worked as a nurse, then as a social worker and physician, before devoting her time to creating a new medical speciality known as palliative care. Her vision was to provide an environment where terminally ill patients could be cared for in their final months, weeks or days in an environment that was more a 'home from home' than a hospital ward. Also, that the quality of their life as they were dying would be treated as just as important as the medical care they received.

Saunders opened the world's first purpose-built hospice, St Christopher's, in 1967. There are now more than 200 hospices in the UK.

She died there, in the hospice she had built, in 2005.

23 June ➻ **Summia Tora**

In Vienna on 23 June 2023, Summia Tora – an Afghan campaigner for women's rights and refugee rights – was one of six Afghan women awarded the CEU Open Society Prize. It's a prize awarded annually to an outstanding individual or organization whose work has contributed to a more open society. Tora – together with Pashtana Durrani, Munisa Mubariz, Tamana Zaryab Paryani, Aydin Sahba Yaquoby and Zeba Mirzayye – was honoured for her incredible courage, social activism, journalism and determination to fight gender discrimination in Afghanistan.

24 June ➤➤ Mary Prince

Mary Prince is thought to be the first Black woman to publish her autobiography. She was born in Bermuda in 1788 to an enslaved family of African descent. After being sold several times, she was brought to England as a servant in 1828.

On 24 June 1829, Prince petitioned the British parliament – unsuccessfully – to allow her to return to the West Indies as a free person to be reunited with her husband. She could not read or write, but after the court case, she dictated her life story to a young woman who lived in the home of a leading British anti-slavery campaigner. *The History of Mary Prince* was published in 1831 and her first-hand personal descriptions of the brutality of her life as an enslaved person had a huge effect on the abolitionist movement.

We don't know for certain where, or when, Prince died. There are records of her in 1833, two years after publication of her memoir, but after that there is nothing.

25 June ➛ Eloísa Díaz

The Chilean physician Eloísa Díaz was born on 25 June 1866. She was not only the first female doctor in Chile, but the first female doctor in the whole of South America.

In 1898, she was appointed director of Santiago's School Medical Service and went on to found nurseries and healthcare centres for the poor, school camps and school breakfast services so pupils would not go to the classroom hungry, and waged campaigns against tuberculosis and alcoholism.

26 June ➻ **Margaret Atwood**

Writing in 2012 about the genesis of her groundbreaking novel, the Canadian poet, author, environmentalist and essayist Margaret Atwood explained how she left Berlin in June 1984 with one hundred and fifty pages of a manuscript that would become *The Handmaid's Tale*. These were the dying years of the Cold War and Berlin was still divided. Atwood wrote by hand, then passed the pages over to a professional typist, letting the book take shape. Having returned to Canada, then gone to Alabama where she was teaching, she finished the novel in the early months of 1985. It came out in 1986 and has never been out of print, though it is banned in many US schools. The novel's vision of a totalitarian fundamentalist American Christian community, Gilead, that has stripped women of their rights and is obsessed with a fertility crisis is, in Trump's America in 2025, looking less like dystopian feminist fiction and more like social realism. Put simply, this is how democracy is dismantled and dictatorship takes hold in plain sight.

Atwood is one of the most significant, inventive and thrilling writers of the 20th and 21st centuries. The multi-award-winning author of novels, volumes of poetry, essays, librettos, children's books, graphic novels, non-fiction — including her magnificent book about the craft of writing, *Negotiating with the Dead*, her career spans more than six decades and Atwood shows no signs of easing up. In 2019, the sequel to *The Handmaid's Tale*, *The Testaments*, was joint winner of the Booker Prize for Fiction (with Bernardine Evaristo's *Girl, Woman, Other*) and her autobiography, *Book of Lives: A Memoir of Sorts*, will be published in November 2025.

A brilliant woman of great integrity, Atwood is courageous and bold, using the power of words and reasoned argument to illuminate and change the world. Her wisdom is needed now more than ever.

Margaret Atwood

27 June ➤➤ The Stratford Martyrs

During times of religious civil war, those who follow a different faith are likely to find themselves arrested, persecuted and even executed.

When Queen Mary I ascended to the English throne in 1553, after the death of her half-brother Edward, she attempted to return England to Catholicism and away from the new Protestant religion introduced by her father, Henry VIII. During her five-year reign, thousands of martyrs were burned at the stake for refusing to recant their Protestant faith. It is why she became known as 'Bloody Mary'.

Because their trial and conviction were recorded by theologian and historian John Foxe in his 1563 book *The Actes and Monuments* – commonly known as *Foxe's Book of Martyrs* – the Stratford Martyrs have a particular place in the history books. Eleven men and two women, Agnes George and Elizabeth Pepper (who was pregnant), were brought to trial. After a long process, where repeated attempts were made to force them to become Catholic, the thirteen were executed on 27 June 1556, either at Stratford-le-Bow in East London or possibly Stratford in Essex.

In 1879, a monument was erected in St John's churchyard in Stratford Broadway to commemorate them and others who were executed or tortured in Stratford during the reign of 'Bloody Mary'.

28 June »→ Queen Victoria

Born in May 1819 at Kensington Place in London, Victoria became queen of the United Kingdom of Great Britain and Ireland in 1837, on the death of her uncle, William IV. She was crowned in Westminster Abbey on 28 June 1838.

Victoria was arguably the most famous and powerful woman of her time. She gave her name to an era, the Victorian Age, there are more statues of her in the UK than any other person, and cities, states, lakes, railway stations and waterfalls all over the world are named after her.

When she died on her beloved Isle of Wight in January 1901 at the age of eighty-one, the newspapers were all printed with black edges. Her state funeral at Windsor Castle on 2 February was the largest gathering of European royalty ever and in churches large and small, throughout the British Isles and the British Empire, services were held at the same time.

Victoria had left detailed instructions for her funeral, and mementos of her family and friends were placed in her coffin, including a dressing gown that had belonged to her husband and a plaster cast of his hand, as well as family photos and a lock of hair belonging to her attendant John Brown, who worked as a ghillie – a type of gamekeeper – on her estates in Scotland.

Victoria's death marked the end of an era. The modern world was just around the corner . . .

29 June ➳ Ninette de Valois

Often called the 'Godmother of British and Irish Dance', there are few women who have had more influence in the world of classical dance than Ninette de Valois.

Born Edris Stannus in County Wicklow in Ireland in 1898, she was a teacher, dancer, choreographer and businesswoman. She changed her name, as was the fashion at the time, to sound European.

De Valois set up her first school – the Academy of Choreographic Art in London – at the end of June 1926. She danced with Diaghilev's Ballets Russes, established the Royal Ballet in 1931, then the Royal Ballet School, then the touring company that later became the Birmingham Royal Ballet.

She died in London in March 2001 at the age of 102. Since 2018, the Ninette de Valois Festival of Dance has been held annually in her hometown of Blessington.

Ninette de Valois performing in *Les Biches*

30 June ➤➤ Simone Veil

Born in 1927, feminist icon Simone Veil transformed the lives of French women. She was an activist, a magistrate and a campaigning politician. She is particularly remembered for her support of the 1974 act which gave French women safe access to contraception and for the 1975 act that decriminalized abortion in France and is known as the Veil Law.

Veil was a Holocaust survivor, imprisoned in both Auschwitz-Birkenau and Bergen-Belsen, and this no doubt contributed to her passion to transform the world for the better. She was the first woman to hold the position of President of the European Parliament and served as President of the Fondation pour la Mémoire de la Shoah for seven years.

She died in Paris on 30 June 2017. The following year, Veil became only the fifth woman to be buried in the Panthéon in Paris after a petition of many thousands of people demanded the government acknowledge her exceptional contribution to France.

Boys Can Be Feminists Too

It was 1985. I was twenty-three, living in London and I bought myself a ticket to a feminist conference. I remember the huge hall, stuffy in winter, maybe a thousand women. I remember the buzz of excitement and adrenaline, the sense that, together, we could change things. I was on my own and, I suppose, a little nervous about dipping my toe in the waters of collective action rather than just reading books about feminism and worrying about the state of the world. I was ready to think, to be part of something. To act.

The woman chairing the session had a new baby and, during the course of the session, her male partner brought the baby on to the stage so she could breastfeed. Then something awful happened. Some of the audience booed, they actually booed at the presence of a man in the room, even though he was being a supportive partner and the baby clearly needed to be fed.

I didn't understand their behaviour, not realizing that some women didn't feel that men should be included in feminism. I was also embarrassed and, worse, disappointed. More than anything, the incident taught me, as an idealistic young campaigner, that not all feminists think the same, that there are prejudices and bigotries in any group. It showed me that it was all right for me to agree with some of what was being said and disagree with other things.

My strong reaction to this seemingly small incident also confirmed in me a belief that, whatever the current feminist thinking was about collaboration, unless women and men worked together to change the world, to make things fairer for women, girls, non-binary and trans people, nothing fundamental would change. Divide and rule is how those in power protect their privilege, by encouraging those who should be working together in the face of injustice to turn on one another.

Today we call this being an ally. Being an ally is not about speaking *for* a group to which you do not belong, but rather using your voice to support justice and using your power and influence (if you have any) to make space for others to speak for themselves. This can be a tricky line to walk, but it's better to try, and get it wrong, than not to try at all. It is this form of advocacy that the UN campaigning organization HeForShe pursues. It invites men and people of all genders to stand in solidarity with women to create a bold, visible and united force for gender equality. So far, they have built a community of some two billion activists, supporting everything from reproductive rights to equal access to education.

Throughout history, there have always been men who have respected women and girls, who have fought for them to be treated fairly and have equal opportunities. I was lucky enough to have a wonderful father, and I have a brilliant husband and son, brothers-in-law and son-in-law, as well as male friends, all of whom support me and cheer me on.

Who are those men or boys in your life? Or, if you're a boy or a man, a father, brother, uncle, friend or teacher reading this book, does this sound like you? Are you someone who believes that everybody, whoever they are, whatever they look like, deserves the same chances, the same respect? Or do you feel intimidated and bullied into silence when you hear others around you saying offensive things about girls? Do you feel bad about not challenging sexist behaviour?

So, as we hit the half-way point in our celebration of feminist history for every day of the year, this seems the right place to give a shout-out to some of the fabulous male allies throughout history who understand that every man and boy has the power to work for what is good and fair, rather than allow themselves to be drawn into a world that sees women and girls as the enemy (looking at you, Taliban and Andrew Tate).

Nine hundred years ago in 12th-century Jerusalem, King Baldwin II was the father of four daughters. Rather than put his wife aside and marry again, in order to try to have a son and heir, Baldwin schooled his exceptional eldest daughter, Melisende (see 11 September), in the ways of ruling and the court, so that she could inherit the kingdom from him. This would be rare in some countries today, let alone for a medieval Crusader State.

> 'The principle which regulates the existing social relations between the two sexes – the legal subordination of one sex to the other – is wrong in itself, and now one of the chief hindrances to human improvement; and that it ought to be replaced by a principle of perfect equality, admitting no power or privilege on the one side, nor disability on the other.'

John Stuart Mill wrote these words in 1869. He was a 19th-century British political and social philosopher, a member of the Liberal Party and founder – along with his wife Harriet Taylor Mill – of much feminist economic thought. When they married in 1851, Mill refused to take possession of his wife's wealth and inheritance – as men were allowed to do under Victorian law of the time – and they worked together on books including *The Subjection of Women*, which argued that gender inequality was both a moral injustice and economically short-sighted. Mill was the second MP to call for women's suffrage after Henry Hunt.

A contemporary of John Stuart Mill was the African American abolitionist, social reformer, writer and civil rights activist Frederick Douglass. A former enslaved person – he escaped his captors in 1833 – he was one of the men present at the Seneca Falls Convention, outside New York, in 1848, the first-known suffrage meeting in the USA arguing for women's right to vote (see 19 July). Douglass was the only Black person who spoke that day, male or female.

In the same year, Jyotirao and Savitribai Phule established India's first school for girls in Pune, Maharashtra (see 24 September). Savitribai was only nine years old and illiterate when she was married to Jyotirao. He taught her to read, then supported her goals to become a teacher. There is no doubt their partnership, built on mutual respect and admiration, transformed educational opportunities for girls in India.

In 1903, the Nobel committee intended to ignore Marie Skłodowska-Curie's (see 7 November) contribution to her husband's work in physics. Pierre Curie, the French scientist, refused to accept the Nobel Prize in Physics unless Marie was honoured equally. Other male scientists were not so honourable and claimed their female colleagues' work as their own . . .

Living male allies include Ziauddin Yousafzai, who founded a series of girls' schools in Pakistan and spoke out against the Taliban when they started to deny girls an education. He is perhaps best known in the UK for being the father of Malala (see 9 October), and is the co-founder and board member of the Malala Fund. He remains a fierce advocate for women's rights and education rights for all.

The Chilean-American actor Pedro Pascal – star of *The Mandalorian*, *The Last of Us* and *The Fantastic Four: First Steps* – is an outspoken feminist and a vocal trans ally too. At the London premiere in April 2025 of the film *Thunderbolts*, Pascal wore one of designer Conner Ives's 'Protect the Dolls' T-shirts ('doll' is an affectionate nickname for transwomen and ultrafeminine transpeople, originating from the Black and Latino ballroom dance culture in America during the 1980s).

There is still a significant pay gap between men and women in film and television, but several male actors have spoken out against it. When interviewed by the *Radio Times* in 2018, British actor Benedict Cumberbatch said: 'Ask what women are being paid, and say: "If she's not paid the same as the men, I'm not doing it."' And in 2019 *Black Panther* star Chadwick Boseman, who died in 2024 from colon cancer, was actor and producer on *21 Bridges*. When the studio refused to pay his co-star Sienna Miller a decent amount of money, he took a cut in his own salary and shared it with her.

When Scottish tennis star Andy Murray was interviewed in 2017, after losing in the quarter-final of the Wimbledon Championships to American Sam Querrey, Murray called out a reporter in the post-match press conference who began his interview by saying: 'Sam is the first US player to reach a major semi-final since 2009.' Murray immediately corrected him, noting that he was the first *male* player – not the first player. It wasn't the first time he'd corrected journalists determined to overlook the exceptional achievements of Venus and Serena Williams. Murray, who declared himself a feminist, also said: 'I have been involved in sport all my life and the level of the sexism is unreal.' It was these, and other moments, that led the *Independent* newspaper to run a feature in 2019 called 'Andy Murray's 10 best feminist moments'.

Sticking with sport, British footballer Ian Wright, who played for Crystal Palace, Arsenal and England before becoming a television pundit, has spoken about the effects of domestic violence and is an outspoken and passionate supporter of the women's game. Ben Hurst, Head of Facilitation and Training at Beyond Equality, is an activist and educator who advocates for gender equality and is admired for his work on challenging toxic masculinity. And journalist Matt Shea is doing brilliant work exposing harmful online misogyny, and the ways in which teenage boys are being targeted and manipulated by influencers seeking to make money out of peddling hate of women and girls.

It's hard for everyone – girls, boys, non-binary and trans – to work out who they are when being constantly bombarded with lies and misinformation via social media, designed to prey on insecurities and to breed fear. It's why it's so important that men and boys who are trying to make a difference should be supported in their attempts to make a change for good in the world alongside the brilliant campaigning women and girls. It's not about us versus them – that's what those who want to benefit themselves at the expense of the rest of us want us to believe. Rather, it's about seeing the good and rejecting the bad.

Most of all, it's all about using your voice, about having the courage to speak out when you see sexism or misogyny – in the classroom, on the train, online – and about having the bravery to stand against prejudice and unfairness.

United we stand, divided we fall. Boys can be feminists too.

JULY

July

1 July ➤➤ **Kimpa Vita**

This was the last night on Earth for the Congolese mystic and religious leader, Kimpa Vita.

Born in 1684, she founded her own Christian sect, Antonianism, preaching that Christ, and other Christian leaders, in fact originated from the Kingdom of Kongo in central Africa rather than the Holy Land.

The Kingdom of Kongo was a flourishing country rich in ivory, copper, salt and cattle, which meant in the 16th and 17th centuries it became a battleground between rival indigenous tribes and Portuguese and Dutch colonizers. Many consider Vita an early anti-slavery campaigner and she challenged the male priests and governors of the time. She was finally caught, tried for crimes against the Crown and condemned as a heretic. She was burned at the stake on 2 July 1706.

2 July ⇒ Nawal El Saadawi

At 6.30 p.m. on 2 July 2016, the Egyptian feminist, psychiatrist and author Nawal El Saadawi took to the stage at the British Library in London with publishing genius Margaret Busby. The session was called 'On Being a Woman Writer' and it was the headline event of the 2016 Africa Writes festival. A hushed silence fell over the packed audience as the eighty-five-year-old El Saadawi came into view.

Born in a village outside of Cairo in 1931, El Saadawi wrote more than fifty books, including *Woman at Point Zero*, her groundbreaking work of feminist criticism; *Women and Sex*, which was banned in Egypt for almost two decades after

El Saadawi protesting on her 80th birthday in 2011, as part of the Egyptian Revolution

its publication; and *Memoirs from the Women's Prison*, written on toilet paper with a smudged eyebrow pencil.

Throughout her life, El Saadawi faced exile and death threats. She founded several campaigning organizations, including the Egyptian section of the Arab Women's Solidarity Association. She was a brilliant thinker and teacher who grew more, not less, radical with age. In 2020, the year before she died, *Time* magazine named her as one of the hundred most influential women of the 20th century.

WOMEN are half the society.
YOU CANNOT HAVE A REVOLUTION WITHOUT WOMEN.

YOU CANNOT HAVE DEMOCRACY WITHOUT WOMEN.

YOU CANNOT HAVE EQUALITY WITHOUT WOMEN.

YOU CANNOT HAVE ANYTHING WITHOUT WOMEN.

Nawal El Saadawi

3 July ⇥ Joan Littlewood

In July 1963, the epic, satirical, groundbreaking musical *Oh! What a Lovely War* had just begun its West End run, having transferred from Theatre Royal Stratford East. The show was developed by the legendary theatre director Joan Littlewood and her ensemble at the Theatre Workshop. It played at Wyndham's Theatre for more than a year, then went on to triumph Broadway and in productions all over the world.

Known as the 'Mother of Modern Theatre', Littlewood was born in London in 1914 and was an outspoken, vibrant, energetic theatre maker determined to put working-class and under-represented voices on the stage. She trained as an actor at the Royal Academy of Dramatic Art, though it didn't suit her, and quickly realized that setting up her own ways of working would be the way to radicalize post-war theatre. She believed in culture being for everybody, and in diversity of expression. Because of her socialist beliefs and support for the Communist Party of Great Britain, Littlewood was for many years on MI5 and Special Branch's list of people to keep an eye on.

Working with an ensemble of actors, her Theatre Workshop lived and breathed the plays they were creating, among them Shelagh Delaney's 1958 *A Taste of Honey*, which premiered at Stratford East in 1958. She also directed and played the lead in the UK premiere of Bertolt Brecht's *Mother Courage and Her Children*.

Littlewood died in London 2002.

4 July ➤➤ **Rebecca Lenkiewicz**

In a large room not far from Waterloo Station in July 2008, the cast of *Her Naked Skin* was rehearsing for a world premiere. Outside, torrential rain and thundery downpours were forecast, and blustery winds were turning the umbrellas inside out on the South Bank in London. Inside, the atmosphere was electric. For Rebecca Lenkiewicz's play – set partly in Holloway Prison and centred on the lesbian affair between two women caught up in the suffragette movement across the class barrier – was to be the first original play by a female writer to be performed in the Olivier Theatre of the Royal National Theatre. The stakes could not be higher.

Her Naked Skin opened three weeks later, on 24 July. Directed by Howard Davies, with Lesley Manville and Jemima Rooper in the leading roles, it firmly planted a feminist flag in the heart of the British theatre establishment.

5 July →→ **Sarah Siddons**

Let's go back in theatre history to the 18th century to the start of what we might call 'celebrity culture'.

At the heart of it was the Welsh actress Sarah Siddons. Newspapers printed pictures and ran gossip columns about her private life, and thousands of people knew her name, even though most of them had never seen her act. Nearly four hundred artists painted her portrait, including Joshua Reynolds and Thomas Gainsborough.

Portrait of Sarah Siddons playing Euphrasia in *The Grecian Daughter* at the British Theatre, 1771

Siddons was born on 5 July 1755 in Brecon into a theatre family, at a time when theatre was becoming respectable. Before that, actresses were seen as little better than prostitutes. She came to London in 1782 and quickly became known as the 'Queen of Drury Lane', after London's most prestigious theatre. She was famous for her portrayal of Lady Macbeth and other tragic roles. Though accused of promiscuity and of being a bad mother to her seven children (for working rather than staying home to look after them), Siddons cleverly used her own domestic experiences in her portrayal of the characters she played and often appeared on stage when she was pregnant. This was all but unheard of at the time.

After a long and fabulous career, Siddons died in London in 1831. In 1876, she became the first woman to be honoured by a blue plaque in York Place (now Upper Baker Street). Sadly, when the house was demolished in 1905, the plaque was lost.

6 July ➤➤ Frida Kahlo

Frida Kahlo is one of the most influential, and original, artists of all time.

Born on 6 July 1907 in Mexico to a German father of Hungarian descent and a mother of Spanish and First Nation American descent, Kahlo suffered from polio when she was a child. Then a serious bus accident when she was eighteen left her in chronic pain with many medical problems that would last for the rest of her life.

Photograph of Frida Kahlo

Despite this – or perhaps because of these challenges – Kahlo produced extraordinary art. She nearly studied medicine and her interest in the human body is evident in much of her work, particularly her uncompromising and brightly coloured self-portraits. They are unsettling, visceral and challenging. Look at the 1932 work *Henry Ford Hospital*, where she pictures herself bleeding on a hospital bed.

Kahlo took inspiration from Mexican popular culture and folk art to explore gender, sex, class, race, identity, suffering, mixing her own story with fantastical and fantasy elements. After her marriage to fellow artist Diego Rivera in 1929, she started to wear the traditional Tehuana dress that became her trademark – a flowered headdress, a loose blouse, a long, ruffled skirt and gold jewellery.

Their marriage was tumultuous – Rivera was repeatedly unfaithful, and Kahlo also had affairs with both women and men – and she self-medicated with drugs and alcohol. Her already fragile health declined yet further. Although her first solo exhibition was in New York in 1938, her first solo exhibition in Mexico was not until 1953, shortly before her death at the age of forty-seven the following year.

7 July ⇥ Sandra Day O'Connor

Born in Texas in 1930, the lawyer, Republican politician and judge Sandra Day O'Connor was the first woman in America to lead a state senate, the first woman to have her name attached to a law school and, on 7 July 1981, was the first woman nominated to the Supreme Court in the United States of America. She served until 2006.

Her appointment was significant for the lives of women and girls. Though conservative by nature, O'Connor was fiercely independent and a passionate advocate for the rule of law. She was also a shining example of how to work constructively with people you disagreed with. She was known for being courteous and listening to other people's points of view, even when she was opposed to what they were saying. When she was proposed for the Supreme Court, the Senate voted 99 in favour and 0 against, showing how all political sides respected her. O'Connor was also a strong believer in mentoring and leading by example. A true role model of how people working together for the common good is more effective than simply opposing anything said by another political party.

O'Connor died in Arizona in 2023.

Even in my OWN TIME and in my OWN LIFE, I HAVE WITNESSED A REVOLUTION.

Sandra Day O'Connor

8 July ➤➤ Artemisia Gentileschi

Meet another of the world's most significant and influential painters, the Italian artist Artemisia Gentileschi.

She was born in Rome on 8 July 1593. When she was seventeen years old, she was raped by a friend of her father. Against all traditions of the time, she refused to be shamed into silence. Instead, Gentileschi took her rapist to court. She was tortured with a thumbscrew to 'verify' her evidence, but she held firm and won her case.

Gentileschi channelled her own experience of male violence and injustice into her magnificent, bold paintings. She produced works inspired by scenes from the Bible and classical literature, but seen through a female lens, such as *Judith Slaying Holofernes* and *Jael and Sisera*. In her retelling of *Susanna and the Elders*, two older men are whispering and looming over a young woman. The threat is clear.

Gentileschi painted herself into history too, for example with *Self-Portrait as Catherine of Alexandria*, and was the first woman elected to the prestigious Accademia delle Arti del Disegno in Florence.

We don't know exactly when she died – though she was still accepting commissions in 1654 – but it's possible she was a victim of the plague that swept through Naples in 1656. She has a place setting in Judy Chicago's *The Dinner Party* (see 20 July).

9 July ➤➤ Chloe Cooley

Sometimes narrowing down on the real-life experience of one person is a more effective way to change public opinion. It makes something personal, not theoretical or abstract.

This was the case with Chloe Cooley, who was a young Black enslaved woman living in Upper Canada in the late 18th century. The area where she lived was being taken over by settlers from the United States. Against Cooley's wishes, her owner forced her into a boat in 1793 to cross the Niagara River in order to sell her in the United States. She was terrified, tied up with rope and begging not to be taken. A bystander witnessed this abuse and reported Cooley's owner to the authorities. Although charges against him were dropped, this shocking incident helped towards getting the Act to Limit Slavery in Upper Canada passed in July that same year.

Sadly, nothing is known about what happened to Cooley after the court case – and there are no known images of her – but sometimes one story, one human story, can make a huge difference.

10 July ➤➤ Jane Grey

Jane Grey was the grand-niece of the Tudor king Henry VIII. After Henry died in 1547, his son Edward VI became king. But he was still a child, and sickly, and only ruled for six years. After his death, the throne should have passed to his half-sister Mary. But since she was a Catholic and England was now a Protestant country, Grey's ambitious father-in-law hatched a plan to put Jane on the throne instead and persuaded the dying Edward to write a will removing his half-sisters from the succession.

To start with, it looked as if the plan would work and Jane was proclaimed queen on 10 July 1553. But support for Mary was growing; most of Jane's supporters abandoned her and the men who ruled England – the Privy Council – changed their minds and nine days later declared Mary the rightful queen. Since then, Jane has been known as the 'Nine Day Queen'.

She was held prisoner in the Tower of London. In November 1553, she was found guilty of treason and handed a death sentence. Mary wanted to spare her life, but the continued plotting of Jane's father-in-law made that impossible. Jane was executed on 12 February 1554. She was only sixteen, or perhaps, seventeen years old.

11 July ➤➤ Harper Lee

One of the biggest-selling, most studied, most loved novels of all time is Harper Lee's *To Kill a Mockingbird*.

It is a coming-of-age story of a young American girl, Scout, telling of her life with her brother and father in a predominantly white, small Southern town. Her father, Atticus Finch, is an attorney, who believes in justice and racial equality. But his faith is shaken when he finds himself called upon to defend a Black man, Boo Radley, falsely accused of rape, before an all-white jury. The book lays bare the roots and consequences of racism and prejudice, and how good and evil can exist side by side in a community, or even in one person.

The novel was published on 11 July 1960.

In 2025, certain US states have removed *To Kill a Mockingbird* from the school curriculum. Some of the reasons given are that the language and themes are too serious, that it is racist, and even that it makes people feel uncomfortable! It's as if they don't understand that the purpose of a great book is not only to entertain, but to help readers better understand the world in which we live and how to right the wrongs of the past . . .

12 July ➻ Olive Morris

Born in Jamaica in 1952, Olive Morris came to the UK as a young woman. A radical Black feminist committed to ending racial, sexual and class oppression, she was a member of the British Black Panther movement, was pivotal in the campaign for squatters' rights, was a member of the Manchester Black Women's Cooperative and a Co-Founder of the Brixton Black Women's Group.

Morris died on 12 July 1979 at the age of twenty-seven, having made a huge impact in her short life. In 1986, Lambeth Council in south London named its new building on Brixton Hill after her and the Remembering Olive Collective (ROC) set up the Olive Morris Memorial Awards in 2011 to offer financial support to young women of Asian or African descent. She was also one of eight Black women named in *The Voice* magazine in 2018 who have contributed hugely to the development of Britain.

13 July ➛ Annie Nightingale

On 13 July 1985, in London and Philadelphia, the largest ever charity concert took place after months of planning – Live Aid. Bringing together many of the greatest performers of the time, Live Aid was the brainchild of the Irish singer-songwriter and campaigner Bob Geldof.

More than 1.5 billion people worldwide tuned in to watch the seventy-plus artists and bands strut their stuff. Performers in London included U2, Paul McCartney, Queen, David Bowie and the Band of the Coldstream Guards. Then coverage switched to Madonna, Phil Collins, The Beach Boys and Joan Baez in Philadelphia.

The anchor for the BBC's broadcast of the Philadelphia show was the British DJ Annie Nightingale. In her long career, she transformed the careers of countless musicians and bands, and changed the opportunities for women in the music industry. She was the first female presenter on BBC Radio 1 in the 1970s, she was the first female presenter for BBC's landmark music show *The Old Grey Whistle Test*, and was the longest-serving female broadcaster of all time.

14 July ➵ **Pema Chödrön**

Pema Chödrön was born Deirdre Blomfield-Brown in New York City on 14 July 1936.

A Tibetan Buddhist nun and teacher, she was the first American in the Vajrayana tradition – a form of Buddhism that dates back to India in the 6th century BCE – to become a fully ordained nun. She has published a dozen books, including the global bestseller *When Things Fall Apart*, which came out in 1996.

15 July ➤➤ **Berta Cáceres Flores**

Honduras is one of the most dangerous countries in the world to be an environmental or human rights activist, as the Lenca leader Berta Cáceres Flores discovered to her cost.

Cáceres was born in 1971 and was a co-founder and coordinator of the Council of Popular and Indigenous Organizations of Honduras (COPINH), an organization set up to fight the growing threats to Lenca communities by illegal logging and theft of their territory. In 2006, she helped mount a campaign against the building of the Agua Zarca Dam, protesting peacefully against national government and local mayors.

For years, COPINH managed to disrupt development, but finally approval for the dam was given. In 2013, Cáceres organized a road blockade to prevent work taking place. On 15 July, soldiers of the Honduran military opened fire on protesters.

Despite repeated intimidation, death threats and false charges brought against her, Cáceres successfully kept the construction equipment out of the proposed site of the dam. In the end, having failed to silence her, gunmen burst into her home on 3 March 2016 and shot her down in cold blood. Two years later, a Honduran court ruled that the executives of the company building the dam had ordered her assassination. In 2019, seven men were convicted of her murder. In 2022, the former president of the company attempting to build the dam was convicted of organizing the assassination plot. The banks financing the dam construction pulled their funding from the project, but the Lenca continue to fight for their land.

16 July ➤➤ Ida B. Wells

The barnstorming 19th-century African American investigative journalist, campaigner, civil rights leader and teacher Ida B. Wells was born into slavery in Mississippi on 16 July 1862. Six months later, on New Year's Day 1863, the Emancipation Proclamation was passed, freeing all enslaved people in the Confederate States. But because America was still in the grips of a civil war, most African Americans did not gain their freedom until after the Union victory in 1865.

Wells started to write for a local paper in Memphis, Tennessee, covering stories of racial segregation and inequality. Later, she became co-owner. She gave lectures about women's suffrage and was one of the loudest voices against lynching – a widespread practice of hanging those accused of a crime rather than allowing them a trial, almost always an act of violence against Black men. Wells published pamphlets and books demanding an end to the vile practice. A

Photograph of Ida B. Wells, circa 1890s

white mob destroyed her offices, but she continued to speak out.

Six years after Wells's death in 1931, a Jewish-American teacher called Abel Meeropol published a poem called 'Strange Fruit' as a protest against lynching, which was still happening. In 1939, the song was recorded by the singer Billie Holiday and became a worldwide hit. It helped bring about an end to this form of violence that had been allowed to continue for a century and more.

Wells was a woman of great courage and stamina. In 2020, in honour of her many achievements, she was awarded a Special Citation by the Pulitzer Prize 'for her outstanding and courageous reporting on the horrific and vicious violence against African Americans during the era of lynching'.

17 July ➤➤ Eunice Newton Foote

Would it surprise you to learn that the phenomenon known as global warming was first identified as far back as 1856?

The American suffragist, scientist and inventor Eunice Newton Foote was born in Connecticut on 17 July 1819. In 1856, she discovered what we now call 'greenhouse gases'. Having done experiment after experiment to double and triple check her findings, she tried to persuade the American scientific community to let her speak. They would not listen and, in August of that year, Foote was forced to sit in the audience at an AAAS (American Association for the Advancement of Science) meeting while a male scientist presented her research. He did a terrible job! He failed to recognize the implications of her discovery – that's to say that increased carbon dioxide in the atmosphere would cause global warming – so he didn't get across how important Foote's discovery was.

Frustrated, Foote tried again. But because she couldn't explain exactly *how* the greenhouse effect worked, when another scientist figured out that piece of the puzzle three years later, the discovery was credited to him rather than her. It wasn't until 2011, 123 years after her death, that her critical role was acknowledged.

18 July ➡ Nadia Comăneci

On 18 July 1976 there was a heatwave in Britain, Elton John and Kiki Dee were at the top of the charts with 'Don't Go Breaking My Heart' and, at the summer Olympics in Montreal, Canada, a fourteen-year-old gymnast from Romania became the first person to score a perfect 10 on the uneven bars. Nadia Comăneci went on to receive six more perfect 10s, on her way to winning three gold medals.

Four years later at the 1980 Moscow summer Olympics, Comăneci took another two gold medals and scored two more perfect 10s. She holds the record as the youngest ever gymnastics all-round champion, and since the eligibility rules have been revised, it's a record that can now never be broken.

At the Paris summer Olympic games in July 2024, American-Romanian Comăneci was one of five iconic sporting legends – along with French footballer Zinedine Zidane, Spanish tennis player Rafael Nadal, American sprinter Carl Lewis and tennis superstar Serena Williams – to carry the Olympic torch during the opening ceremony.

19 July ➳ The Seneca Falls Convention, 1848

Advertising itself as an opportunity to discuss the 'social, civil and religious condition and rights of women', the Seneca Falls Convention was the first women's rights conference in America.

Held at the Wesleyan Methodist Chapel, it opened on 19 July in the little town of Seneca Falls, in upstate New York. Many of the leading lights of the American suffrage movement – including Lucretia Mott, Elizabeth Cady Stanton, Amelia Bloomer and Eunice Newton Foote – were there. The African American abolitionist and social reformer Frederick Douglass also spoke, the only Black person allowed a platform.

At the end of the second day, a 'Declaration of Sentiments' was published with 100 of the 300 people who attended signing the document. Despite the fact that the voices of Black women and other women of colour were excluded, it is considered the beginning of the national women's suffrage movement in America.

Copy of the signature page of the Declaration of Sentiments, U.S. Library of Congress

20 July ▶▶ Judy Chicago

Finally, we get to meet Judy Chicago, the American artist who was born on this day in 1939 and created the iconic 1979 artwork *The Dinner Party*.

A magnificent piece of installation art, Chicago created place settings at the table for thirty-nine mythical and historical famous women, including Kali, Boudica, Hypatia, Trota of Salerno, Christine de Pizan, Artemisia Gentileschi, Caroline Herschel, Ethel Smyth, Sacajawea, Sojourner Truth, Theodora of Byzantium and Georgia O'Keeffe. As well as a hand-painted plate, ceramic cutlery and glass, or goblet, each place also has a napkin with an embroidered golden edge that represents the achievement, or character, of the woman who might sit there.

On the Heritage Floor on which the table stands, there are white handmade porcelain tiles with the names of another 998 notable women (and one man, included by mistake!). Drawing on traditional female art forms such as textile arts and painted china, banners were hung in the doorway as you went into the exhibition intending to 'express the belief and hope that once reverence for the feminine is re-established on Earth, a balance will be restored to human existence'.

The work is powerful, idealistic and, although perhaps not as diverse as it would be if Chicago was making it today, it is a stunning tribute from one female artist to the amazing women of the past. More than anything, it is an illustration of how art can put women back into history.

In the summer of 2023, there were only two topics of conversation in the film world – *Oppenheimer*, starring Cillian Murphy, Robert Downey Jr and Emily Blunt, and the feminist comedy *Barbie*. Both films were released in the United States on 21 July and went head-to-head. The phenomenon 'Barbenheimer' was born, with audiences turning up to cinemas to watch both as a double bill.

The co-writer and director of *Barbie* was thirty-nine-year-old California-born American actress, screenwriter and director Greta Gerwig. Girls, boys, women, men, everybody flocked to see Margot Robbie bring the pretty-in-pink Mattel Barbie Doll to life. It had a brilliant soundtrack – with vocals from Lizzo, Dua Lipa and Charli XCX – and the all-star cast included Ryan Gosling, America Ferrera and Helen Mirren as the narrator.

Barbie was a triumph. And Gerwig became the first solo female director to gross more than $1 billion worldwide.

22 July ➻ Mary Magdalene

According to the gospels of the New Testament, Mary Magdalene was a woman who travelled with Jesus as one of his followers and witnessed his Crucifixion and Resurrection. She is mentioned by name twelve times in the Bible, more than most of the male apostles and more than any other woman in the gospels except for those in Jesus's family. She was important, powerful and respected.

However, in the centuries after the Crucifixion – which was the form of execution used by the Romans in the countries such as the Holy Land they had occupied – commentators tried to destroy her reputation by portraying her as a 'fallen' woman, that's to say a prostitute. In 591 CE, Pope Gregory gave a sermon identifying Mary Magdalene as the 'sinful woman' mentioned in the gospel of Luke. This trashing of her character – perhaps out of fear, perhaps out of the developing Christian Church wanting to exclude women from positions of leadership – continued until 1969, when another Pope (Paul VI) stamped on the gossip and ruled that Pope Gregory had been wrong.

It's impossible to know who the real Mary Magdalene might have been. But she was made a saint in the Catholic Church before the Reformation in the 15th century, and is the patron saint of apothecaries, of penitent sinners, tanners, glovers and even hairdressers . . .

Her feast day is 22 July.

23 July ⇒ Jane Goodall

Over the page are the words of the pioneering English zoologist and anthropologist Jane Goodall, who, in July 1960, arrived in Gombe Stream National Park in Tanzania to study chimpanzee behaviour in the wild. She is the world's leading primatologist – that's to say, a scientist who studies primates like monkeys and apes.

Goodall was born in London in 1934. Travelling the world armed with little more than a notebook, binoculars and a passion for wildlife, her love affair with Africa began when she visited Kenya in 1957. But it was her research in Tanzania, observing how chimpanzees made and used tools, that revolutionized attitudes to animal behaviour. In more than sixty years of groundbreaking work, Goodall has campaigned to protect chimpanzees from extinction and has redefined species conservation to embrace environmental needs.

In January 2025, Goodall was presented with the Presidential Medal of Freedom by Joe Biden. Of the nineteen recipients, three other trailblazing women were also honoured: the magazine editor and fashion guru Anna Wintour, the politician Hillary Rodham Clinton and Fannie Lou Hamer, a founder of the Mississippi Freedom Democratic Party, a leading civil rights activist challenging the exclusion of Black voices who laid the groundwork for the 1965 Voting Rights Act.

THERE IS STILL so much in the WORLD WORTH fighting for. So much that is BEAUTIFUL, SO MANY people WORKING TO reverse the HARM, to HELP ALLEVIATE the SUFFERING.

And SO MANY young PEOPLE DEDICATED to making this a BETTER WORLD.

Jane Goodall

24 July ⇢ Matilda of Tuscany

The Italian medieval queen, Matilda of Tuscany – also known as Matilda of Canossa – died on this day in 1115.

Like most nobly born women of the time, her life was a succession of marriages for influence, and to secure succession, and she had little choice in the matter. At the same time, Matilda was also one of the most powerful women in the medieval era and became a leading political figure in medieval Europe. She was a military commander and expert negotiator in the murky world of territorial and papal conflicts of the time, she founded many churches, monasteries and nunneries, and even found time to encourage the growing of the Lambrusco grape to make wine. These days, the annual blind wine-tasting in Italy to determine the best Lambruscos is called the *Concorso Matilde* or the Matilda Awards.

So, let's raise a glass to Matilda – and all the strong women of history – who take control of their own lives and refuse to allow others to order them around . . .

25 July ➻ Louise Joy Brown

This is a very special birthday. Because on 25 July 1978, a little girl called Louise Joy Brown was born at Oldham and District General Hospital in the Pennines. She was the very first baby in the world to be conceived via IVF (in vitro fertilization).

At the time, Brown was described as a 'test tube baby' – the actual jar is kept on display in the Science Museum in London – but she prefers the term IVF. Her birth was nerve-racking for everybody involved: the scientists who'd pioneered the technique, the doctors and nurses at the hospital, and most of all the family themselves. She was born by Caesarean section – where the baby is removed surgically from the womb rather than being born vaginally – and the operation was filmed by the doctors, to prove to the world that IVF was not a hoax. Some religious groups campaigned against the procedure, others criticized the Browns for letting the cameras record it, but no one denied it was a groundbreaking moment in medical history.

One of the three people – with Robert Edwards and Patrick Steptoe – involved in pioneering IVF treatment was British nurse, lab technician and embryologist Jean Purdy. Though she was co-founder of Bourn Hall Clinic, the world's first IVF clinic, her contribution was overlooked for thirty years, despite Edwards' attempts to have her acknowledged too, and her significance only really became more widely known in the 2010s. She (and Steptoe) also missed out on a Nobel Prize – though Edwards was honoured – because a Nobel cannot be awarded posthumously. Purdy died from skin cancer in 1985 at the age of only thirty-nine.

Once it was clear that IVF worked, women queued up for the treatment. The fortieth baby born through IVF, in 1982, was Louise's sister, Natalie. It's now estimated that perhaps as many as twelve million children have been born through IVF and other assisted reproductive technologies worldwide, bringing joy to so many families and friends.

Perhaps you are one of them?

26 July ⇝ The First Women's Cricket Match, 1745

The world's first recorded women's cricket match was played on Gosden Common near Guildford, Surrey, on 26 July 1745 between 'eleven maids of Bramley' and 'eleven maids of Hambledon'. Both teams dressed in white, but the Bramley lasses wore blue ribbons and the Hambledon ladies wore red. Hambledon won. The match was reported in the *Reading Mercury* and attracted a large, and enthusiastic, local crowd.

Now, women's cricket is one of the most popular sports worldwide. Stars include India's Venkatacher Kalpana, Australian Belinda Clark, New Zealander Sarah Illingworth and Pakistan's Sajjida Shah, who made her international debut in 2000 at the age of twelve. In 2009, England's Claire Taylor was named as one of *Wisden*'s five cricketers of the year. *Wisden* is the bible of the cricketing world and it was the first time in its 120-year-history that a woman was included.

27 July ➤➤ Jeanne (Jean) Baret

The French plant collector, explorer and natural scientist Jeanne (Jean) Baret was born on 27 July 1740. She is the first woman known to have circumnavigated the globe on a ship.

Passing as a man, and calling herself Jean, Baret enlisted as a valet and assistant to the naturalist, Philibert Commerçon, on board an expedition ship. Jean was an expert botanist herself. The expedition headed first to Uruguay, then arrived in Tahiti in 1768. This part of her story is a little sketchy, but it seems that it was here she was revealed to be a woman. However, she was not thrown off the expedition and continued on to Papua New Guinea, Indonesia, Madagascar and Mauritius.

After Commerçon's death, Baret seems to have run a tavern in Port Louis (we know this because she was fined for selling alcohol on a Sunday) before returning to France around 1774 or 1775. In 1785, she was given a pension by the Marine Ministry, suggesting that her reputation as a botanist was secure in her own lifetime. A variety of nightshade – *Solanum baretiae* – is named after her.

28 July ➤➤ Beatrix Potter

Beatrix Potter was born in London on 28 July 1866, but her heart belonged to the Lake District. She is world-famous for writing thirty books — twenty-three of them for children, including *The Tale of Peter Rabbit* and *The Tale of Mrs Tiggy-Winkle* — but Potter was also a natural scientist, an illustrator, an expert in mycology (fungi such as mushrooms) and a conservationist.

Thanks to a legacy from an aunt, and her huge success as a writer, Potter was able to buy a farm near Sawrey, between Hawkshead and Lake Windermere, in 1905 and devote her time to the protection of the natural landscape.

When she died in 1943, she left almost everything to the National Trust — some 4,000 acres of land, herds of cattle and Herdwick sheep, sixteen farms and cottages. This generous gift forms a huge part of what is now the Lake District National Park.

29 July ➵ Im Yunjidang

Born in 1721, Im Yunjidang is considered one of the first female Korean philosophers – although she was probably not acknowledged as such during her lifetime. Her work could be said to be a form of early feminism, based on the teachings of the Chinese thinker and philosopher Confucius. Confucius was born in 551 BCE and his ideas have profoundly influenced not only Chinese civilization, but other East Asian countries and beyond. At the heart of Confucian philosophy is the idea that certain ethical, moral and social standards might form the basis of a good life.

Writing thousands of years after Confucius, Im's writings were based on the thesis that since women and men were equal in human nature, there was no reason that a woman should not become a Confucian master.

Thirty-five pieces of her work have survived, all published after her death in 1793. On 29 July 2022, Cambridge University Press published her combined writings in English, a key moment in opening up her work to a much wider readership.

30 July ➻ **Maria Anna Mozart**

In Salzburg, on this day in 1751, a musical genius was born. No, not Wolfgang Amadeus, but his older sister Maria Anna Mozart, who was also a child prodigy. Often nicknamed Nannerl, her father taught her the harpsichord and took her all over Europe with her little brother, performing in cities such as Paris and Vienna.

Once Nannerl reached an age where she might be married, her father refused to let her continue performing in public and she was sent home to Salzburg. From 1722, she worked as a piano teacher, but there is plenty of evidence that she continued to compose. The siblings remained close and several letters from her brother compliment her compositions. Sadly, none of them has survived.

31 July ⇒ Evonne Goolagong Cawley

The Wiradjuri Aboriginal Australian star tennis player Evonne Goolagong was born in New South Wales on 31 July 1951. She was the first player of Aboriginal descent to play at Wimbledon, and in 1980 she became the first mother to win at Wimbledon in sixty-six years.

At the age of nineteen, Goolagong won the French Open singles and the Australian Doubles championship with fellow Australian, Margaret Court. She went on to win fourteen Grand Slam titles and eighty-six singles titles in her career. She was inducted into the International Tennis Hall of Fame in 1988 and the Aboriginal Hall of Fame in 1989. She now leads the Goolagong National Development camp for indigenous boys and girls and has been a sports ambassador for Aboriginal and Torres Strait Island communities since 1997.

The Shamers and the Trolls

In the autumn of 2024, a French rape trial filled newspapers and online news channels all over the world. It was not only the horrifying details of the case involving a husband and fifty men in Provence, but because his wife, Gisèle Pelicot, did something extraordinary. Rather than insist on privacy she asked for the trial to be held in an open court – that's to say that she decided that she would not be anonymous and would allow the details of what had been done to her to be revealed.

Why? Because as the seventy-two-year-old Madame Pelicot explained, she wanted to bring the issue of violence against women and girls into the light and to change society:

Gisèle Pelicot

'When you're raped there is shame,' she said, 'and it's not for us to have shame, it's for them.'

All fifty-one men were convicted of rape or sexual assault in December 2024.

Shame is a powerful emotion and an undermining one, inducing self-loathing and regret. It's different from embarrassment, which can bring with it a sense of fun and amusement. Shame bullies people into silence and into the shadows.

Throughout history, nation states, kings, emperors and generals, have shamed their enemies in victory. In the 1st century CE, the Roman Empire paraded Zenobia, queen of the Palmyrene Empire (modern-day Syria), through the streets after they had defeated her in battle. In France, in the weeks after the country had been liberated from Nazi occupation, women who were accused of collaborating with the Nazis had their heads shaved to make their shame visible.

What makes the 21st century different is social media platforms and mobile phones. It is now possible for people to shame or troll – posting or commenting online with the intention of deliberately upsetting someone else – anyone, at any time, anywhere. You don't have to know the person, or live in the same street or even town as them. When pretty much everyone carries a computer in their pocket in the form of a mobile phone, photographs, lies, misinformation can be shared at the click of a button or swipe of a screen. Anyone can post a bullying message, or try to make someone feel ashamed for something they might (or just as often might not) have done.

In our interconnected modern world, it is almost impossible to escape. Every one of us has had that sinking feeling at one time or another that everyone is talking about you, or that someone's spreading rumours about you. Worse still, that people might be sharing inappropriate or fake photos of you to make you look stupid or ashamed.

A survey by University College London in 2020 showed that 76 per cent of girls aged between twelve and eighteen had been sent unwanted, and unasked-for, photos of boys' body parts. Deep-fake images or films are commonplace.

Why do people do it? Well, it's about power. Trying to belittle or ridicule someone to make yourself feel stronger, or more popular, or more successful. Some of those doing the trolling or bullying might feel unconfident and unhappy themselves. They diminish other people because that is what has been done to them.

Perhaps you have been tempted to send an unpleasant message yourself. If you have, why? Was it out of jealousy, or betrayal, or a sense of wanting to get your own back on someone who made you feel bad? Did you regret it? And did it make you feel triumphant at first, then ashamed for having behaved unkindly?

How can we break this spiral of shame and online bullying? Well, it's tough and requires confidence not to give in. The biggest lesson Gisèle Pelicot teaches us is that if the 'victim' refuses to be shamed into silence, then the bullies have lost. It is not a question of just ignoring malicious comments, but rather about refusing to let yourself be defined by someone else or be silenced by someone else.

Turn shame into resilience.

By standing tall, you can reflect back the shamers' and trolls' words on them. You will be taking back your own agency. It's hard, I know, but it is the only way not to hand over your power to someone else.

Above all, be proud of yourself. Think about who you are, all that you are and all the good you do in the world. Think about your real friends and how they stand by you. Send shame back to the shadows where it belongs.

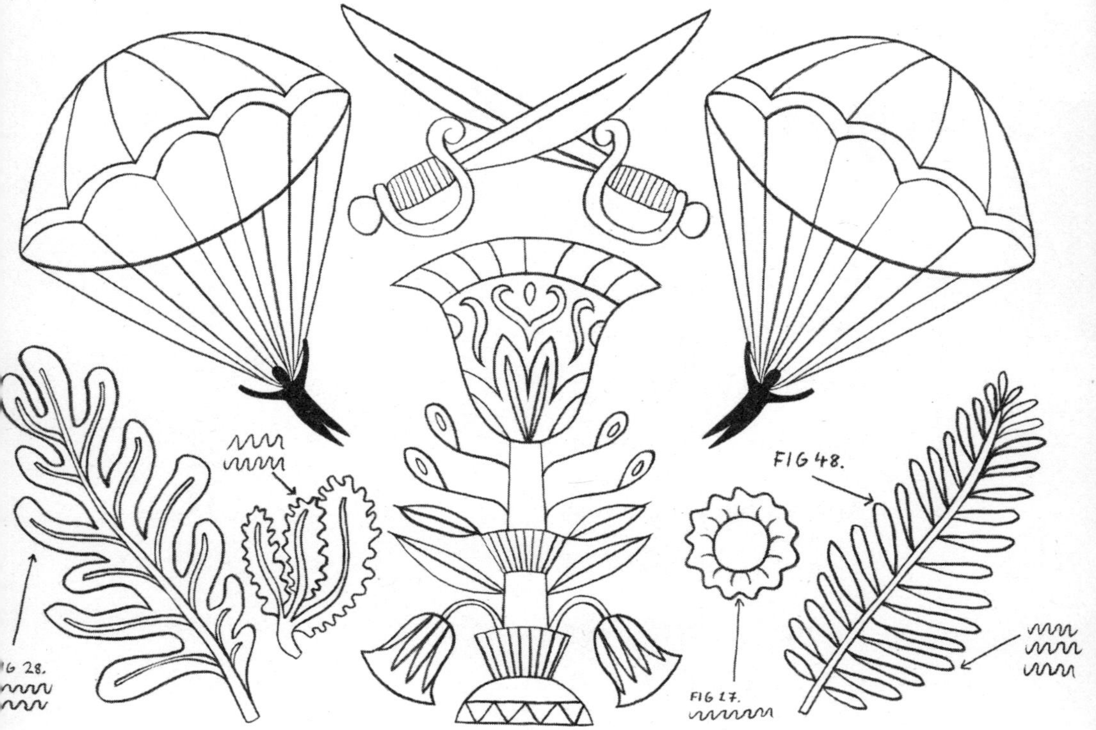

AUGUST

August

1 August ➳ Gerda Taro

On 1 August 1937, thousands of mourners lined the streets of Paris to pay tribute to one of the great war photojournalists, Gerda Taro.

Born Gerta Pohorylle, into a Jewish family in Leipzig, Germany, she moved to Paris in 1933. There she met the Hungarian photojournalist Endre Friedmann. They began working together under the pseudonym Robert Capa, with Friedmann pretending to be the agent of this fictitious American photographer to sell both his own and Pohorylle's work. Later, when they began to publish separately, Friedmann continued using the Capa name while Pohorylle took a new pseudonym – Gerda Taro.

Taro covered the Spanish Civil War, embedded with the Republican side fighting against Franco's Nationalists. In July 1937, the car she was travelling in, with wounded Republican soldiers, collided with a tank and she was fatally injured. She was the first female photojournalist to be killed on the frontline and Taro became a martyr, seen as a woman who'd sacrificed her life to bear

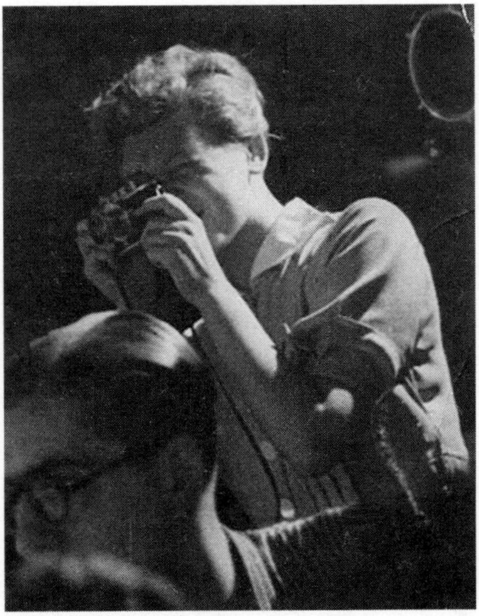

Gerda Taro, 1937

witness to the suffering of troops and civilians.

Unfortunately, as Friedmann's fame grew under their once-shared pseudonym of Robert Capa, her role as the original other half of the famous photographer was largely forgotten. It was only at the beginning of the 21st century that Taro's contribution to war photography began to be properly acknowledged and her brilliance appreciated.

2 August ➾ Jeanne de Clisson

Jeanne de Clisson, who was born in 1300, was known as the 'Lioness of Brittany'.

When her husband was executed for treason by the French king on 2 August 1343, she vowed revenge. She sold her estates, raised a force of about 400 soldiers and started to attack French forces in Brittany. With the assistance of the king of England, who was also no fan of the king of France, de Clisson bought three warships. She named her flagship *My Revenge*, painted all three vessels black and fitted them out with red sails, then launched a thirteen-year reign of terror against ships in the English Channel.

After a long life as a pirate, and a fourth marriage, Jeanne settled in the Castle of Hennebont, a port town on the Britanny coast, and died there in December 1359.

3 August ➻ **Josephine Cochrane**

Everyone should lay flowers on the grave of the American inventor Josephine Cochrane, who died on 3 August 1913.

Cochrane lived in Chicago. One day, presumably because she was fed up with clearing up after everybody else, she went to a shed at the bottom of her garden and with the immortal words (overleaf), she set about designing the prototype of what is pretty much the dishwasher we have today.

Working with a mechanic, George Butters, who became one of her first employees in the Garis-Cochrane Manufacturing Company (Garis was her name before she married), Cochrane's patent for an automatic dishwater was issued on 28 December 1886. She was inducted into the American National Inventors Hall of Fame in 2006.

Josephine Cochrane

4 August ➳ Anbara Salam Khalidi

Born in Beirut on 4 August 1897, Anbara Salam Khalidi was a Lebanese feminist, translator and author who played a significant role in promoting women's rights in the Arab-speaking world.

Khalidi was in the Society for Women's Renaissance and worked to establish schools for girls, advocating for girls' and women's education. In 1927, she was invited to speak about her time studying in the UK. Once she was up on stage, she removed her veil, making her the first Muslim woman in Lebanon to publicly abandon the veil. Her memoir was published in 1978 and translated into English in 2013 under the title *Memoirs of an Early Arab Feminist.*

5 August ➡ Anne Mackintosh

Known as 'Colonel Anne', Anne Mackintosh was one of the very few known female military leaders during the 18th century Jacobite Uprising and the first woman to hold the rank of colonel in Scotland. The Jacobite Uprising of 1745 was an attempt by Charles Stuart – known as Bonnie Prince Charlie – to regain the British throne for his father. Though Mackintosh never actually led troops into battle, the name 'Colonel Anne' stuck.

In an early skirmish on 5 August, Jacobite forces captured British troops. Two weeks later, on 19 August, Bonnie Prince Charlie raised the Royal Standard at Glenfinnan in the Scottish Highlands. Anne was instrumental in gathering more than 350 men to fight on the Jacobite side. When Charles was defeated at Culloden on 16 April 1746, she was arrested and held at Inverness for six weeks, but was later released.

She died in Leith in 1787.

6 August ➤➤ Fanny Blankers-Koen

Nicknamed the 'Flying Housewife' by the press, the Dutch athlete Fanny Blankers-Koen was the star of the Austerity Olympics, so called because plenty of things were still rationed in the UK after the Second World War and food was scarce. They were held in London in the summer of 1948.

Thirty years old, and pregnant with her third child, Blankers-Koen won four gold medals and set world records in long jump, high jump, hurdles and sprint. Her achievements serve as a reminder that there is nothing that a woman cannot do, pregnant or not.

Fanny Blankers-Koen competing in the hurdles

7 August ➤➤ Nancy Wake

On 9 February 1943, the leader of the Free French in exile, Charles de Gaulle, established the Médaille de la Résistance to honour those who had shown exceptional courage in fighting against the Nazis. Medals were presented to about 38,000 living people and nearly 25,000 who had been killed in the conflict, though relatively few were given to women. Of those that were, most were to women from outside of France.

New Zealander Nancy Wake was one of them. She was born in Wellington in 1912 and worked as a journalist and a nurse before joining the SOE. Given the code-name 'Hélène' – though known as 'Andrée' by the Resistance and 'White Mouse' by the Gestapo – Wake was a courier and a vital part of the network smuggling Allied airmen out of France to Spain.

After the war ended, Wake worked for the Intelligence Department at the British Air Ministry, then relocated with her second husband back to Australia. She published her autobiography, *The White Mouse*, in 1985. She emigrated back to London after her husband died, and died at the age of ninety-eight on 7 August 2011.

8 August ⇢ Ascensión Chirivella Marín

Born in Valencia in 1894, Marín was the first female law graduate in Spain to practise as a lawyer. She began her career in 1922, specializing in civil law and promoting women's rights within the context of the promises that the new Spanish government had made to women, such as the right to vote, to hold political positions, to divorce and to receive child support.

Marín died on 8 August 1980 in Mexico, a heroine in the Spanish-speaking world.

9 August ➤➤ Lillian Ngoyi

Lillian Ngoyi – known as 'Ma Ngoyi' – was one of the leaders of the Pretoria Women's March on 9 August 1956. The march was convened to protest against the extension of the hated South African Pass Laws – which required all Black men to carry passbooks and controlled their right to travel freely – to women over the age of sixteen, too.

A seamstress, a nurse and an anti-apartheid campaigner, Ma Ngoyi was held under house arrest in Soweto for fifteen years. She was the first woman elected to the executive committee of the African National Congress (ANC).

Lillian Ngoyi

10 August ➺ Edna O'Brien

On 10 August 2024, the Irish novelist, playwright, essayist and force of nature Edna O'Brien was buried on Holy Island in Lough Derg.

O'Brien was born in December 1930 in County Clare. Her first novel, *The Country Girls*, was published in 1960 and it scandalized the Catholic Church. No one had written before so frankly about sexuality and Irish girls' lives. It, and several other of O'Brien's novels, were banned by the Irish Censorship Board.

It made not a scrap of difference. O'Brien kept writing her brilliant, truthful novels putting ordinary women and girls' lives on the page, laying bare the hypocrisy in the treatment of women and men at the heart of Irish society. There was no subject she would not tackle. She won award after award and changed the face of Irish writing, and women's writing worldwide. Her last novel, *Girl*, was published in 2019.

11 August ➤➤ Edith Wharton

From an Irish literary legend to an American one, albeit a century earlier, in the shape of Edith Wharton. She, too, put the lives of women on the page, though in her case it was the gilded lives of American socialites in New York and Newport rebelling against the restrictions of their privileged lives.

In 1921, Wharton was the first woman to win a Pulitzer Prize for Fiction for her novel *The Age of Innocence*. Despite not publishing her first novel until she was forty, she notched up twenty-two novels and novellas, as well as eighty-five short stories, poetry, books on design, travel, literary and cultural criticism and a memoir, *A Backward Glance*. She was also the author of brilliant ghost stories, the queen of what she called 'the thrill of the shudder'.

Wharton loved dogs and had her own pet cemetery at her home in Massachusetts, and many photographs show her with her beloved companions.

Edith Wharton with her dogs Miza and Mimi

My favourite is one with two tiny chihuahuas balanced on each of her shoulders beneath the brim of her straw boater hat . . .

After the collapse of her marriage, Wharton moved to Paris in 1913. During the First World War, she nursed refugees and tuberculosis sufferers, then after the war was over, she bought a small villa, the Pavillon Colombe, in a village in northern France. She died there on 11 August 1937.

12 August ➻ Cleopatra

Although this book is about putting brilliant, often unknown, women and girls in the spotlight, there are a few who need no introduction. One of those is the queen of Egypt, Cleopatra, who died on 12 August (or possibly 10 August) 30 BCE.

Cleopatra has been immortalized on the big screen and the small, on stage and in print, in paintings and sculptures. In her lifetime, she was one of the most famous people in the world and her legend has persisted ever since. But, as with Joan of Arc, it's hard to glimpse the real woman behind the hype.

So, what do we know about the queen of Egypt who was so powerful and so beautiful that both the Roman leaders Julius Caesar and Mark Antony were prepared to sacrifice their reputations and their status to be with her? Well, we know that she was Cleopatra VII and the last female Pharaoh of Egypt. We know that by the age of twenty she had been crowned, deposed, reinstated, married two of her half-brothers and ordered the execution of a half-sister. We know that her affair with Mark Antony led to his rival attacking their combined forces at Actium in 31 BCE. We also know – and this is one of the most famous deaths in history – that after she was taken captive by the Romans in Alexandria, and fearing she would be publicly paraded before her execution, Cleopatra chose to poison herself rather than allow herself to be humiliated.

13 August ➤ **Florence Nightingale**

In recent years, the 'Lady with the Lamp' has gone from being seen as a British heroine to something of a controversial figure thanks to her appalling views on race. And they were appalling, extreme even by the standards of the time.

But, for all that, Nightingale should not be cancelled. When putting women and girls back into history, we cannot leave out those we don't agree with or don't like. Women, like men, contain contradictions and if we include all men in the history books, the sinners as well as the saints, we have to be courageous enough to include all the women too.

She was born in the Italian city of Florence in 1820 (hence her name). Nightingale is often portrayed as passive and maternal, a mother-like figure who cared for soldiers in the Crimean War. But, in fact, she was someone who helped revolutionize modern nursing and gave millions of women the opportunity to have a professional career outside the home. Thanks to Florence Nightingale and Mary Seacole, the 1901 census recorded that there were about 68,000 nurses working in the UK.

She was also a gifted mathematician and statistician – she invented the pie chart – and, in 1856, Nightingale was admitted to the Royal Statistical Society. This side of her character was continually underplayed by the press, who wanted only to present her as a silent woman walking around the wards at night with her oil lamp in her hand looking after wounded soldiers. But her letters reveal her to be outspoken, short-tempered and frustrated by the restrictions put upon her because of her sex.

She died in London on 13 August 1910.

14 August ➻ Faye Schulman

Faye Schulman was born into a Jewish family in November 1919 in a small town called Lenin on the Russian–Polish border (in what is now Belarus). At the age of ten, she was apprenticed to her brother, who was a photographer.

This would save her life.

The population of Lenin was mostly Jewish and lived side by side with their Catholic neighbours until the Nazis invaded and forced the Jewish families into a ghetto.

On 14 August 1942, everyone was herded out of the ghetto at gunpoint into the forest, and shot. This is known as the Lenin Ghetto Massacre. The Nazis spared only twenty-eight people, Schulman among them, because they wanted her to photograph the mass graves.

Schulman with three other soldiers in the Molotov Brigade in Naliboki Forest, Belarus, December 1944

Grieving and set on revenge, Schulman managed to escape and fled into the forest, where she joined Russian guerrilla soldiers known as the Molotov Brigade. There is an extraordinary photograph of her in the snowy forest in a leopard-print coat with three Russian partisan soldiers, and another where she is clutching a machine gun.

After the war, Schulman lived in a displaced persons camp, then emigrated to Canada in 1948, where she dedicated her life to making sure that everyone knew the truth of the Holocaust.

Schulman died at the age of 101 in Toronto in 2021.

Faye Schulman

15 August ➤➤ **Rabia Balkhi**

On 15 August 2021, the Taliban retook Kabul in Afghanistan – after the withdrawal of British and American troops – and recommenced their campaign of terror. One of their first acts was to erase – literally – images of the inspirational Afghan poet-princess and role model for Afghan women, Rabia Balkhi.

Born in northern Afghanistan in the 10th century, Rabia Balkhi is one of the very few female writers of medieval Persia to be recorded by name (she also wrote in Arabic). Her tomb in Balkh, known as the 'mother of cities', was a much-visited site, and many hospitals and universities are named in her honour. Portraits of her wearing a blue khimar with a book, inkwell and quill were everywhere in Afghanistan.

But since the Taliban were determined to deny girls the right to write and learn, there were multiple accounts of Taliban soldiers destroying images of Balkhi. It was part of a broader campaign to erase women and girls from public life.

But women in Afghanistan continue to write and organizations such as Untold Narratives in the UK are working to bring their powerful words to readers.

16 August ➤➤ **Ellen Hutchins**

On 16 August 2025 a festival was held in County Cork in Ireland celebrating the life of the 18th-century botanist Ellen Hutchins.

Born in Bantry Bay in 1785, Hutchins was responsible for finding and cataloguing many plants new to science. She specialized in seaweeds, lichens, mosses and liverworts, identifying hundreds of species and producing the most beautiful botanical illustrations.

Hutchins was always a sickly child and young woman, and her many letters – to her brothers and fellow botanists – are full of details about her declining health as well as her work. She died on 9 February 1815, at the age of twenty-nine, and was buried in an unmarked grave in Bantry churchyard.

Thanks to the determination of the Hutchins family, a plaque in her honour was erected in 2002 and, on the bicentenary of her death in 2015, a public memorial was placed in the Garryvurcha Graveyard, Bantry.

Hutchins' seaweed illustrations

17 August ➤ Ruth First

The anti-apartheid activist Ruth First was the daughter of Jewish immigrants, who had come to South Africa from Latvia in 1906. They were founding members of the Communist Party of South Africa.

First was a courageous and fearless investigative journalist, married to a fellow activist, Joe Slovo. She was one of the 156 defendants in the Treason Trial of 1956–1961. This was a landmark case, held in Johannesburg, where many of those fighting against the introduction of increasingly repressive measures against Black people were accused of treason by the apartheid government. Other defendants included Nelson Mandela, Walter Sisulu, Helen Joseph, Bertha Gxowa and Joe Modise, Joe Slovo and Lillian Ngoyi. The trial began in December 1956 and lasted until 1961, when all defendants were found not guilty.

Even though First was acquitted, she was listed and banned from attending political meetings. Two years later, she was arrested again, the first white woman to be detained under the Ninety-Day Detention Law. Introduced in 1963, as a response to the increase in protest by the ANC, the law allowed police to detain a person suspected of a politically motivated crime for up to ninety days without a warrant or access to a lawyer. In response, First wrote a brilliant account of her confinement – *117 Days* – a book that was reissued in 2010 with an introduction by her daughter, the novelist, author and playwright Gillian Slovo.

First was forced into exile in 1964. She lectured at the universities of Manchester and Durham, then went to Mozambique in 1978 to take up a position as director of research at the Centre of African Studies in Maputo. It was there, on 17 August 1982, after a lifetime of campaigning against the evils of apartheid, that First was assassinated. She opened a parcel bomb sent to the university on the orders of the South African police, and was killed instantly.

18 August ➻ The Married Women's Property Act, 1882

In the summer of 1882, the 1870 Married Women's Property Act was extended to allow English, Welsh and Irish married women to have complete control over their own property (Scottish law is and was separate, and a similar law was passed there in 1881). The 1882 Act also protected women from being liable for debts incurred by their husbands, their employees and other creditors, and allowed women to petition the courts if they felt they were being unfairly treated.

This was one of three major pieces of legislation passed during the Victorian period in Britain thanks to the work of Caroline Norton, Barbara Bodichon and others. In all, between 1870 and 1964, there were seven Married Women's Property Acts passed affecting women in England, Ireland and Wales that put married women on an equal basis with their husbands. Similar provisions were extended to women in Scotland in 1880 under the Married Woman's Policies of Assurance (Scotland) Act.

19 August ➤➤ The Samlesbury Witches

If you've studied Shakespeare's *Macbeth* or read Arthur Miller's *The Crucible*, you'll know that in the 17th century there was an obsession with witches.

In the UK, almost everyone accused of being a witch was female, often an independent unmarried woman who was not afraid of speaking her mind. Accusations of witchcraft were used to settle old scores, to silence people who were speaking out about anything, such as unfairness in taxes to assault or theft. It created a nervous atmosphere up and down the country.

The problem was that it was almost impossible to prove that you *weren't* a witch. One of the harshest measures was dunking, where the accused was tied up and thrown into a river or lake. If she (or occasionally he) floated, it was taken as proof they were in league with the devil and guilty. If they drowned, they were innocent.

A classic no-win situation.

Certain parts of the country, such as East Anglia and Lancashire, had more witch trials than others. On 19 August 1612, three women from Samlesbury in Lancashire – Jane Southworth, Jennet Brierley and Ellen Brierley – were put on trial, accused of practising witchcraft. The accuser was Ellen's niece and Jennet's granddaughter, though her motives were not entirely clear. The three women were found guilty. However, suspicions began to surface that Ellen had been coached in what to say by a Catholic priest. Exceptionally for a witch trial, the verdict was overturned and the three women were acquitted on the grounds that it was a papist plot to send Protestant women to their deaths.

The Pendle Witches – perhaps the most famous witches put on trial during this time in England – were also held in Lancaster Castle. They were less lucky. Ten of the eleven accused were found guilty of charges including murder, witchcraft and talking to dogs. They were hanged at Gallows Hill in Lancaster on 20 August 1612.

20 August ➼ Greta Thunberg

The first School Strike for Climate took place on 20 August 2018. The Swedish activist Greta Thunberg was fifteen years old when she refused to go to school and, instead, sat outside the national parliament with a sign that announced she was on strike to protect the planet. Soon, she said that she would never go to school on Fridays until the voices of young climate activists were listened to.

The global 'Fridays for Future' movement was born.

Young people across the world took up the challenge. A global strike on 15 March 2019 saw more than a million schoolchildren walk out of lessons in protest at their governments' lack of action on climate change.

From Nigeria to Germany, Brazil to Canada, Italy to Alaska, the Netherlands to Japan, India to Australia, the strikes have attracted young people from all communities determined to protect our planet. In 2019, Thunberg became the youngest person ever to be named *Time* person of the year.

Greta Thunberg outside the Swedish parliament, 10 January 2020

21 August →→ Lisa del Giocondo

You might not think you know this 16th-century Italian noblewoman, but think again. For Lisa del Giocondo is the woman who inspired one of the most famous, most written about, most analysed paintings of all time.

I'm talking, of course, about the *Mona Lisa*, painted by the Italian artist Leonardo da Vinci, probably between 1505 and 1506. We are not sure why da Vinci never gave the painting to the Giocondo family, since the portrait had been commissioned by Lisa's husband, but it was subsequently bought by Francis I, king of France, after da Vinci's death in 1519.

The painting was put on display in the Louvre in Paris in 1797 and remained there until 21 August 1911, when a former employee stole it. He was an Italian nationalist and believed the painting should be returned to Italy. He kept it in his apartment for two years, then was caught in November 1913 when he tried to sell it to an art dealer in Florence.

The story made the front page of newspapers all over the world. *Mona Lisa* was returned to her place on the wall of the Louvre in January 1914, where she still hangs, smiling her enigmatic smile . . .

22 August ➠ Anne Bonny

Irish-born 'she-captain' Anne Bonny is one of the most notorious female pirates in history.

On or around this day in 1720, Bonny stole a ship with the help of fellow pirate Mary Read – who lived most of her life as a man – and another pirate called Calico Jack. Together, they began their reign of terror as pirates of the Caribbean. (Keira Knightley's character in the movies is said to have been inspired by Bonny and Read.)

After a few months, their luck ran out. In October 1720, their ship was captured by British forces. Calico Jack and the male crew members were hanged, but Bonny and Read were

both spared by 'pleading the belly' – that's to say, they told the court they were pregnant. We know that Read died in jail sometime in April 1721, possibly in childbirth, but we have no idea what happened to Anne Bonny. I like to think of her still out there, a ghostly pirate sailing the waters of the Caribbean on a haunted ship . . .

23 August ➻ Regina Jonas

The German-Jewish teacher and theologian Regina Jonas is thought to be the first female rabbi.

Born in Berlin in August 1902, Jonas felt her rabbinical calling when she was young. In 1930 she wrote a paper based on biblical, Talmudic (the Talmud is the central text of Judaism after the Hebrew Bible) and rabbinical sources putting forward her case for women to be rabbis.

After five years of teaching, lecturing and giving unofficial sermons, in 1935 a liberal rabbi agreed to ordain Jonas. Although many orthodox Jews would not accept a female rabbi, others did. As the persecution of Jewish people intensified and male rabbis were arrested, Jonas was able to bring support to the embattled Jewish community within Germany.

In November 1942, Jonas was arrested by the Gestapo and deported to Theresienstadt prison camp in Czechoslovakia (now the Czech Republic), where she became part of the Jewish Council. The councils – *Judenräte* – were set up by the Nazis in occupied areas, camps and ghettos. They were in the impossible position of having to implement the regime's instructions as regards the treatment of Jewish people. In June 1944, Jonas was deported, with the majority of her fellow council members, to Auschwitz concentration camp. There, six months later, Jonas was gassed.

It's bewildering why none of the hundreds of people who must have heard Jonas lecture in Theresienstadt wrote or talked about her. As a result, her place in history was lost until a throwaway comment in an article in 1973, following the ordination of the first American female rabbi, Sally Priesand, mentioned her name. In 1991, after communism had collapsed in East Germany and the Berlin Wall came down, research in the newly opened archives unearthed Jonas's rabbinical dissertation, various lectures and two photographs that had survived.

Forgotten no longer.

24 August ⇥ Tilly Shilling

On 24 August 1934, the motorcycling, motor-racing celebrity Beatrice 'Tilly' Shilling lapped the track at Brooklands, Surrey, at over 100 miles per hour. A record-breaking motorcyclist, as well as racing-car driver, she was one of the very few women to be awarded the Brooklands race-track gold star.

Shilling was also an award-winning engineer and inventor who saved the lives of countless British fighter pilots in the Second World War. She studied electrical and mechanical engineering and, in 1940, discovered that fitting a tiny brass washer in the shape of a thimble would prevent planes from stalling and plummeting from the sky.

Her invention became known as 'Miss Shilling's Orifice'.

25 August ➛ **Errollyn Wallen**

On 25 August 2024, the Belize-born British composer Errollyn Wallen was announced as Master of the King's Music. It's a role broadly equivalent to that of the Poet Laureate in the world of classical music, where the composer is part of the Royal Household and produces music for significant royal and national events.

The first person to hold the title of Master of the King's Music was Nicholas Lanier in the 17th century. The first woman to hold the role was Wallen's immediate predecessor, Judith Weir, who composed music for the state funeral of Queen Elizabeth II in September 2022.

Wallen is the first Black person to hold the position. She was also the first Black female composer to have music played at the Proms. Full of life, inspirational and vibrant, she is a breath of fresh air in the world of classical music.

26 August ⇒ Katherine Johnson

Katherine Johnson was another of the trailblazing African American female mathematicians who worked for NASA after the Second World War – others include Dorothy Vaughan and Mary Jackson. Their story was told in the 2016 film *Hidden Figures.*

Johnson was born on 26 August 1918 in West Virginia. She was a child genius and, by the age of fifteen, was already at college despite segregation laws that discriminated against Black students. At NASA, Johnson's calculations were essential to the American space programme and she was instrumental in saving the lives of the astronauts on the Apollo 13 mission, quickly recalculating their route back home after their spacecraft malfunctioned. When Johnson died at the age of 101 in 2020, NASA tweeted that 'her pioneering legacy will never be forgotten', and the US Space Agency issued a statement talking of her 'legacy of excellence' that broke down racial and social barriers.

27 August ➤➤ Laura Bates

Born on 27 August 1986, Laura Bates is a British activist, writer, speaker and journalist. In 2012, she founded the Everyday Sexism Project to raise awareness of sexism and provide an empowering space for survivors' stories to be heard – and believed. So far, there are more than 200,000 testimonies of shaming and inequality on the site.

Bates was moved to start the project after a week in which she experienced numerous different forms of harassment, including being shouted at in the street and followed home. Afterwards she asked herself: 'Why am I so used to being made to feel uncomfortable, unsafe and unhappy because I am a woman?'

Does this sound familiar to you?

Bates has been subject to online abuse – including deep-fake pornography images – but she continues to campaign and is always unfailingly articulate, warm and inspirational. She has published several game-changing books, including *Everyday Sexism*; *Fix the System, Not the Women*; *Men Who Hate Women* and *The New Age of Sexism*, as well as a number of adventure novels for younger readers. Her 2025 study *The New Age of Sexism: How the AI Revolution is Reinventing Misogyny* is essential reading for all young people, their teachers, parents and politicians.

28 August ➤➤ Mairead Corrigan Maguire and Betty Williams

In despair at the endless violence and tit-for-tat reprisal killing in their home city of Belfast, on 28 August 1976 Mairead Maguire and Betty Williams led a peace rally of about 200 Protestant and Catholic women through the streets of Belfast. This grew into an organization known as Women for Peace (later renamed the Community of Peace People), dedicated to promoting a peaceful resolution to the bitter conflict between mostly Catholic Republicans and mostly Unionist Protestants in Northern Ireland, known as 'the Troubles'. The Troubles began in the 1960s and lasted until the signing of the Good Friday Agreement on 10 April 1998.

In 1977, Maguire and Williams received the 1976 Nobel Peace Prize. Maguire was only thirty-two at the time and, until Malala Yousafzai was awarded the Prize in 2014, she was the youngest ever Nobel Peace Prize laureate.

29 August ➤➤ Sarah Storey

The Paris Summer Paralympics opened on 29 August 2024. One of those taking part in the ten-day competition was the British multi-medal winning swimmer and cyclist Sarah Storey.

Born in Manchester in 1977, Storey is Britain's most successful Paralympian of all time. She has won thirty medals in her career – including nineteen golds – and also holds many World and European records for cycling, both on the road and in the stadium, in both the para class and the able-bodied class.

An amazing athlete and role model.

30 August ➤ Beryl Gilroy

One of Britain's very first Black headteachers, Beryl Gilroy was born on 30 August 1924 in Guyana (then British Guiana). She went to teacher training college in Georgetown, then came to England in 1951.

To start with, she found it hard to find employment as a teacher. But she studied for a diploma in child development, then took a BSc degree in psychology, and these additional qualifications helped kick-start her teaching career in London. In 1968, she was appointed as a deputy head and, the following year, became one of the first Black female headteachers in London, alongside Islington's Yvonne Connolly.

Gilroy's autobiography, *Black Teacher*, was published in 1976. She published an adult novel – *Frangipani House* – in 1986, followed by other works of fiction and a collection of poems. Her final novel was published after her death in London in 2001.

31 August ➤➤ Maria Montessori

Perhaps you went to a childminder when you were little? Or maybe you were at home with your siblings? Or perhaps you went to a Montessori nursery? Chances are, whether you went to one or not, that you will have heard the name.

What you might not know is that Montessori nurseries were set up by an Italian doctor, Maria Montessori, who was born on 30 August 1870. She devised a radical and new form of education for pre-school children rooted in play-based learning, believing that allowing children to develop at their own pace, and through play rather than regimented and controlled lessons and exercises, was better.

She opened her first Montessori school – the *Casa dei Bambini*, or Children's House – in Rome in January 1907. Now there are thousands of Montessori nurseries all over the world, and her ideas form a fundamental part of other types of pre-school education, too.

Warrior Queens

We've already met warrior queens who took up arms and led armies into battle – from Boudica to Velu Nachiyar, Nakano to Joan of Arc.

Most countries have their own versions of Joan of Arc – it's a kind of shorthand to describe any visionary female military leader – though each woman is her own unique self. Aurora Mardiganian survived the Armenian genocide of the First World War and is sometimes called the 'Armenian Joan of Arc'. The 'Russian Joan of Arc' is Alyona Arzamasskaia, who, like the Maid of Orléans, also dressed as a man and was one of the leaders of the Peasants' Revolt in Russia in 1670. The 17th-century 'Congolese Joan of Arc' is Kimpa Vita. The 18th-century Filipina resistance leader Gabriela Silang was often referred to as the Joan of Arc of Ilocandia. There is even a Vietnamese Joan of Arc, the 3rd-century warrior queen Triệu Thị Trinh, who lived 1,200 years before La Pucelle.

But there is more than one way to be a warrior queen and more than one kind of bravery. Sometimes it takes more courage and strength to stand against your own government than to face an enemy on the battlefield.

We've already come across the Pass Laws in South Africa, which required all Black men over the age of sixteen to carry passbooks, and how, in 1955, the government had ordered the law be extended to all Black women over the age of sixteen, too. Having seen the pain and anguish the law caused to their sons, brothers, friends, husbands, community leaders, women prepared to protest.

On 9 August 1956, nearly 20,000 women set out to march to the Union Buildings in Pretoria. One of the many iconic photographs of that day shows Lillian Ngoyi with Rahima Moosa, Helen Joseph and Sophia Williams-De Bruyn, with stacks of petitions in their hands. Other protesters included Motlalepula Chabaku, Bertha Gxowa, Albertina Sisulu, Amina Cachalia and Fatima Meer, women from all parts of South Africa – Black, brown, white, mixed race – standing shoulder to shoulder.

They waited in silence at first, then began to sing the women's protest song '*Wathint'abafazi, wathint'imbokodo*' ('You strike women, you strike a rock'), before handing over a petition of nearly 14,000 names. But it made no difference. The government did not listen. As we know, the *dompas* would lead to the Sharpeville Massacre in March 1960. It would not be until July 1986 that the requirement for Black South Africans to carry passbooks was lifted.

Apartheid formally ended in South Africa in 1994 with the formation of a democratic government headed by the ANC and heralding elections in which all citizens were allowed to vote. The first president was Nelson Mandela.

Women's March 1956 in Pretoria, South Africa

SEPTEMBER

September

1 September ⇒ Agnes Beckwith

On 1 September 1875, watched by London's press and cheering fans, fourteen-year-old swimming sensation Agnes Beckwith made history by diving from a boat at London Bridge and swimming to Greenwich in one hour and seven minutes.

Beckwith was a celebrity in Victorian England and beyond, touring the world with her entertainment troupe, a kind of 19th-century synchronized swimming team. Here's the fantastic poster for her 1885 show at the Royal Aquarium, Westminster, in her bathing suit, all ruffles and frills. It looks more like the costume a can-can dancer in Paris might wear than a swimming champion. Ellie Simmonds and Sarah Storey would be horrified!

Greatest Woman Swimmer in the World advert in 1885

On 2 September 1998, a young woman called Martha Lane Fox co-founded a company that revolutionized travel and holidays. It was called lastminute.com and Lane Fox, and her business partner Brent Hoberman, were aiming to help people find cheaper holiday deals and flights. She was only twenty-six and, at the time, most people weren't convinced that buying things off the internet would work.

Lane Fox and Hoberman launched lastminute.com the following month and, by January 2000, the site had more than 500,000 regular users. Now a Baroness in the House of Lords, Lane Fox is a philanthropist, a Digital Tsar, a serial entrepreneur (she also founded the karaoke sensation Lucky Voice) and Chancellor of the Open University. She set up a new governmental digital service that built gov.uk, one of the achievements of which she is most proud. An advocate for human rights, women's equality and social justice, she is an inspirational woman who uses her platform to stand up for others and succeeds in bridging the worlds between tech and ethical business practice like no one else.

Think
BIG.
That's what i've
always been
ENCOURAGED
TO DO
AND IT WORKS.

Martha Lane Fox

3 September ➤ Fatima bint Muhammad al-Fihriya

On 3 September 1965, the al-Qarawiyyin Mosque in Morocco was named a university. It had been established as a mosque and place of learning by Fatima al-Fihriya in 857–859 CE. What little we know of Fatima's life comes from the work of a medieval writer and scholar writing hundreds of years after her death, so it is hard to substantiate. But it's thought she was born into a privileged family in Tunisia who moved to Morocco when she was a child. Inheriting a large fortune on the death of her father and then her husband, al-Fihriya used her wealth to improve society. Known as the 'mother of boys', or sometimes the 'mother of children', because of her focus on learning, the al-Qarawiyyin Mosque is the oldest continuing education institution in the world.

And founded by a woman . . .

4 September ➤➤ **Beyoncé**

'Crazy in Love', 'If I Were a Boy', 'Single Ladies' . . .

Beyoncé Knowles was born on 4 September 1981 in Houston, Texas. She is one of the few women in history to achieve more than twenty top 10 songs as a solo artist, as well as ten as a member of the girl group Destiny's Child. A cultural icon, she's also a businesswoman, an advocate for Black Lives Matter and women's rights, an actress and multi-award-winning artist.

Simply, 'Queen Bey' . . .

5 September ➻ Hillary Rodham Clinton

On 5 September 1995, Hillary Rodham Clinton was in Beijing and delivered an iconic speech about women's rights. One of America's most successful – and most attacked – female politicians, she was brave enough to use her opportunity to speak out against injustice, to encourage women and girls to stand together and to campaign for equality, calling on them – us – to 'resist, insist, persist, enlist'.

Clinton would go on to be the first former FLOTUS to be elected to the US Senate in 2000 and also the first woman elected statewide in New York. She served as Secretary of State from 2009 to 2013 and, in 2016, she ran for president for the Democratic Party.

Since leaving political office, Clinton has produced podcasts and documentaries. She is Chancellor of Queen's University Belfast and a Professor of Practice at the School of International and Public Affairs at Columbia University. In 2025, she was awarded the Presidential Medal of Freedom as one of a group of nineteen people who 'are great leaders who have made America and the world a better place. They are great leaders because they are good people who have made extraordinary contributions to their country and the world.'

6 September »→ Martina Navratilova

The Czech-American tennis player Martina Navratilova is one of the most successful sports sensations, male or female, of all time.

Born in Prague in communist Czechoslovakia in 1956, on 6 September 1975 she asked for political asylum in the United States. She was only eighteen years old and already attracting headlines worldwide for her skill on the court.

Navratilova dominated the women's tennis scene in the 1980s – winning all the major singles titles, thirty-one women's doubles titles and what is called the 'boxed set' – the mixed doubles, doubles and singles titles at all the Grand Slam events, namely the Australian Open, the French Open, the US Open and Wimbledon. She became a US citizen in 1981 and is a regular commentator on television. An LGBTQIA+ icon, she is married to *Real Housewives of Miami* star, the Russian former model and actress Julia Lemigova.

Elizabeth I, the last Tudor monarch, was born on 7 September 1533 at Greenwich Palace in London. Her childhood was unsettled to say the least. When she was two, the marriage between her parents Henry VIII and Anne Boleyn was annulled and Elizabeth was declared illegitimate.

There was no reason to suspect she would ever rule England – she had a younger half-brother (Edward) and an older half-sister (Mary) – but yet, in 1558, that's what happened.

Elizabeth hit the ground running. Though she formally established the English Protestant Church, she was more moderate and pragmatic in terms of faith than either her father or her half-sister Mary, having seen how religious conflict could bankrupt a country. During her reign, there were countless conspiracies and challenges to her throne, but she always came out on top.

When it became clear that Elizabeth did not intend to marry and produce an heir, she became something of a legend, not least because of the defeat of the Spanish Armada at the hands of the English fleet in 1588. During her reign, theatre thrived, sea exploration became a key part of the imprinting of England on the rest of the world and she acquired a host of nicknames including the 'Virgin Queen', 'Good Queen Bess' and 'Gloriana'. Her words to the troops at Tilbury Docks on 9 August 1588 (overleaf) are some of the most quoted in English history.

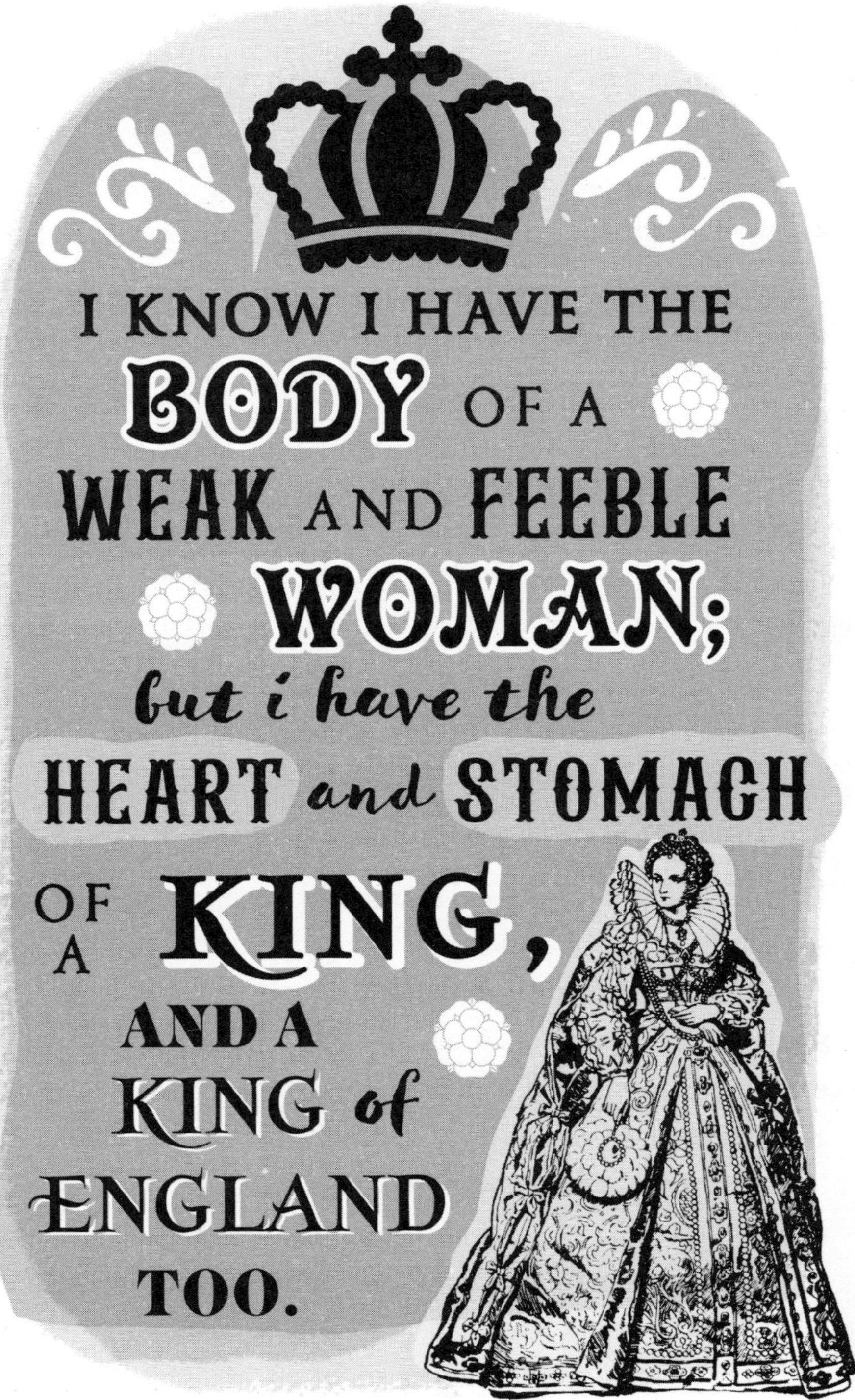

Queen Elizabeth I

8 September ⇒ Oprah Winfrey

From one queen to another, in the shape of the superstar broadcaster, influencer, chat show host, businesswoman, actress and producer Oprah Winfrey. The first episode of *The Oprah Winfrey Show* was broadcast on 8 September 1986 from Chicago, and it went on to become one of the most successful television series of all time.

Born to a teenage single mother in Mississippi, Winfrey credits her tough childhood with giving her the resilience and determination to succeed. She created a more emotional, personal and confessional style on television that connected with millions of viewers. Between 1986 to 2011, while *The Oprah Winfrey Show* was on air, she interviewed most of the world's leading entertainers and thought-leaders – from Barack and Michelle Obama to actress Elizabeth Taylor, Ellen DeGeneres (who came out as lesbian on the show), Tom Cruise and Celine Dion – and won every major broadcasting award several times over. Since then, of course, she has continued to interview global household names such as Prince Harry and Meghan Markle and former vice president Kamala Harris.

One of the richest women in the world, Winfrey was named *the* richest African American woman of the 20th century and was once the world's only Black billionaire.

9 September ➳ Senedu Gebru

On 9 September 1957, the writer, freedom fighter and founder of the Ethiopian Red Cross, Senedu Gebru, took up her seat in the Ethiopian parliament. She was the first woman to be elected.

Gebru was born in Addis Alem in January 1916. Educated in Switzerland and France, she returned to Ethiopia (then Abyssinia) in 1933 to take up a teaching post. During the Second World War, her country was invaded by Italy, which was allied with Nazi Germany. Gebru, and other members of her family, were part of the anti-fascist resistance. She was caught, interrogated, but released following the liberation of Ethiopia in 1941.

In 1943, she became assistant director of the first girls' school in Ethiopia and was appointed headmistress two years later. Gebru wrote more than twenty plays for the girls at her school, works often inspired by Ethiopian history. In 1950 she published her own book, *Book of My Heart*, which contained plays and poems.

She died in 2009.

10 September ➻ Marie Laveau

It's time to meet the Queen of Voodoo . . .

The Creole herbalist and voodoo practitioner, Marie Laveau, was born on 10 September 1801 in New Orleans, Louisiana. Voodoo is a West African religion and magic tradition that originated in Louisiana, mixed with a smattering of Catholic Christianity and Haitian folklore and practice.

Laveau was born a free woman of colour in the French quarter and built a reputation as a wise woman and a healer. She cared for the sick during the yellow fever epidemic of 1878 with herbal remedies and prayer, but also ran a beauty parlour and was known as a clairvoyant.

There are many songs inspired by Laveau and paintings alleged to be of her (though, so far as we know, she never sat for a portrait). She was the inspiration for novels including Robert Tallant's *The Voodoo Queen* and in Charlaine Harris's *True Blood* series a character is lured to her death at the site of Laveau's tomb.

11 September ➵ Melisende

One of the most significant, but least well known, of the medieval Crusader queens is Melisende, who ruled Jerusalem between 1131 and 1152.

The eldest of four daughters of Baldwin II in the Holy Land, Melisende was raised from the earliest age to rule, and her name appeared alongside her father's on official documents. Although she married a wealthy French crusader, Fulk of Anjou, her father held a coronation ceremony investing the kingship of Jerusalem three ways – between his beloved daughter, Fulk and his grandson.

However, after Baldwin II died, Fulk refused to accept his wife as his equal. Melisende had no choice but to go to war against him to secure her rights. Extraordinarily for the times, the bishops and nobility of the Holy Land supported her.

She won . . .

Melisende and her husband were back together by 1136 and it's thought that the exquisite Melisende Psalter – a manuscript which is held in the British Library in London – was commissioned by Fulk as an apology. Certainly, when he died in a hunting accident in 1143, she seems genuinely to have mourned him.

During her reign – and Melisende also served as regent for her son – she endowed many convents and religious institutions, and was a great supporter of art and artists.

Thanks to her, Jerusalem became a flourishing and vibrant cultural city.

She died on 11 September 1161.

12 September ➺ Maria Pronchishcheva

The world's first female polar explorer, Maria Pronchishcheva, died on 12 September 1736 at the age of twenty-six.

In 1735, Pronchishcheva joined the Great Northern Expedition with her husband. Three separate explorations had been set up by the Russian Admiralty in 1732 to map the coastline and the eastern landmass of Siberia, and to investigate a sea route to America and Japan. The Pronchishchevs sailed down the Lena River from Yakutsk in Siberia, recording what they saw. Yakutsk lies only about 240 miles south of the Arctic and is said to be the coldest city on the planet.

Despite difficulties, and illness in many of their crew, they reached their destination in 1736. But their luck did not hold. They both were struck down by scurvy and died on the way home.

13 September ⇒ **Noor Inayat Khan**

We've already mentioned the courageous Anglo-Indian SOE agent codenamed 'Madeleine' (see 15 June). Here is her extraordinary – and tragic – story.

Noor Inayat Khan was the first female wireless operator to be sent into Occupied France during the Second World War. A wireless operator was the link between an aircraft on active mission and the command base back at home. They also transmitted messages in Morse code and sent vital information to the Allies fighting the Axis forces. At that time, the life expectancy of a wireless operator was only about six weeks.

But her network had been compromised and Khan was betrayed. Captured by the Gestapo on, or around, 13 October 1943, she was taken to their headquarters and interrogated. Courageously, she refused to give anything away. Khan managed to escape, but was recaptured and imprisoned, before finally being transferred to Dachau concentration camp. There, on 13 September 1944, she was executed by firing squad. Her final word, as the soldiers raised their weapons, was '*liberté*' – 'freedom'.

Khan was posthumously awarded the George Cross and the Croix de Guerre. In 2012, a statue was unveiled to her in Gordon Square in London, after a campaign by her biographer, and founder of the Noor Inayat Khan Memorial Trust, Shrabani Basu.

14 September ➻ Whina Cooper

One of the most inspirational women's voices of the 20th century was the activist and Māori elder (or *kuia*) Whina Cooper.

Born Hōhepine Te Wake in 1895 in Te Karaka, Aotearoa, Cooper was a historian, teacher and influential campaigner who joined the campaign against an area of leased mudflats on New Zealand's North Island in 1914. The crisis was precipitated by the farmer who rented the land deciding that he wanted to drain the estuary for farming. But this would have prevented local Māori people from being able to live their lives according to tradition, so they tried to stop the work. Cooper and her fellow protesters were charged with trespass, but they managed to prevent the project from going ahead.

In 1949, Cooper moved to Auckland. Two years later, she was elected the first president of the Māori Women's

Whina Cooper at Māori March, 1975

Welfare League. When her term of office was over, she was given the title *Te Whaea o te Motu* – 'Mother of the Nation'.

But the best was yet to come. On 14 September 1975, at the age of seventy-nine, Cooper set off at the head of a month-long march from the tip of the North Island to the New Zealand parliament in Wellington to protest at the loss of Māori land and to demand acknowledgement of Māori property rights. Here is a wonderful photograph of her addressing crowds in Hamilton in her *kahu huruhuru* – feather cloak – and a magnificent pink headscarf.

Cooper died in March 1994 at the age of ninety-eight.

15 September ➤ Agatha Christie

Happy birthday to the 'Queen of Crime', the one and only Agatha Christie, who was born in Torquay on 15 September 1890.

In her wildly successful career, Christie created iconic characters such as Miss Marple, Hercule Poirot, Tommy and Tuppence in novels such as *And Then There Were None, Sleeping Murder* and *Murder on the Orient Express*. In all, she published sixty-six detective novels, fourteen short story collections, six romance novels written under the pseudonym Mary Westmacott, an autobiography and several plays, including *The Mousetrap*, which opened in London's West End in 1952 and is the world's longest-running play.

Christie is the world's biggest-selling fiction author of all time, having sold more than two *billion* copies. Dame Agatha, writers and readers everywhere salute you . . .

A young Kurdish-Iranian woman, Mahsa Amini, was looking forward to her twenty-third birthday when she was arrested in Tehran for opposing the mandatory hijab laws. What happened next is disputed by the Iranian morality police, but Amini died in police custody on 16 September 2022.

Her murder sparked protests throughout Iran and beyond, against all forms of discrimination and oppression of women. Women ripped off their hijabs in solidarity, others set their headscarves on fire and called for the overthrow of Iran's governing system. Soldiers used shotguns and assault rifles to fire on protests, killing many and injuring even more.

Before the Iranian Revolution in 1979, it was not compulsory for women to cover their hair, though many women chose to do so. It was only when Iran became an Islamic theocracy that women's personal freedoms in the matter of clothing were significantly rolled back. It reminds us that the rights of women and girls can go backwards as well as forwards.

In 2024, a 'hijab removal treatment clinic' was announced in Tehran to 'cure' women in breach of Iran's mandatory dress code. A chilling development in the war against women.

17 September ➨ Hildegard of Bingen

The idea of the 'Renaissance Man' – someone who excels at many things from art to philosophy, sport to politics – dates from 15th-century Italy. But what about the Renaissance Woman? She had been around for even longer. Meet the extraordinary Hildegard of Bingen.

Born around 1098, Hildegard was a renowned composer, a poet, a Christian mystic, and a prolific writer on a wide range of natural and scientific studies including botany and medicine.

She entered a convent at the age of fourteen and became a great religious leader. Using herbs from the convent garden to treat ailments, Hildegard is considered Germany's first female physician and herbalist. In 1150, she produced a book, *Physica*, cataloguing the use of herbs in medical treatments.

Hildegard also founded other religious communities throughout Germany and conducted preaching tours. Her writings – which include 400 letters, a morality play and many musical compositions – make up one of the largest surviving collections of work from the medieval era. Even now, nearly one thousand years later, her music speaks to us down the ages.

She died on 17 September 1179.

Known as the 'Notorious RBG', Ruth Bader Ginsburg was the first Jewish-American woman to serve on the US Supreme Court. Appointed in 1993, she was a powerful voice advocating for women's rights and spoke up for equality and fairness under the law. Her death on 18 September 2020 paved the way for the devastating rolling back of women's reproductive rights in America that is still ongoing, now RBG is no longer there to defend them.

Ginsburg in the US Supreme Court,
Washington, DC, USA in 1993

19 September ➤➤ Kate Sheppard

On 19 September 1893, the governor of New Zealand consented to the Electoral Act. This made New Zealand the first self-governing country in the world where all women had the right to vote in parliamentary elections.

This achievement was the result of years of work by campaigners, including Kate Sheppard. Sheppard was born in Liverpool in 1847, but emigrated to New Zealand with her family in 1868 and became a leading voice in the women's suffrage movement. Between 1891 and 1893, Sheppard and her fellow campaigners organized a series of petitions calling on parliament to grant the vote to women.

That spirit of inclusivity has lasted: in 2023, 51 per cent of MPs in Aotearoa New Zealand were female and women have held all of the country's key positions – Prime Minister, Governor-General, Speaker of the House of Representatives, Attorney-General and Chief Justice.

In 1993, a bronze sculpture by Margriet Windhausen was unveiled in Christchurch. Called the Kate Sheppard Memorial, it honours women who campaigned for women's suffrage in Aotearoa New Zealand, including Meri Te Tai Mangakāhia, Amey Daldy, Ada Wells, Harriet Morison, Helen Nicol as well as Sheppard herself.

20 September ➤➤ Dorothy Vaughan

Here is another of the amazing African American 'human computers' who worked at NASA to develop America's space programme.

Born on 20 September 1910 in Kansas City, Dorothy Vaughan was an exceptional mathematician. Battling against racism as well as sexism, in 1949 Vaughan became acting superintendent of the West Area Computers at NASA, the first African American woman supervisor. Later, she headed the programming section of the Analysis and Computation Division at NASA's Langley Research Centre.

Vaughan's leadership and advocacy not only advanced NASA's missions, but also paved the way for a more diverse and inclusive workforce in the traditionally white and very male space industry.

21 September ➤➤ Amy Johnson

In September 1934, the British celebrity and pioneer pilot, Amy Johnson, was elected President of the Women's Engineering Society, the youngest president in its history.

Johnson was born in 1903 in Yorkshire, then moved to London after university to work as a secretary in a legal office. It was there that she became interested in planes. Johnson learned to fly at the London Aeroplane Club in the winter of 1928–29 and, soon, her hobby took over. Determined to show women could be as brilliant as men in the very male world of flying, she became the first British-trained female ground engineer – for a while, she was the only female GE in the world.

On 5 May 1930, she set off alone from Croydon Aerodrome outside London in a Gypsy Moth plane (called *Jason*) to fly to Australia, an epic journey of 11,000 miles. She landed in Darwin on 24 May, making her the first woman to fly solo to Australia. Other records followed, including setting a new record flying from England to Cape Town, solo, in 1932.

Johnson worked as a pilot for Hillman Airways London-Paris, but her commercial flying ended with the outbreak of the Second World War in 1939. She joined the Air Transport Auxiliary, ferrying aircraft from factory airstrips to RAF bases. It was during one of these flights on 5 January 1941 that Johnson crashed into the Thames Estuary and was killed. She died as she lived, doing what she loved up in the clouds.

Born on 22 September 1953 on a French military base in Dakar (now the capital of Senegal), Ségolène Royal developed her socialist and feminist politics at the famous *Institut d'études politiques de Paris* (known as Sciences Po). She put her politics into action when she was nineteen, suing her father – an army officer – because he refused to divorce her mother or pay alimony and child support to finance his children's education (Royal had seven brothers and sisters).

Royal stood as the Socialist Party candidate for the presidency of France in the 2007 election. Though she was not elected, she was the first woman to be nominated as a presidential candidate by a major political party in France.

23 September ➤➤ Suzanne Valadon

Staying in France, let's say *bonjour* to the artist Suzanne Valadon, who was born on 23 September 1865. Valadon was the first female painter admitted to the Société National des Beaux-Arts (the National Society of Fine Arts) in Paris. She left school when she was only eleven, and did a fair range of jobs including working in a milliner's workshop making hats, in a factory making wreaths for funerals, selling vegetables and as a waitress. She even worked in the circus as an acrobat.

But her great passion was drawing and painting. Valadon began to work as an artists' model in Paris to fund her art, watching their techniques and teaching herself. Unusually for women at the time, she painted female nudes, as well as still lifes and landscapes – occasionally, she even painted male nudes, which was seen as scandalous in 19th-century Paris.

Valadon died in 1938.

24 September ➻ Savitribai Phule

One of the mothers of the feminist movement in India is the education pioneer, poet and social campaigner Savitribai Phule. On 24 September 1873, she founded the Truth Seekers' Society.

Born in 1831, Phule is considered the first professional female teacher in India. Despite huge opposition, she and her husband set up one of the earliest girls' schools in India in 1848 and went on to set up another seventeen. She also established a care centre for pregnant rape victims and campaigned for the rights of widows, who often found themselves impoverished and outcast when their husbands died.

When plague swept through Maharashtra in 1897, Phule opened a clinic for sufferers. She died there, a victim of illness caught from those she was trying to save.

An extraordinary woman.

25 September ⇒ amina wadud

The American Muslim theologian, academic and 'Lady Imam' amina wadud made headlines the world over in 2005 when she led mixed prayers – that's to say, a congregation of both women and men – in a mosque in New York City. Although many supported her, traditionalists did not believe a woman should lead men in prayer and they protested.

Born Mary Teasley in Bethesda, Maryland, in 1952, she was the daughter of a Methodist minister. When she converted to Islam twenty years later, she chose the name amina wadud and decided to spell it without capital letters because they don't exist in the Arabic language.

As a scholar and activist, wadud has held professorial roles in Malaysia and the USA, focusing on Islam, justice, gender and sexuality. She advocates for gender equality in Islam and supports the LGBTQIA+ community. Her books include the groundbreaking *Qur'an and Woman: Rereading the Sacred Text from a Woman's Perspective.*

26 September ➤➤ Wangarĩ Maathai

On 26 September 2011, news was spreading of the death of the Kenyan activist, and biological and environmental scientist, Wangarĩ Maathai, the previous day.

Maathai was the first female professor in Kenya, the first woman in all of east and central Africa to receive a doctorate in biology and the first woman from Africa to win a Nobel Prize, which she was awarded in 2004 for her work with the Green Belt Movement.

The Green Belt Movement was founded in 1977 to challenge the deforestation threatening the livelihoods of rural communities in Kenya by encouraging women to plant trees. Since then, a whopping fifty million-plus trees have been planted throughout Africa and over 30,000 women have been trained in sustainable trades.

27 September ➡ Rachel Carson

The book that changed writing about the environment – *Silent Spring* by Rachel Carson – was published on 27 September 1962.

One of the mothers of the modern environmental movement, Carson was a marine biologist by training. She began her career in the US Bureau of Fisheries, but the success of her trilogy of books written in the 1940s and 1950s telling the story of our oceans – *Under the Sea-Wind, The Sea Around Us* and *The Edge of the Sea* – enabled her to give that up and become a full-time writer.

Carson's skill was to make science accessible and gripping for the general reader. Writing articles under the gender-neutral R. L. Carson to get her pro-environmental message across, in the late 1950s she turned her attention to the study of conservation and pollution, especially pollution caused by the indiscriminate use of synthetic pesticides, which can be harmful to humans and the environment.

When *Silent Spring* came out it took the world by storm and brought environmental destruction to widespread public attention. The chemical companies tried to discredit her, and the media attacked her on the grounds of her health and her sexuality, but ordinary people responded to her message of the importance of protecting our Earth.

Carson's courage in weathering these storms, and her refusal to back down, helped bring about a reversal in national pesticide policy in the USA. In turn, this led to a nationwide ban on DDT (the first modern synthetic insecticide) and other pesticides.

Carson suffered from ill health for much of her life and, by 1963, she had been diagnosed with breast cancer. Weakened by radiation treatment, she died in February 1964 from a heart attack. Her letters to her close friend – possibly partner – Dorothy Freeman were published by Freeman's granddaughter in 1995.

28 September → Althea Gibson

Althea Gibson was a star of paddleboard, golf and tennis. In 1956 she was the first Black tennis player to win the French Open, she then won the US Open in 1957 and 1958, and lifted the Wimbledon trophy twice. She was inducted into the Tennis Hall of Fame in 1971.

Gibson was also the first Black female professional golfer, taking up the sport after her tennis career was over. That she thrived in a time when segregation and the Jim Crow laws in America relegated Black people to second-class citizens is incredible.

Venus Williams is just one of the contemporary stars of the sport who have named Gibson as an inspiration. Born in South Carolina in 1927, Gibson died in New Jersey on 28 September 2003.

The first female Prime Minister of Australia, Julia Gillard, was born in Barry, in Wales, on 29 September 1961. Her family emigrated to Adelaide in 1966. She was the first female deputy leader of the Labor Party and the first, and to date only, female leader of the Australian Labor Party and prime minister.

For her entire career, Gillard put up with attacks on her ability and whisperings about her personal life – she wasn't married, she had no children. What was even more dispiriting was that some of the attacks on her came from men within her own party.

Finally, on 9 October 2012, she'd had enough. When the male leader of the opposition accused her of sexism in parliament, quick as a flash, Gillard fought back . . . and her words went viral. Now known as the 'Misogyny Speech', it is one of the most watched speeches of all time on social media and a masterclass in how to turn an attack to your favour.

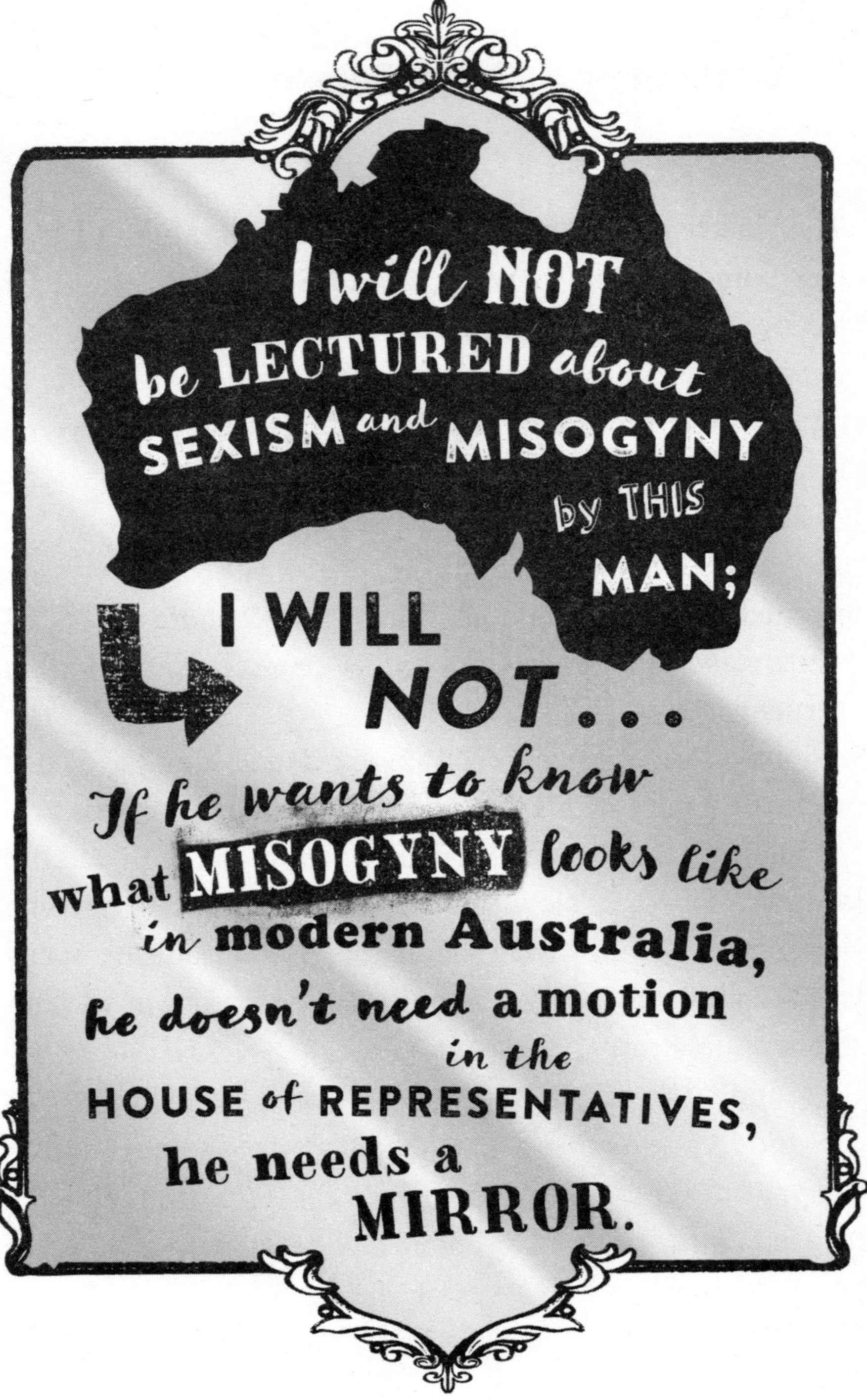

Julia Gillard

30 September ➤➤ **Zohra Drif**

We've talked about putting all women back into history, the sinners and the saints. We've also seen how one person's freedom fighter is another person's terrorist, depending on whose side you might be on. Real life is more nuanced than it appears on social media, which favours simplistic, clickbait slogans over explaining all sides of a situation without bias.

Algerian activist Zohra Drif was only twenty-one years old when she planted a bomb in a busy ice-cream parlour in Algiers, killing three young women and injuring others. At this stage, Algeria was engaged in a war with France for independence, a conflict that lasted from 1954 to 1962. Drif was a member of the National Liberation Front (NLF), and on 30 September 1956 her unit was directed to carry out a bombing. The atrocity became known as the Milk Bar Bombing. In 2012, one of the French women who survived the bombing, Danielle Michel-Chich, published an open letter to Drif about the effects of the bombing on her life.

After the atrocity, Drif continued working for the NLF, campaigning to bring women into the movement and focus the world's attention on the 'Algerian Question'. She evaded capture until September 1957, when she was arrested and held in solitary confinement, before being sentenced to twenty years' hard labour on charges of terrorism in August 1958. She was later pardoned by the French president Charles de Gaulle when Algeria gained independence in 1962.

Drif later became a highly respected criminal lawyer and

was one of the first women elected to the Algerian Council of the Nations. Years after the events of that day, Drif wrote of still feeling justified in her action as part of a campaign to rid her country of years of colonial repression and violence.

A complicated figure, both inside Algeria and France, she published her memoir, *Inside the Battle of Algiers: Memoir of a Woman Freedom Fighter*, in 2017. Read it and decide for yourself . . .

Our Bodies, Ourselves

In every period of history, and in almost every culture, societies have tried to control women's reproductive rights. These are battles that are still raging today. At the time of writing, there are twenty countries that ban abortion altogether, even in cases of rape or incest, even if the woman's life is at risk: Andorra, Malta, Jamaica, El Salvador, Honduras, Senegal, Egypt, the Philippines, Laos, the Dominican Republic, Haiti, Iraq, Madagascar, Nicaragua, and Suriname. Others have been attempting to limit women's choices. At the same time, in recent years, some sixty countries have liberalized their laws on abortion, including Ireland in 2018.

In the UK, the right for a girl or a woman to decide what she should do with her own body if pregnant is protected by the 1967 Abortion Act. This allows abortions up to twenty-four weeks into a pregnancy, provided the procedure is performed by a registered medical practitioner in an NHS hospital or other approved premises and verified by two independent doctors. In very occasional circumstances, a later abortion could be performed if the mother's life is at risk or the child would be born with an extreme, life-limiting disability. Despite this, some people – for reasons of faith or a belief that they should have the right to determine what a woman does with her own body – try to intimidate women and medical professionals outside abortion clinics.

Having to end an unwanted pregnancy can be distressing and no one wants to have to have an abortion. But, in some circumstances, it is the only or the best option – the health of the mother or the foetus, a pregnancy that is the result of a rape or sexual assault, poverty, economic hardship, emotional distress. In the end, it should be up to each individual woman to choose. There is no law in the world that restricts men and boys' rights over their own bodies, so why should women and girls be treated differently?

When abortion provision is not legal, it leads to unsafe procedures – what are often known as 'backstreet abortions' – and women's and girls' lives are put at risk. Making abortion provision illegal doesn't stop abortions, it just means that desperate women and girls are forced to seek out unsafe and often life-threatening alternatives. Those from lower income brackets and ethnic minority backgrounds are more likely to be affected. This has become a crisis in the US.

Roe v. Wade was the landmark piece of legislation in America that gave women and girls the right to make decisions over their own bodies. It came about because of the courage of a twenty-five-year-old woman, Norma McCorvey. Using the pseudonym 'Jane Roe', in 1969 she challenged the criminal abortion laws in Texas. Texan lawmakers claimed abortion was unconstitutional, except in cases where the mother's life was in danger. Defending the anti-abortion ban was a lawyer called Henry Wade.

McCorvey's appeal went before the Supreme Court in 1973. By a vote of seven to two, the court ruled that pregnant women could choose an abortion during the first three months of their pregnancy, while keeping some restrictions and bans in the second and third trimester. They judged that a woman's right to end her pregnancy was protected by the US Constitution. On 22 January 1973, Roe v. Wade was passed.

Fifty years later, after highly financed campaigns by anti-abortion activists – supported by right-wing Christians and many Republicans, not least of all President Donald Trump – the Republican-dominated Supreme Court overturned Roe v. Wade on 24 June 2022 and paved the way for individual states to make their own decisions about abortion provision. Since then, fourteen states have introduced near total abortion bans, while four – Georgia, South Carolina, Florida and Iowa – have banned abortion after six weeks of pregnancy, when most girls and women don't even know they are pregnant.

In 2025, the anti-choice lobby is not only continuing to try to pressure other states into full abortion bans, but is also attempting to limit access to contraception and to IVF treatments, too. At the time of writing, it's deeply alarming to see authoritarian attitudes in all areas taking hold in America – bigotry, a lack of compassion, dishonesty, intolerance, lack of respect for any people not inside a very white, very privileged, painfully ill-informed, technocratic inner circle – and, as with all authoritarian regimes throughout history, an attempt to control women's bodies is at the heart of that. After Trump's election victory, on social media some boys and men even perverted the rallying cry of the 1970s women's movement to 'Your body. My choice'. It reveals the truth of things – that this is not about the rights of an unborn child, but rather the desire to control women.

But, though the situation seems – and is – bleak (it's

always depressing when progress stalls), it's also important to remember that in fact the USA is one of only four countries globally who have made their laws stricter in the past thirty years. More than sixty countries have liberalized, acknowledging that women's rights are human rights. The fight for women and girls to have the same rights as men will never stop until everyone is treated equally and fairly under the law.

Our bodies, ourselves. A woman's right to choose.

OCTOBER

October

1 October ➤➤ Kathleen Ollerenshaw

Meet another Renaissance woman, the mathematician, astronomer, scholar and politician Kathleen Ollerenshaw.

Ollerenshaw was born in Manchester on 1 October 1912. She was seriously ill as a child and, though she recovered, she became D/deaf at the age of eight. She was taught how to lip-read, but astonishingly didn't get her first hearing aid until she was in her thirties. Throughout her life, Ollerenshaw refused to let what was then seen as a disability be used as a way to limit her opportunities. So, in her interview for Oxford University to read maths, she didn't even tell them she was D/deaf until she'd been offered a place.

After graduating, Ollerenshaw joined the staff of the Shirley Institute as a statistician, then worked at the University of Manchester as a lecturer, where she became an honorary member and vice president of the Manchester Astronomical Society. Not content with two careers, Ollerenshaw began a third. In 1956, she was elected as a Conservative councillor for Rusholme, a position she held until 1981. She was Lord Mayor of Manchester, High Sheriff of Greater Manchester and one of the key movers in the creation of the Royal Northern College of Music.

On top of all of this, she was an extraordinary sportswoman: lacrosse, cricket, hockey, a keen skier and mountain climber, a figure skater and an ice dancer. Her autobiography –

gloriously called *To Talk of Many Things* – was published when she was ninety-two.

2 October ➳ Marie Stopes

Here is another of our complicated heroines, that's to say a woman who did life-changing things for women (or, at least, some women), but who had other views that might give us pause for thought.

Born in Edinburgh in 1880, Marie Stopes was a pioneer. Her book *Married Love*, published in 1918, which was both controversial and influential at the time, brought the subject of women being able to control their fertility into the light. Stopes founded the first birth control clinic in Britain in 1921 and gradually built up a network across the UK, run by midwives and supported by visiting doctors. The clinics were free and open to all married women – though not to unmarried women – and gave advice on all aspects of birth control. Stopes transformed women's lives and was part of the Women's Freedom League, which campaigned for women's suffrage and sexual equality.

But, at the same time, she was against abortion and was a eugenicist, believing that only certain people should be allowed to have children. She advocated sterilization for poorer people, people of different races and those with disabilities, and was against mixed-race marriages.

So, Stopes was someone who did a huge amount for women at the same time as holding awful opinions and promoting racist views. Should she be written out of history? Of course not. Like many people, she did good and bad, and it is good history to acknowledge both.

Stopes died on 2 October 1958.

3 October ➤➤ **Nadine Gordimer**

On 3 October 1991, the South African activist, international award-winning novelist and short-story writer, Nadine Gordimer, was awarded the Nobel Prize in Literature.

The daughter of a British-Jewish mother and a Lithuanian-Jewish father from Tsarist Russia, Gordimer was born in a mining town outside Johannesburg in 1923. Her exquisite novels – which shone a spotlight on racial and moral issues, particularly under apartheid in South Africa – were often banned, but state criticism and government repression did not silence her.

Gordimer passionately believed in equality and fairness, she campaigned against censorship and was vice president of PEN International. She joined the political party the African National Congress (ANC) when it was still an illegal organization, having been propelled into the fight against apartheid after the arrest of a friend and the Sharpeville Massacre of 1960. She helped Nelson Mandela edit his famous 'I Am Prepared to Die' speech, delivered at his trial on 20 April 1964.

After apartheid was defeated, Gordimer was active in the fight against HIV/AIDS, which was causing a significant health crisis in South Africa. In 2004, she curated a selection of twenty writers to contribute to a book to help raise funds for treatment and research.

Gordimer died in Johannesburg in 2014 at the age of ninety.

4 October ➻ Aloha Wanderwell and Lexie Limitless

On 4 October 2019, the American explorer and YouTuber Lexie Alford – known as Lexie Limitless – reached her final destination in her around-the-world expedition.

Lexie was following in the footsteps of a Canadian-American explorer, Aloha Wanderwell, who'd made the history books a century earlier for being the first woman to circumnavigate the globe by car. I say woman, but actually Aloha was only sixteen when she set out in 1922 in a Ford Model T motorcar to travel more than 500,000 miles across eighty countries, beginning and ending her journey in Nice, France, five years later.

To be honest, Wanderwell's whole life was like a film – and she really did live up to her name and wander well! She

Aloha Wanderwell and her husband, Walter, next to her Ford Model T motorcar

looked like a starlet from the silent movies and, while on the road, she performed on stage, gave lectures and, with her husband, made films of her travels.

Lexie herself is no less intrepid, travelling to 196 countries before she was twenty-two and writing herself into the history books in the process. Sharing her experiences with her millions of followers, Lexie is a brilliant example of living your dreams.

5 October ➤ The Women's Bread March, Paris, 1789

We're heading back to Paris in the grips of the French Revolution for the Women's Bread March.

Also known as the October March, on 5 October 1789, women in the markets of Paris downed tools to protest about the high price of bread. The Revolution had been threatening for two years, and would continue until 1799. It was a conflict between the people of France and the nobility, who lived privileged lives while the majority of their subjects were starving.

Armed with pitchforks, sticks and anything else that came to hand, the women set off to march to the Palace of Versailles, about thirty kilometres away, where the royal family was in residence. It turned out to be a significant turning point in the Revolution, forcing King Louis XVI and his wife Marie Antoinette to return to Paris to face the wrath of the people. It's often misquoted – and it's not sure she even said it at all – but it's where the phrase attributed to Marie Antoinette, 'Let them eat cake', is supposed to have come from (cake, as opposed to bread) . . .

It was the beginning of the end of the French monarchy, which was abolished in 1792. Both Louis and Marie Antoinette were condemned to death and executed in 1793.

6 October ➤➤ Barbara Castle

The Labour MP Barbara Castle was born in Chesterfield on 6 October 1910. Castle was one of the most dogged and longest-serving MPs of the 20th century. She was elected as the Labour MP for Blackburn in the historic Labour 1945 landslide, having only been included on the shortlist when the women of Blackburn Labour Party threatened to resign if there were only male candidates! The world was changing and women wanted to be part of it.

Tireless, and always true to her principles, Castle served as Minister for Transport, First Secretary of State (the first woman to hold the post), Secretary of State for Employment, and for Health and Social Security. Castle introduced many measures we take for granted today – such as speed limits on British roads, compulsory seat belts and breathalyser tests as well as measures that made a huge difference to the lives of women and girls (see page 460 in the essay A Woman's Place is in the House).

But trouble was brewing.

In 1969, when she was Secretary of State for Employment and Productivity, Castle tried to take on the trade unions and limit their power with her 'In Place of Strife' proposed legislation. Britain was being brought to its knees by strike after strike, but Castle faced opposition from within her own party as well as from union leaders. One of the proposals was that unions would have to ballot their members before a strike was held.

Castle stepped down at the 1979 election and was elected to the European Parliament instead. She served as an MEP from 1979 to 1989, then became a member of the House of Lords in London.

She remained active in politics until her death in 2002, at the age of ninety-one.

I will FIGHT for what i BELIEVE in until I drop DEAD. And THAT'S what keeps you ALIVE.

Barbara Castle

7 October ➻ Mary Kingsley

Mary Kingsley was an English explorer, science writer and ethnographer, a woman who – like Lexie Limitless and Aloha Wanderwell – believed that the world was there to be discovered. An ethnographer is someone who studies specific groups of people to understand and illuminate their traditions, culture and customs better.

Kingsley was born in London in 1862. Like many middle-class Victorian girls, she did not attend school, but she had the run of a library at home and particularly enjoyed reading science and travel books.

Her adventures began in 1892 after the death of her parents, when she decided to stop being an armchair traveller and visit West Africa in person. She left England in 1893, landing first in what is now Sierra Leone and then heading south to what is now Angola. She collected – or bought – scientific specimens which proved to be invaluable in the understanding of the flora and fauna of the region.

Bitten with the travel bug, Kingsley returned to Africa in 1894, this time staying in what is now Nigeria, before heading to Gabon, a country little visited at that time by European explorers. Armed with extraordinary specimens – insects, shells, plants, reptiles, fish – Kingsley returned to the UK on 7 October 1895 to a hero's welcome.

She lectured widely and published books, including *Travels in West Africa* in 1897, campaigning not only for a greater understanding and respect of West African culture, but against the colonialism that characterized and had scarred Britain's relationship with much of that continent.

Kingsley died in Cape Town in 1900.

8 October ➻ Ursula von der Leyen

The German politician Ursula von der Leyen was born in Brussels on 8 October 1958. She was the first woman to serve as Germany's Minister of Defence and, in July 2019, became the first woman to be elected President of the European Commission. She was re-elected in 2024 for a second five-year term.

Ursula von der Leyen speaking during a media conference after a meeting of the College of Commissioners at EU headquarters in Brussels, Belgium in 2023

9 October ⇥ **Malala Yousafzai**

On 9 October 2012, a masked gunman forced his way onto a bus in north-west Pakistan demanding to know which of the girls was Malala. When she replied, the Taliban terrorist shot her in the head. Why? For the crime of speaking up for the rights of girls to an education.

Before the Taliban took over their town in the Swat Valley, Malala's father had run a girls' school. But when the Taliban took charge, they not only banned things such as owning a television or playing music, but decreed that girls could not go to school past the age of eleven. Malala refused to accept this and became an outspoken, and well-known, advocate of girls' education. This made her a target.

The brutal shooting of a fourteen-year-old girl simply for wanting to learn made headlines the world over and the Taliban was denounced for its violent and misogynist ideology. At the time, Malala herself was unaware of this. She was flown to Birmingham, in England, and woke up ten days later in hospital. Two years of surgeries and rehabilitation followed before she was well enough to join her family in their new home in the Midlands.

Known all over the world simply as 'Malala', she realized she had a choice: to keep quiet or to continue to speak up about the right of girls to an education. She set up the Malala Fund and, in December 2014, was awarded a Nobel Peace Prize when she was seventeen years old. This made her the youngest ever Nobel laureate.

With the rights of girls and women being rolled back in Pakistan and Afghanistan, and with nearly 130 million girls out of school against their wishes, Malala is an inspiration and testament to how one person can make all the difference.

Malala Yousafzai

10 October →→ The Founding of the WSPU, 1903

We've heard a lot about the Women's Social and Political Union, the organization founded by Emmeline Pankhurst, and her daughters Christabel and Sylvia. As we know, the women-only WSPU would become known for civil disobedience and direct action and played a leading role in getting women the right to vote.

Let's go back to the beginning and why the WSPU came to be set up. Frustrated that the Independent Labour Party (ILP) was not taking women's concerns seriously, or prioritizing them, on 10 October 1903, Emmeline Pankhurst invited a group of female ILP supporters to meet at her house in Nelson Street, Manchester.

The rest, as they say, is history.

It's likely you won't know the Victorian writer Lily Watson, even though she was a famous novelist in her day.

Lily was born on 11 October 1849 in Taunton, Somerset, the eldest daughter of a Baptist minister and his wife. Her grandmother was descended from French Huguenots, who'd fled as refugees to England in the 17th century. Watson wrote fourteen novels, devotional poetry and stories for children, and was a correspondent for the magazine *The Girl's Own Paper*. She was the Prime Minister William Gladstone's favourite writer. But, despite being well-known in her day, after her death her voice fell into silence.

Lily Watson is my great-grandmother, but it wasn't until 2022 that I started to find out anything about her. Surprised by how quickly she'd disappeared from the history books, she was the inspiration for *Warrior Queens & Quiet Revolutionaries*, my memoir putting one thousand women back into history. That, in turn, was the starting point for *Feminist History for Every Day of the Year*.

How much do you know about the women in your family? Have you asked your mother, or carer, or grandmother or aunt about their lives and the lives of their mothers and grandmothers? You might be amazed at what you discover . . .

12 October ➢ Toshiko Kishida

Toshiko Kishida – who wrote under the pen name Shõen – was one of Japan's first feminists. She was born in 1863, a time where the country was starting to open up to new reforms and new ideas. In 1882, Kishida gave a speech called 'The Way of Women', urging that women should be allowed to be educated as a basis for equality. But it is for her speech 'Daughters in Boxes' that she is most remembered.

Delivered on 12 October 1883, the speech criticized the family system in Japan that treated girls as second-class. In it, Kishida said, the girls were like creatures kept confined in boxes and even if they did have a voice, they were unable to use it.

Nothing she said could be denied, but her words were more radical than the authorities were prepared to accept. Kishida was arrested, taken to court and fined. It seems Japan was keen to modernize some aspects of society, but not transform the lives of women.

13 October ➤➤ The Arrest of the Knights Templar, 1307

This may be the origins of why Friday the 13th is considered an unlucky day. For it was on Friday, 13 October 1307 that there was a mass arrest of Knights Templar in France on the order of the king, Philip the Fair, probably because they had refused to allow him to join their elite order (and he owed them a lot of money and was trying to avoid repaying his debts!). The warrior knights were tortured and executed and the order was destroyed, bringing to an end two hundred years of tradition.

The Order of the Knights Templar had been founded during the early 12th century to protect European travellers on pilgrimage to the Holy Land and to carry out secret operations. It grew into an incredibly powerful and wealthy institution. In those times, it was believed that only men could be knights – it was both a military position and a social one – but when the Templars wrote down a list of their rules, sometime around 1129, the mandates mentioned that women had, in fact, been admitted to the Order in the past.

There is no record of any of the knights rounded up on 13 October 1307 being a woman. All the same, it's another example of always digging a little deeper and realizing that history can go backwards, in terms of equality, as well as forwards. And players of the historical-adventure video game *Assassin's Creed* will know that there is a female Templar knight in the first game of the series.

14 October ➤ The Salsa Soul Sisters

The first march for lesbian and gay rights in Washington, DC, took place on 14 October 1979. Estimates vary as to how many took part, but there might have been as many as 120,000 lesbians, bisexuals, gay men, transgender people and straight allies marching together to demand equal civil rights and to urge legislation that did not discriminate on the grounds of sexual preference or gender.

Carrying the official banner, the march was led off by the Salsa Soul Sisters, one of the first lesbian organizations created by and for Black women and women of colour.

Salsa Soul Sisters Harriet Alston and Shirley Carvin at Gay Pride March, 1978

15 October ➤➤ Isabella Bird

Meet another extraordinary Victorian explorer.

Isabella Bird was born in Boroughbridge in Yorkshire on 15 October 1831. Despite always suffering from ill health, she became an explorer, naturalist and writer. Bird was the first woman elected a fellow of the British Royal Geographical Society and rode over 800 miles of the Rocky Mountains in the US on horseback, which formed the basis for *A Lady's Life in the Rocky Mountains*. The book made her a celebrity, though she threatened to sue *The Times* of London for suggesting she wore trousers while undertaking her epic journey. She also travelled in Hawaii, through China, Japan and Malaysia.

In her late fifties, Bird studied medicine in order to become a missionary. She arrived in India in February 1889, where she founded a hospital. Still full of enthusiasm and curiosity, she travelled to the border with Tibet, then journeyed on through Persia, Kurdistan, Armenia and Turkey.

In 1897, though in her sixties and with her health deteriorating, she sailed the Yangtze River in China and the Han River in Korea, then saw in the new century in Morocco. There, she became seriously ill and had no choice but to return home. She died in Edinburgh on 7 October 1904.

16 October ➤➤ Alice Oseman

Are you a fan of the LGBTQIA+ *Heartstopper* graphic novel series? Have you read *Loveless* or *Solitaire*? They all come from the pen of YA author, illustrator and TikTok sensation Alice Oseman, who puts the lives, loves and challenges of teenage life on the page.

Oseman, who was born on 16 October 1994, got her first publishing deal at the age of seventeen, before she had even started at university. She also talks openly about her own mental health issues. She's won awards, seen her work adapted for Netflix, and has been awarded an honorary degree from the University of Kent . . . and she's still only thirty!

17 October ➠ Mother Teresa

On 17 October 1979, a Catholic nun – born in North Macedonia in 1910 – was awarded the Nobel Prize for Peace.

In 1950, Mother Teresa founded the Missionaries of Charity, an order dedicated to looking after the 'poorest of the poor' in Calcutta (now Kolkata), in India. She was named a saint in 2016 and the anniversary of her death, 5 September 1997, is observed as her feast day.

Over many years, the Missionaries of Charity has grown to operate in more than 133 countries, with more than 4,500 nuns running homes for those dying from HIV/AIDS, leprosy and tuberculosis, as well as running soup kitchens, dispensaries, mobile clinics, orphanages and schools. There is no doubt Mother Teresa made a huge difference to the lives of millions, though her views were also challenging – she opposed contraception, abortion and divorce. Access to any or, better, all of these three things would have made a substantial difference to the lives of some of the poorest women she cared for.

18 October ➤➤ **The Famous Five**

Also known as the 'Alberta Five', in the early years of the 20th century, five women in Canada – Emily Murphy, Nellie McClung, Irene Parlby, Louise McKinney and Henrietta Muir Edwards – went to court to demand that they be considered 'persons'.

On 18 October 1929, the court ruled in their favour.

The battle had begun in 1916 when lawyers said that Emily Murphy, as a woman, did not count as a 'person' under Canadian law. She – and others – began a campaign to challenge the wording, and to pave the way for Canadian women to vote. Finally, after many setbacks and a successful appeal to the British government, the Famous Five were victorious.

19 October ➛ Jacqueline du Pré

One of the most joyful and brilliant musicians and performers of the 20th century, Jacqueline du Pré, died on 19 October 1987.

She started to play the cello at the age of four – encouraged by her mother, who was a pianist and composer – and made her television debut at the age of fourteen. She made her professional debut in 1961 with a recital at London's Wigmore Hall, and her Proms debut the following year.

In her short career, du Pré studied with, and played with, the greatest musicians of the time and performed with the world's leading orchestras. On Christmas Eve 1966, she met the acclaimed conductor and pianist Daniel Barenboim. A few months later, she flew to Jerusalem, converted to Judaism, and they married in July 1967.

In 1971, du Pré began to lose sensitivity in her fingers and, after two desperate years trying to find out what was wrong, she was diagnosed with multiple sclerosis. Her illness made it harder and harder to play. She gave her last public concerts in New York in February 1973.

Du Pré died in London and is buried in Golders Green Jewish Cemetery. A star who burned briefly, but burned bright.

20 October ➤➤ Kamala Harris

I am honoured to share a birthday with Kamala Harris.

Harris was the first female vice president of the US, as well as the first African American and the first Asian American to hold the position. A member of the Democratic Party, she was the second woman to run for the presidency of the United States, after Hillary Clinton.

Born in Oakland, California, on 20 October 1964, Harris studied law. She was elected as Attorney General of California in 2010, then was re-elected in 2014. Again, she was the first African American and first Asian American to hold the office.

A passionate supporter of women's rights and equality, when she was defeated in the US presidential election of November 2024 – having campaigned on a platform in favour of women's reproductive rights, LGBTQIA+ issues and in support of environmental protections – Harris gave an elegant concession speech encouraging her supporters not to give up hope. As the reality of Trump's second presidency sinks in – and so many of the things Harris warned about are coming true – let's hope that she, or another woman dedicated to inclusivity, honesty and harnessing the best of all the citizens of the United States, will run for President next time around.

Let us FILL the sky with the LIGHT of a billion brilliant stars. The light of OPTIMISM, of FAITH, of TRUTH and SERVICE.

Kamala Harris

21 October ➤➤ Edmonia 'Wildfire' Lewis

In October 1876, visitors were continuing to flock to the Centennial Exposition held in Philadelphia to celebrate the hundredth anniversary of the signing of the Declaration of Independence. One of the highlights of the exhibition was a monumental white marble sculpture by the artist Edmonia 'Wildfire' Lewis called *The Death of Cleopatra*. Lewis was the only Black artist represented at the exhibition.

Of First Nation American and African American heritage, Lewis was born free in upstate New York in 1844, and she took her inspirations from leading figures in history and historical events. Her marble masterpiece *Forever Free* commemorated the Thirteenth Amendment to the US constitution, which ended slavery.

But racism in America forced her to move to Europe. She lived in Rome, then went to Paris in 1896, before settling in London. Lewis died there in 1907 and is buried in the same cemetery in Kensal Green where Mary Seacole and Christine Granville (whose birth name was Krystyna Skarbek) both lie.

Forever Free by Edmonia Lewis, 1867

22 October ➻ Inez Milholland

Inez Milholland is one of the best known of the American suffrage leaders. There is a glorious photograph of her leading the major women's suffrage procession in Washington in March 1913 on a white horse – Grey Dawn – wearing a long white cloak and crown. She looks rather like a Knight Templar!

Milholland came from a wealthy background and graduated from Vassar College in 1909. She was already involved in the suffrage movement, but after she heard Emmeline Pankhurst speak, she was inspired to become a lawyer and campaign for the labour rights of children and women in New York City.

Milholland collapsed during a speaking tour of the US on 22 October 1916, and died weeks later. Her sudden death made her a martyr. Her last words of the tour were addressed to President Woodrow Wilson: 'Mr President, how long must women wait for liberty?'

Inez Milholland leading the women's suffrage procession, Washington, March 1913

23 October ➵ **Soong Mei-ling**

Soong Mei-ling was a leading Chinese political figure of the 20th century. Born in Shanghai in 1897, she was educated in the United States, which would prove essential in 20th-century Sino–American relations. She was married to Chiang Kai-shek, who led the Chinese Nationalists against both the Japanese Empire in the Second World War and against the communists in the Chinese Civil War, and worked with him to form alliances with the West.

During the Second World War, she wrote many articles on China for American journals. In 1943, during a visit to the United States, she became the first Chinese person – and only the second woman – to address a joint session of the US Congress, where she asked for increased support for China in its war against Japan – and got it!

When the Nationalist forces were defeated in the Civil War in 1949, Soong and her husband fled to Taiwan, a former Japanese colony China had seized after the Second World War. There he established his government-in-exile. Still highly influential, Soong continued to seek support from the United States, and her efforts helped sway the US government's policy toward China and Taiwan.

Soong died in New York City on 23 October 2003.

24 October ➻ Virginia Woolf

One of the most significant pieces of writing about women's creativity is Virginia Woolf's essay *A Room of One's Own.* First published on 24 October 1929, it was based on two lectures she had given at Newnham and Girton women's colleges at Cambridge University the previous year.

Born on 25 January 1882, into a wealthy middle-class family in London, Woolf is one of the greatest 20th-century English writers. A novelist and essayist, a diarist, critic and co-founder of publishing company the Hogarth Press, she wrote about feminism, aesthetics, culture, economics, pacifism, sexuality, art and literature, and was always analysing and questioning the world in which she lived. She pioneered a technique called 'stream of consciousness', a style of writing where the characters' thoughts, feelings and reactions are put down on the page without being interrupted by dialogue or objective description. Her novels – including *Orlando, To the Lighthouse* and *The Waves* – are beloved by readers and studied by students the world over.

Woolf struggled with depression and poor mental health all her life. Finally, on 28 March 1941, she died by suicide in the River Ouse near Lewes, in East Sussex, close to where she lived. She left behind a huge body of writing that still inspires readers today. Every year, a Wednesday in mid-June is celebrated as 'Dalloway Day' in honour of the day in Woolf's novel *Mrs Dalloway*, when her lead character takes her famous walk around London.

25 October ➳ Margery Kempe

On 25 October 2024, the exhibition *Medieval Women: In Their Own Words* opened at the British Library in London. On display were countless treasures, including a precious signed letter from Joan of Arc never before seen outside of France, a birthing girdle – a kind of soft belt that women wore during labour with prayers, incantations and words of encouragement written on it – and the skull of a lion! Among the many manuscripts, including Melisende's Psalter, was a rare surviving copy of *The Book of Margery Kempe.* It is considered to be the first autobiography in the English language.

Kempe was an English mystic who was born around 1373. Unlike most mystics of the time, she was married (she had at least fourteen children) rather than being a nun. She began to have visions, and because she couldn't read or write she dictated her dreams to be transcribed. She described everything from her pregnancies, births, illnesses, domestic issues in the town of Lynn where she lived (now King's Lynn) to her pilgrimages to holy sites in Europe and the Holy Land. Sometime around 1413 or 1414, we also know she visited the mystic Julian of Norwich to get her blessing for her writings.

Kempe died in 1438 and the manuscript of the book was copied shortly before 1450, but then was lost for centuries.

In 1934, what appears to be the only surviving manuscript of *The Book of Margery Kempe* was found at the back of a cupboard in a private library in England. It is now safe at the British Library in London.

26 October ➛ Nicola Adams

Born on 26 October 1982 in West Yorkshire, Nicola Adams helped make women's boxing popular. Fighting in the flyweight division, she was the first female boxer to win an Olympic gold medal in 2012, the year women's boxing was included at the Games for the first time. When Adams returned home after her victory, it was to discover that post boxes in her home town of Leeds had been painted gold in her honour.

Adams became the first double Olympic champion at the Rio Olympics four years later, when she won a second gold medal. She turned professional in 2017. Adams also won the World Boxing Organization (WBO) female flyweight title in 2019 and retired that same year, undefeated.

Since then, she has appeared on many television shows – including *Strictly Come Dancing* – and hasn't ruled out a return to the boxing ring when the time is right!

27 October ➻ Lise Meitner

The physicist and chemist Lise Meitner is another victim of the 'Matilda Effect' (see 28 February).

Often referred to as the 'German Marie Curie' (though she was actually Austrian), Meitner was one of the first women to graduate from the University of Vienna and the first woman to become a full professor of physics in Germany. She lost her position in the 1930s because of discrimination and mounting violence against Jewish people. In 1938, she fled to Scandinavia and later became a Swedish citizen.

But long before that, in 1917, Meitner and a colleague, Otto Hahn, discovered the isotope of protactinium (a key element in nuclear fission). Years later, when Hahn was given the Nobel Prize in Chemistry for his work, he failed to acknowledge Meitner's role in their joint discovery.

The story didn't end there. Between 1924 and 1948, Meitner was nominated nineteen times for a Nobel Prize in Chemistry, and she was nominated a whopping twenty-nine times for a Nobel Prize in Physics between 1927 and 1965. But never won. She is surely the most important scientist consistently overlooked by the Nobel committee.

Meitner died on 27 October 1968 in Cambridge, England.

28 October →→ Émilie du Châtelet

On 28 October 1740 the French natural philosopher and mathematician Émilie du Châtelet published her groundbreaking *Foundations of Physics*. In it, she tackled three of the major issues concerning natural philosophers in the 18th century and it's considered one of the – if not *the* – first physics textbooks.

Turning accepted thinking about forces and energy on its head, she also promoted intellectual free-thinking rather than following the ideas of 'great men'. She rejected established philosophical authorities and championed the notion that women, like men, should develop their minds and take part in intellectual pursuits. The book was circulated widely and translated into other languages. Du Châtelet also translated *Newton's Principia Mathematica* from Latin into French. Published in 1759, ten years after du Châtelet's death, it remains the standard translation even today.

29 October ➤➤ Ellen Johnson Sirleaf

Sometimes known as 'Africa's Iron Lady', a reference to the nickname of British Prime Minister Margaret Thatcher, today is the birthday of the Liberian politician and peace campaigner Ellen Johnson Sirleaf.

Born in Monrovia in 1938, to a Gola father and Kru-German mother, Sirleaf was president of Liberia from 2006 until 2018, the first elected female head of state in Africa. She led her country through recovery after its long and bloody civil war and, in 2011, was awarded a Nobel Peace Prize in recognition of her efforts to include women in the peacekeeping process. In 2016, Sirleaf was elected chair of the Economic Community of West African States, again the first woman to hold the position.

30 October ➤➤ Florence Nagle

Sometimes called the 'Mrs Pankhurst of British horse racing' – because of her determination to fight for women to be part of the British training world on the same terms as men – Florence Nagle was a horse trainer, and an award-winning breeder of racehorses and pedigree dogs.

Nagle bought her first Irish Wolfhound in 1913 and went on to own, or breed, twenty-one United Kingdom Champions – in other words, dogs that had won show and certification certificates. She was also the first woman to have a driving licence in Berkshire!

She trained her first racehorse in 1920. At this time, women had to employ men to hold a Jockey Club trainer's licence on their behalf (or to have licences in their husbands' names). Steadily and forcefully, Nagle challenged the gentlemen's clubs of the racing and canine worlds over their gender inequality. Finally, in 1966, she became one of the first two women in the United Kingdom licensed to train racehorses in her own name (the other was Norah Wilmot).

Frustrated by the lack of opportunities for women jockeys, Nagle sponsored the Florence Nagle Girl Apprentices' Handicap, first run in 1986 at Kempton Park. She died at her home in West Sussex on 30 October 1988.

31 October ➻ Zaha Hadid

Described by *The Guardian* as 'the Queen of Curves', for her swooping, elegant, non-angular buildings, the Iraqi-British architect Zaha Hadid was born in Baghdad on 31 October 1950. An architect, artist and designer, she is a key figure in architecture of the late 20th and early 21st centuries.

Hadid studied maths at university, then enrolled at the Architectural Association School of Architecture in 1972 with a vision of doing things differently. The first woman to win the prestigious Pritzker Architecture Prize in 2004, she went on to win the UK's biggest architectural award, the Stirling Prize. She was also the first woman to be individually awarded the Royal Gold Medal from the Royal Institute of British Architects.

Hadid's most famous works include the London Aquatics Centre for the 2012 Olympics, the Broad Art Museum in Michigan, Rome's MAXXI Museum and the Guangzhou Opera House. When she died unexpectedly in March 2016 from a heart attack, several of her buildings were still under construction, including the Daxing International Airport in Beijing.

A Woman's Place is in the House

The UK General Election of 2024 saw the highest ever proportion of female Members of Parliament elected. Forty-two per cent of MPs – nearly 50 per cent of the House of Commons – were women, including the first ever female Tamil MP, Uma Kumaran, and the first ever Chinese-born MP, Yuan Yang. There was a female Deputy Prime Minister, in the shape of Angela Rayner, and the position of Chancellor of the Exchequer was occupied by a woman, Rachel Reeves, for the first time in history. Eluned Morgan was elected Welsh Labour's first female leader and all three Deputy Speakers of the House were women. Can you imagine how delighted those early suffragettes would have been to see such a thing? It's a reminder of how, even if things take a long time, working together to shift the dial can work.

Hope matters. Change matters.

But why does it matter so much that there are more women in the House (of Commons and the Lords)?

Technically, the laws we live by in the UK apply to everybody equally. At the same time, there are certain laws that impact more on the lives of women and girls than they do on men and boys, such as reproductive rights or those covering health, equal pay, domestic violence, childcare and caring, because the vast majority of those working in the care sector, paid and unpaid, are women. It was the Labour politician Barbara Castle who put through the Equal Pay Act in 1970 and also oversaw the introduction of a Carers'

Allowance, both policies critical to improving women's lives. On IWD each year, the Labour politician Jess Phillips stands up in the House of Commons and reads out the names of all the women who have died in the previous year as a result of domestic violence. To have women lawmakers, working alongside their male allies, is the surest way to make sure the specific needs of women and girls are not overlooked.

Mary Robinson

We've met some of the first female MPs from around the world, from Constance Markievicz to Senedu Gebru, and learned the stories of some of the first female heads of state. Here are a few more names to remember.

Mary Robinson was Ireland's first female president. Serving from 1990 to 1997, her presidency was transformational. Having campaigned successfully on several liberal issues as a senator and as a lawyer, Robinson was part of the drive to decriminalize homosexuality, to legalize contraception, to make divorce available and enable women to sit on juries. Vigdís Finnbogadóttir was the first female democratically elected president of Iceland. Serving from 1980 to 1996, she remains the longest-serving elected female head of state in history.

Vigdís Finnbogadóttir

Elisabeth Domitien was Prime Minister of the Central African Republic from 1975 to 1976, the first and only woman so far to hold the position, as well as being the first woman prime minister of a country in Africa. Maria de Lourdes Pintasilgo was the first woman to serve as Prime Minister of Portugal. Agathe Uwilingiyimana is to date the only female prime minister of Rwanda, serving from 18 July 1993 until her assassination on 7 April 1994.

Elisabeth Domitien

But there is more work to do. In 2025, only twenty-six out of 195 countries are led by a woman and some 113 countries have never had a woman at the helm. It's why campaigns like Ask Her to Stand – encouraging women in the UK to put themselves forward at all levels, from local councils to being a prospective Member of Parliament – are so important. The wider the diversity of voices, the truer the representation will be.

The UK has had three female prime ministers, all from the Conservative Party. The first was Margaret Thatcher, who was prime minister from 1979 to 1990; Theresa May served from 2016 to 2019; and Liz Truss was prime minister for

Maria de Lourdes Pintasilgo

forty-nine days, from 6 September to 25 October 2020 (making her the shortest-serving prime minister in British history). In November 2024, Kemi Badenoch was elected as Conservative Party leader, making her the first Black leader of a major British political party and the first Black Leader of the Opposition.

The Scottish National Party (SNP), the Green Party and Plaid Cymru have all had female leaders, and Wales, Northern Ireland and Scotland have all had female first ministers. But neither the Labour Party nor the Liberal Democrats have managed a female leader . . . so far!

Could it be you?

NOVEMBER

November

1 November ➤➤ Margaret Thatcher

On 1 November 1990, Britain's first female prime minister, Margaret Thatcher, had to listen as one of her longest-serving colleagues issued a challenge to her leadership in the House of Commons. To her dismay, many of her supporters deserted her, and she was left with no choice; she resigned three weeks later.

Margaret Thatcher was born above her parents' grocery shop in Grantham, Lincolnshire, on 13 October 1925. She studied chemistry at Oxford University, but politics was her passion. She worked briefly as a research chemist, then worked as a barrister while trying to further her political ambitions. After years of trying to be selected as a Conservative Party candidate – partly because many Conservative Associations did not think women with young children should have careers or be MPs – she was selected to fight the seat of Finchley in north London. In 1959, she was elected to Parliament.

Over the next fifteen years, Thatcher held several important governmental positions, including Secretary of State for Education, but she was aiming higher. In 1975, she won the contest to become leader of the Conservative Party, making her the first woman to lead a major political party in the UK. Four years later, when the Conservatives won the General Election of 1979, Thatcher became the first ever female prime minister of the UK.

Her nickname was the 'Iron Lady'. She liked this nickname, determined as she was to prove she was tough enough to do the job. Even today, more than thirty years after she stood down in 1990, many female leaders the world over are compared to Margaret Thatcher.

But she was a highly divisive figure – beloved by many, reviled by others. Some of that was sexism, pure and simple, but much of it was because of her policies and attitudes. She led Britain into a war over the Falkland Islands in 1982. On her watch, the miners' strike divided and hollowed out communities throughout the UK, and the hated Poll Tax brought people onto the streets in protest. In October 1984, the Provisional IRA bombed the hotel in Brighton hosting the Conservative Party annual conference in an assassination attempt. Thatcher escaped unhurt, but others were killed or injured.

She was one of the most recognized political figures in the world and her popularity abroad helped keep her in power at home. But there were storm clouds on the horizon. The thorny matter of closer relations with Europe was starting to split the Tories and, in the end, it was her own party that brought her down.

The thing to bear in mind is this. Whether you like her politics or oppose them, Thatcher broke the glass ceiling – that's to say, simply by being a woman in a powerful position, she made it more likely that other women would follow.

2 November ➦ Dawn French and Jennifer Saunders

Although great comic actresses are celebrated – think of Doris Day, Lucille Ball, Victoria Wood, Patricia Routledge, Miranda Hart, Mindy Kaling, Aubrey Plaza, Ali Wong, Kate McKinnon, Quinta Brunson, Ayo Edebiri, Maya Rudolph – comedy has always been a tough gig for women. Sexist preconceptions about women not being funny, and a tradition of performers cutting their teeth in working men's clubs on the comedy circuit (where the audience was almost always entirely male) meant that comediennes had to work twice as hard.

Two of the trailblazing and most versatile women in comedy are Dawn French and Jennifer Saunders. On 2 November 1982, which was Channel 4's first night on air, they appeared in the opening episode of *The Comic Strip Presents: Five Go Mad In Dorset*. Both would go on to have hugely successful careers, together and separately, in shows such as *French and Saunders*, *The Vicar of Dibley* (French) and *Absolutely Fabulous* (Saunders).

3 November ➤➤ Jennie Lee

'Behind every great man stands a great woman,' as the old saying goes.

Step forward the Scottish politician Jennie Lee, who was married to Nye Bevan (who laid the foundations for the National Health Service) and is often overlooked in favour of him.

The daughter of a coalminer, Lee became a Labour MP when she was only twenty-four. Her victory meant she was the first Labour woman to represent a Scottish seat in the House of Commons. Having lost her seat and been out of government, she was returned to Parliament in Clement Attlee's landslide victory in 1945 representing Cannock in Staffordshire. Lee was the UK's first arts minister in Harold Wilson's government in 1964; she played a key role in setting up the Open University and campaigned all of her life to improve the living conditions and opportunities of working-class women and men.

Born in Fife on 3 November 1904, Lee died in 1988.

4 November ➤ Ruth Handler

We've already celebrated the *Barbie* movie, but what about the creator of the actual doll herself, American business tycoon and inventor Ruth Handler?

Born in Colorado on 4 November 1916, Handler was the daughter of Polish-Jewish immigrants. She worked at Paramount film studios in Los Angeles, where she fell in love with furniture-making. After she married, she suggested to her husband they should start their own business, and they came up with the name Mattel for their company. When materials were scarce during the Second World War, they went from manufacturing furniture to manufacturing toys. Handler later noticed her daughter and her friends playing with paper dolls, and inspired by the German Bild Lilli doll, the idea for Barbie was born.

The first Barbie was launched on 9 March 1959 and cost $3. She came with either blonde or brown hair, worn in her signature high ponytail, and wore a black-and-white swimming costume. She was an instant hit. Mattel later added a boyfriend for Barbie – Ken, named after Handler's son – and then more and more dolls, until there were more than 125 Barbies with all sorts of different careers.

Although there had been Black and brown friends of Barbie from the 1960s (including Francie, Christie and Julia), Mattel's first Black Barbie was launched in 1980 with the slogan: 'She's Black. She's beautiful. She's dynamite!' She was designed by Mattel's first Black designer, Kitty Black Perkins.

Ruth Handler, Mattel Inc. Co-Founder and Barbie Doll Inventor, 1994

5 November ➻ Violet Barclay

The world of comic books is seen as a boys' club. But there are plenty of female comic-strip artists, key among them the American artist Violet Barclay.

Born on 5 November 1922, Barclay was part of the golden age of comic books in the 1930s and 1940s. She attended the School of Industrial Art high school in New York City, then she got her break at the age of seventeen, when a penciller for Timely Comics (the forerunner of Marvel Comics) said he could get her a job as an inker – an artist who adds solid lines and extra details to the initial pencil drawings for a comic or graphic novel. Barclay became a full-time member of staff in 1942. The *Who's Who of American Comic Books* credits her with having inked stories for *Super Rabbit*, *Ziggy Pig* and *Silly Seal*, as well as the comedy series *Nellie the Nurse*.

After leaving Timely Comics in 1949, Barclay freelanced and worked on the crime comic *Exposed*, and for DC Comics, mostly in the romance genre.

She died in 2010 in New York.

6 November ➵ **Louise Labé**

Meet the 16th-century cross-dressing poet Louise Labé.

Born around 1522 in Lyon, Labé is one of the most important French Renaissance poets. Sometimes known as *la belle cordière* – the beautiful ropemaker (because of her father's job, though he was also a butcher and a surgeon, as well as a ropemaker) – not much is known about her early life and schooling. She received some education in Greek, Latin, Italian and Spanish, as well as music, and she learned to play the lute. She was also a brilliant horsewoman and archer, which led to another nickname, *la belle*

amazone, after the female warriors from Greek mythology. Contemporary records have her dressing in men's clothing and competing in tournament jousts alongside the men. This was enough to make some critics accuse her of being immoral.

After Labé married, she hosted literary salons in Lyon, which was a cultural centre in the 16th century. In 1545, she began writing her own poetry. In March 1555, she received permission from the king to protect her exclusive right to publish her own work, and her collected works were published around 6 November that same year.

7 November ➠ **Marie Curie**

Her name has come up many times, but it's time now properly to celebrate the most famous female scientist of all time, Marie Curie. The Polish-French physicist and chemist was the first woman to win a Nobel Prize, the first person to win a Nobel Prize twice, and the only person to win a Nobel Prize in two scientific fields.

Born on 7 November 1867 in Poland, Curie was forced to go to Paris to study because the University of Warsaw would not accept women. That was lucky, as it turned out, as it was at the Sorbonne University in France that she met her future husband and lifelong scientific partner. In 1903, they were jointly awarded the Nobel Prize in Physics, months after she became the first woman in France to earn a PhD. In 1911, Curie won the Nobel Prize in Chemistry (this time on her own). She was the first woman to be honoured for her own achievements in the Panthéon in Paris in 1995. (Sophie Berthelot was the first woman buried there in 1907, but her remains were only moved when her husband, a famous chemist, died and their family insisted they be laid to rest together.) Curie's husband Pierre is also buried in the Panthéon, one of seventy-five men honoured, including the writers Victor Hugo and Voltaire. To date, Curie is one of only six women buried there.

Curie's numerous achievements – and her importance as a leading woman in science – have been the subject of numerous biographies, histories, films and plays. This short entry cannot possibly do her justice. But we salute her not only for discovering radioactivity, for her groundbreaking work in the development of nuclear energy and for the treatment of cancer, but also for the way in which her mentorship and success opened up possibilities for so many female scientists coming after her, including her own daughter Irène Joliot-Curie, who jointly won the 1935 Nobel Prize in Chemistry.

Like mother, like daughter.

8 November »» **Dorothea Bate**

In 1898, Dorothea Bate from Carmarthen in south Wales turned up at the door of the Natural History Museum in London and talked her way into a job. She had no formal qualifications and was only nineteen, but she was determined to be a palaeontologist. The museum had almost no women scientists – in fact, women weren't actually allowed to be official members of the scientific staff until 1928 – but Bate was determined.

She worked at first in the Bird Room, where she sorted bird skins into species. Gradually respect for her expertise grew. Her first fossil discoveries were in the cliffs above the River Wye in Wales, where she uncovered fifteen species of mammals and birds dating back to around 10,000 BCE. She published her findings in *Geological Magazine* when she was twenty-two. Between 1901 and 1911, Bate explored Cyprus, Crete and the Balearic Islands and discovered numerous fossil remains of extinct species, then in the 1930s worked in what is now northern Israel.

Bate worked with the Natural History Museum all of her life. She published eighty reports and reviews, and numerous other papers. Born on 8 November 1878, she died in 1951.

9 November ➤➤ **Miriam Makeba**

Often called 'Mama Africa', the South African singer, songwriter, actress and anti-apartheid activist Miriam Makeba was born in Johannesburg in 1932.

She began singing professionally in the 1950s and, after appearing in the anti-apartheid film *Come Back, Africa*, she was invited to perform all over the world. For much of her life Makeba was forced to live in exile, as an outspoken critic of the apartheid government, but her reputation continued to grow. She moved to New York and recorded her first solo album in 1960. It was not until apartheid was defeated in 1990 that she was able to return home to South Africa.

On 9 November 2008, Makeba was performing in Italy when she had a heart attack on stage and was rushed to hospital. They couldn't save her and she died the following day. Paying tribute to her, the former South African President Nelson Mandela said: 'Her music inspired a powerful sense of hope in all of us.'

10 November ➳ Elizabeth Day

One of the most popular and inspirational podcasts is Elizabeth Day's *How to Fail*, where her guests reveal what their failures taught them. The podcast started in 2018 with Phoebe Waller-Bridge as Day's first guest. Since then, a fabulous range of people, from the great American feminist Gloria Steinem, to cyclist Chris Hoy, to actress Kate Winslet, have sat in the famous chair.

Day was born on 10 November 1978, and raised in Northern Ireland. When she was twelve, she became the youth columnist for the *Derry Journal*. After studying history at university, she started to write fiction – and later non-fiction, as a tie-in with her podcast. Listeners and readers love her for relatability – she talks and writes about being a woman in the 21st century, about friendship, and is admired for her courage in sharing her personal challenges, especially her struggles to have children. Day is unfailingly generous and supportive to other women. Her story is a dazzling example of how to create your own, unique career – and have fun while doing it.

11 November ➛ Emma Duffin

At the eleventh hour, of the eleventh day, of the eleventh month, there is a two-minute silence in the UK and the Commonwealth to remember all those who gave their lives and served during the First World War. Some of us wear red poppies, others white.

One of those who served during the First World War was the Irish nurse and diarist, Emma Duffin. She was born in Belfast in 1883. When war broke out, Duffin enlisted in the Voluntary Aid Detachment (VAD) as a nurse. In 1915, she was sent to Alexandria in Egypt. A year later she was dispatched to France, where she remained for the rest of the war.

Although those on active service were not supposed to keep diaries, Duffin did. As a result, we have some of the most important and moving first-hand reminiscences of what it was like to be a woman at war. Her description of Armistice Day on 11 November 1918 is one of the most affecting, and moving, pieces of writing you could read. Borrow her book *The First World War Diaries of Emma Duffin: Belfast Voluntary Aid Detachment Nurse* from your local library and see for yourself. Her humanity, her modesty and her relatability shine through the years.

On IWD 2017, a blue plaque was erected to Duffin at her former home on University Square, Belfast.

12 November ➳ Mary Astell

Mary Astell, who was born on 12 November 1666, has a good claim to be called the first British feminist (though the term 'feminist' didn't come into use for about another 180 years!).

Astell was a thinker, philosopher and writer who advocated for equal educational opportunities for women. In 1694, she anonymously published a paper challenging the arguments men made against women's education. Three years later, she followed it with proposals for female-centred education and, in 1709, she was appointed head of a charity school for girls in London. So far as we know, it was the first school in England to have an elected all-female board of governors.

IF GOD had NOT intended that WOMEN SHOULD USE THEIR REASON, He would NOT have GIVEN them ANY, For HE does NOTHING IN VAIN.

Mary Astell

13 November ➻ Emma Raducanu

British tennis player Emma Raducanu was born on 13 November 2002 in Toronto, Canada. Her Romanian father and Chinese mother moved to England when she was two, so she has joint Canadian-British citizenship. She speaks English, Mandarin and Romanian.

At the 2021 US Open, Raducanu became the first qualifier – that's to say she didn't automatically have a place in the competition – to win a Grand Slam title since the rules were changed in 1968 to allow professional players to compete in major tournaments alongside amateurs. Raducanu was the first British woman to win a Grand Slam tournament since Virginia Wade in 1977.

14 November ➤➤ Nicola Sturgeon

On 14 November 2014 Nicola Sturgeon, the leader of the Scottish National Party (SNP), was elected the First Minister of Scotland. She was the first woman to lead the SNP and the first female First Minister. During her time leading the party, she won eight elections (if you include European and council elections) in a row, an amazing record in the modern era.

Born in Ayrshire, Sturgeon studied law before she was elected to the Scottish Parliament in 1999. She was deputy leader of the SNP until Scotland narrowly voted against independence from the UK in 2014, when the leader of the SNP and the pro-independence campaign, Alex Salmond, resigned. She was elected as SNP leader in November that year and remained in office for nine years, overseeing a surge in party membership and negotiating difficult times, not least during the Covid-19 era. She was one of the rare women on the political stage who was universally known and recognized.

After a series of challenging situations – including allegations of sexual misconduct against her former mentor Alex Salmond and disagreements over trans rights and self-ID (Sturgeon is passionately committed to inclusivity), she resigned in February 2023 and in March 2025 announced she would stand down as an MSP at the next election. An avid reader and writer – her memoir *Frankly* came out in 2025 – she began a new career 'post politics' as a books commentator and interviewer with a series of live book events with the brilliant bestselling Scottish crime writer and Queen of Tartan Noir, Val McDermid. A powerhouse duo.

15 November ➥ Georgia O'Keeffe

The American painter Georgia O'Keeffe was born on a farm in Wisconsin on 15 November 1887. She studied in Chicago and New York, learning the techniques of traditional painting while experimenting to find her own voice as an artist. O'Keeffe mailed some of her abstract charcoal drawings to a friend, who shared them with an art dealer (reader, she married him). In 1916, he was the first to exhibit her work.

By the mid-1920s, O'Keeffe was already acknowledged as one of America's most important modern artists, known for her paintings of New York skyscrapers – a very modern American symbol – as well as for her stunning depictions of flowers. But falling in love with New Mexico in the summer of 1929 inspired a new direction in O'Keeffe's work. For the next twenty years, she spent most summers living and working in New Mexico.

Although her vision started to fail later in life, O'Keeffe kept painting into her nineties, enlisting assistants to help her to continue creating. She died in Santa Fe in 1986.

16 November ➻ Irena Sendler

Saturday, 16 November 1940 was the first full day of incarceration of Polish-Jewish people inside the Warsaw Ghetto. The ghetto had been sealed the day before.

Alongside the many Jewish women and men who worked for the Resistance smuggling people, weapons and food in and out of the ghetto was the Catholic Polish humanitarian aid worker, Irena Sendler. Her code name was 'Jolanta', and it's estimated that she saved as many as 2,500 Jewish children. Despite being arrested by the Gestapo in 1943 after the Warsaw Ghetto Uprising, and tortured, she refused to give up the names of other resistance fighters.

Sendler managed to escape and survive the war. In 1965, she was named as Righteous Among the Nations, an honour given to non-Jewish people who helped Jews escape persecution during the Holocaust. Poland has the most recipients, followed by the Netherlands, France and Ukraine.

Sendler died in Warsaw in May 2008.

17 November ➵ **Catherine the Great**

The 18th-century Empress of Russia, Catherine the Great, died on this day in 1796.

Loved, admired and feared, Catherine ruled Russia for more than thirty years from 1762, after overthrowing her husband and taking the throne for herself. She was a modernizing queen and, during her reign, Russia experienced a period of cultural and scientific growth. New cities were established, universities were founded and she was instrumental in changing girls' education by establishing schools for the daughters of both the nobility and the middle-class.

Only eighteen months before her death, Catherine approved the project to build an Imperial Library. The library was to contain not only her own extensive collection, but also valuable books that had been looted from Warsaw after the Partition of Poland in 1794. Because of her policy of brutal conquest and annexation, Russia became one of the great powers in Europe.

18 November ➻ The Edinburgh Seven

This is a story of unintended consequences. On 18 November 1870, seven aspiring doctors – Sophia Jex-Blake, Isabel Thorne, Mary Anderson Marshall, Edith Pechey, Matilda Chaplin, Emily Bovell and Helen Evans – walked to the Surgeons' Hall in the heart of Edinburgh to take their anatomy exam. They were the first female medical students at the university, but many male students, and a fair few male professors, resented their presence.

When the women arrived for their exam, they were greeted by a baying crowd of men hurling insults, mud and worse. But in Hillary Clinton's phrase, they 'resisted and persisted', and managed to get inside. Then, still hell-bent on intimidating their fellow students, the men set loose the university mascot – a sheep – into the examination room.

The first Scottish women to graduate from The University of Edinburgh

The altercation became known as the Surgeons' Hall Riot and it would prove to be a turning point. Many people who had previously been against women training to be doctors were so appalled by the behaviour of the men that public opinion turned in the women's favour. Sophia Jex-Blake, the most famous of the seven, filed a lawsuit against the university for failing to allow them to finish their medical education. Finally, six years later, a new Medical Act was passed, paving the way for women to be doctors.

And what of the Edinburgh Seven? Well, they all passed their exams, some with flying colours. Women were still not allowed to take degrees, of course, but they all went off to study elsewhere and many had glittering careers in medicine. Jex-Blake went on to become the first practising female doctor in Scotland and to co-found the London School of Medicine with Elizabeth Garrett Anderson.

In 2019, on the 150th anniversary of their matriculation at the University of Edinburgh, the Seven were awarded posthumous degrees. A plaque was unveiled at the university and seven contemporary female students accepted the degrees on their behalf.

19 November ➵ **Indira Gandhi**

Indira Gandhi was another controversial leader, whose uncompromising views and willingness to use military force to attack her enemies led to her being called the 'Iron Lady of India'. At the same time, her anti-poverty campaigns in the countryside led to her being known as 'Mother Indira'.

Born on 19 November 1917 in Allahabad (then under British control, now in Uttar Pradesh state), Gandhi was India's first – and only – female prime minister. She served from 1966 until 1977, then again from 1980 until her assassination. She was murdered by two of her bodyguards on 31 October 1984.

On 20 November 1959, the Declaration of the Rights of the Child was adopted by the United Nations (UN). The goal was to ensure that children everywhere were protected and cared for. This declaration was actually based on an earlier one drafted in 1924 by the British humanitarian, social reformer and children's champion, Eglantyne Jebb.

Born in Shropshire in 1876, Jebb founded Save the Children after the end of the First World War to try to help save Austrian and German children dying from hunger. She launched the organization at the Royal Albert Hall in London in 1919. Save the Children helped countless children during the refugee crisis in Greece between 1919 and 1921, and during the Russian Famine of 1921. It was these experiences that led her to draft a document about the need for the international community to consider children's rights.

21 November ➤➤ Rumaitha Al Busaidi

On 21 November 2023, BBC Radio 4's *Woman's Hour* announced their '100 Women List', which celebrated one hundred of the most inspiring and influential women of that year. One of those included was the Omani marine scientist and FIFA activist Rumaitha Al Busaidi. The FIFA Foundation works to improve people's lives through football and by funding social projects and training.

Al Busaidi is a modern-day Renaissance woman. Not only is she a marine scientist and advocate for Arab women's leadership, but she's also a climate change activist, radio presenter, governmental adviser, entrepreneur and footballer (having played briefly for the Omani national team)! She's perhaps the first female football analyst in the Arab world and, as another sideline, also became the youngest Omani woman to trek to the South Pole.

22 November ➻ Gladys Zikusoka

Another wonder woman on the *Woman's Hour* list was the Ugandan vet Gladys Zikusoka. Born in 1970, she founded Conservation Through Public Health, an organization dedicated to the coexistence of endangered mountain gorillas and other wildlife in Africa. In 2009, Zikusoka won the Whitley Gold Award, awards known as the 'Green Oscars', and in 2021 she was named as the United Nations Environment Programme's Champion of the Earth for Science and Innovation.

23 November ➤➤ Natsuko Higuchi

The 19th-century novelist, diarist and short-story writer Natsuko Higuchi – who wrote under the pen name of Higuchi Ichiyõ – was Japan's first professional female writer of modern literature.

A year before her death on 23 November 1896, she became a household name with the publication of her short novel *Takekurabe* (translated into English in 1930 as *Comparing Heights*). The novella tells the story of a group of young people living in the red-light district in Edo (modern-day Tokyo). A study of women's roles and male expectations, it scandalized many, but became a cult classic.

Higuchi Ichiyõ

Have you read *War Horse* or seen the stage show or film? Millions of children worldwide have fallen in love with Joey, the farm horse who becomes a hero on the battlefields of northern France during the First World War.

But more than a hundred years before Michael Morpurgo's novel hit the shelves, another literary horse was taking the world by storm.

On 24 November 1877, Jarrold and Sons of Norfolk published Anna Sewell's *Black Beauty*. Written in the form of an autobiography told from the horse's point of view, it's a beautiful story about kindness to animals and respectful relations between horses and people.

Sewell suffered from ill-health all her life – an accident at fourteen years old left her permanently disabled – and wrote the novel when she was confined to bed. She said she hadn't intended *Black Beauty* to be a children's novel – rather, her intention was to 'induce kindness, sympathy, and an understanding treatment of horses' – but it became an instant children's classic.

Sewell herself died just five months after its publication. With more than fifty million copies sold worldwide, *Black Beauty* is still one of the biggest-selling books of all time.

25 November ⇥ The Mirabal Sisters

You might know that 25 November is International Day for the Elimination of Violence Against Women. But did you know it was prompted by the murder of the three Mirabal sisters – Patria, Minerva and María Teresa – in the Dominican Republic in 1960?

The dictator of the Dominican Republic, Rafael Trujillo, seized power in 1930, and a reign of terror began. Anyone who disagreed with him, or stood against him, was eliminated. He was responsible for the massacre of nearly 30,000 Haitians near the Dominican border in 1937.

After a number of dissidents were tortured and killed by his regime in 1959, the sisters became involved in the 14 June Movement, where they gave out pamphlets revealing the extent of Trujillo's crimes against his own people. Along with their husbands, and many others, they were arrested by the secret police. The women were later released.

On 25 November 1960, a car carrying them to visit the prison where their husbands were still being held was stopped. The 'Butterflies', as Patria, Minerva and María Teresa became known, were beaten to death, along with their driver. The car was then pushed over a cliff in order to make the assassination look like an accident. This fooled no one and the Mirabal sisters became martyrs of the Dominican resistance. Their sister Dedé dedicated her life to caring for their children and later set up a foundation to honour her sisters' legacy.

To honour their memory, the UN General Assembly designated 25 November to be International Day for the Elimination of Violence Against Women.

Mural of The Mirabal Sisters in Paris

26 November ➤➤ Sojourner Truth

One of the most iconic – and inspirational – anti-slavery speeches in all history was given at the 1851 Women's Rights Convention in Ohio, when a formerly enslaved woman known as Sojourner Truth stood up and delivered 'Ain't I a Woman?'. The speech was a plea for Black women to be treated equally and it is one of the most significant abolitionist speeches ever made. The actual text is slightly controversial, in that the first printed version of the speech was not published until twelve years after the event, and there are different versions (in one of them, the phrase 'Ain't I a Woman?' doesn't actually appear), but Truth's conviction and the powerful sentiments behind her words are undeniable. Truth was the only woman of colour who spoke at the convention.

Born Isabella Baumfree in New York state, Truth was first sold at the age of nine. In 1826, when her owner refused to honour his promise to let her go, she walked to freedom with her infant daughter. When the New York Anti-Slavery Law emancipating all enslaved people took effect the following year, Truth sued her former owner for custody of her son – whom she'd had to leave behind – and won. She was the first Black woman to win such a case against a white man.

In 1843, believing she had been spoken to by God, she changed her name to Sojourner Truth and became a travelling preacher. She campaigned for equal rights for women as well as men, Black people as well as white. She never learned to read or write, but with the help of a friend she published her autobiography in 1851, recounting her life as an enslaved woman and her transformation into an activist.

Truth is the first African American woman to have a statue in the Capitol building and the only Black woman to have a place at the table of Judy Chicago's *The Dinner Party* (see 20 July).

She died on 26 November 1883 in Battle Creek, Michigan.

Sojourner Truth

27 November ➤➤ Ada Lovelace

Chances are that you will have used a computer today – to finish homework, to order something online, to check a map, to message a friend.

Step up, Ada Lovelace, the world's first computer programmer.

Born in London in 1815, Lovelace was a brilliant and precocious child, gifted in mathematics. When she was still in her teens, Lovelace met the mathematician Charles Babbage, who was designing a calculating machine. It was Lovelace who created a program for the prototype of a digital computer. Even though the machine was never built, her programs became the basis for much of what we take for granted today – not least in healthcare and medical imaging techniques such as MRI and CT scans – and one of the earliest computer programming languages was named for her. She described herself as an 'analyst and metaphysician'.

Lovelace died of cancer on 27 November 1852 at the age of thirty-six, but her legacy is immense. The second Tuesday in October is known as Ada Lovelace Day, when women working in STEM are celebrated.

28 November ➤➤ Bernardine Evaristo

At the end of November 2021, the British writer Bernardine Evaristo was announced as the President of the Royal Society of Literature. She is the second woman and first writer of colour to hold the position (since the RSL was founded in 1820) and the only President who didn't go to either Oxford or Cambridge University!

The author of a dazzling array of work from fiction, verse fiction, short fiction to non-fiction, poetry, essays, literary criticism, journalism, and radio and theatre drama, her novel *Girl, Woman, Other* won the 2019 Booker Prize amongst many other awards. Evaristo is a bold and generous activist, advocating for inclusion in literature and the arts. She was a co-founder of the Theatre of Black Women in 1982 and, in 2020, was voted one of the top 100 Great Black Britons. Among her numerous awards, fellowships and honorary positions, Evaristo was President of Rose Bruford College of Theatre and Performance, the first Black president of a British drama school, and is currently Professor of Creative Writing at Brunel University of London.

More than anything, she is tireless in promoting other writers, and ensuring that Black British voices and talents do not go unacknowledged.

29 November ➤➤ **Gertrude Jekyll**

The British horticulturist, garden designer, photographer, writer, embroiderer and artist Gertrude Jekyll was born on 29 November 1843.

In her day, Jekyll was one of the most sought-after and prolific garden designers. She created nearly 400 gardens all over the world from Lindisfarne to Connecticut, Taunton to Hestercombe, including her own garden at Munstead Wood in Surrey. She bred many new plants, kept copious notebooks and drawings, published some twenty books and

contributed more than a thousand articles to magazines.

Jekyll was a celebrity and there are many photographs of her, particularly in her later years with her walking stick. Her official painting, by William Nicholson, hangs in the National Portrait Gallery in London and shows a serious woman with wire-rim glasses. Nicholson also did a more playful painting as a gift to fellow painter and architect Edwin Lutyens. Entitled *Miss Jekyll's Gardening Boots*, it shows only a pair of black, shabby boots!

30 November ➤ **Shirley Chisholm**

The first African American woman elected to Congress (though she described herself as a Barbadian-American), Shirley Chisholm, was born in Brooklyn on 30 November 1924.

Chisholm was a politician, an educator and an author, fighting against both sexism and racism. In 1964, she was elected to the New York State Assembly and, four years later, became the first Black woman elected to Congress. In 1972, Chisholm was the first Black candidate to run for a major party nomination and the first woman to run for the presidential nomination for the Democratic Party. She played a key role in the Equal Rights Amendment (ERA), which made it illegal to discriminate based on sex. In 2025, still not all US states have adopted the ERA.

After leaving Congress in 1983, Chisholm resumed her career in education and gave numerous speeches at colleges and universities, always encouraging students to avoid polarization and intolerance. Her mantra was that everyone should accept differences and work together for the common good.

Chisholm died on New Year's Day 2005. On the wall of the mausoleum where she is buried are inscribed the words: 'Unbought and Unbossed.'

Life on a Pedestal

When the statue of Millicent Garrett Fawcett was unveiled in London in April 2018, it was the first statue *of* a woman in Parliament Square and the first statue *by* a woman.

In the UK, only 17 per cent of statues are of real – as opposed to mythical – women, and once you discount statues of Queen Victoria, the figure plummets. Less than 2 per cent of statues honour Black women or other women of colour. In fact, the very first statue of a Black woman, Henrietta Lacks – created by a Black artist, Helen Wilson-Roe – was only unveiled in October 2021. The ratio of women to men is even worse in America, where only 8 per cent of statues commemorate women.

In Edinburgh, there are more statues to animals than to women . . .

But why does it matter if there aren't many statues of women?

It matters because statues are living history. Their presence in public squares and on

Henrietta Lacks by Helen Wilson-Roe

street corners is a symbol of what a particular society values. Statues take people out of the history books and into the real world. So, if we only see statues of men on horseback with weapons, that gives the impression that it's the only thing we think is important. Surely we should honour everyone who has made a contribution?

Statues are also significant in helping demystify the ancient past, when there were either no papyrus or paper records, or when they have not survived. We only know about the existence of the first named female physician in history, Peseshet – who was born around 2613 BCE – because an excavation at a tomb in Giza in Egypt dug up the plinth on which her statue once stood. The Roman female physician Antiochis lived in the hilltop citadel of Tlos (in present-day Turkey). Again, the statue itself is missing, but the pedestal was discovered in 1892.

There is a life-sized statue of the 11th-century Chinese poet and collector Li Qingzhao in her hometown of Jinan. Fashioned from white marble, she is wearing a full-length dress and robe and holds a scroll in her right hand. What we learn, therefore, is not only that she was a famous and admired female poet, but also about the sort of clothes she wore and the kind of writing implements she used.

This is living history.

Statues in public spaces can also provide a focal point for shared celebration and commemoration. In the gardens in Aizu, Japan, there is a statue of 19th-century *onna-musha* Nakano Takeko, holding her weapon – a long wooden stave with a blade at one end. An *onna-musha* was a female warrior and, although they were not part of the official army, we know Takeko led a unit described as the 'Women's Army' at the Battle of Aizu in 1868. Even today, more than 150 years after her death, girls come to her monument during the Aizu Autumn Festival each year to lay flowers.

Nakano Takeko, Jinan, Japan

But if the ratio of men to women is not great, the better news is that we can do something about it, as the campaigns for Mary Anning in Lyme Regis, Mary Seacole in London, Mary Barbour in Glasgow and Gráinne O'Malley in County Mayo prove. Each of these statues have happened because campaigners persuaded the local council to allocate land and to commission an artist to create the work.

Think about where you live. Are there any statues of women? One or two? None at all? What inspirational woman would you like to see in your town square or park? Write a letter, start a campaign, spread the word.

Together, let's put women and girls back into history one statue at a time.

DECEMBER

December

1 December ➤➤ Rosa Parks

On 1 December 1955, in Montgomery, Alabama, Rosa Parks refused to give up her seat in the colored section of the bus for a white passenger. The most famous of the 'freedom riders', Parks was arrested for civil disobedience and violating Alabama's segregation laws. Black women and men had been protesting for years, but Parks was a forty-two-year-old lawyer, she worked for the NAACP, she was politically astute and she was highly respected in the community. In other words, she seemed the perfect candidate to challenge the unjust law.

Just over a year later, in December 1956, Montgomery desegregated the public transport system. It was the beginning of the end for the discriminatory Jim Crow laws.

PEOPLE ALWAYS SAY
THAT I DIDN'T GIVE UP MY SEAT
because i was
TIRED,
BUT THAT ISN'T TRUE.
I WAS NOT TIRED PHYSICALLY,
OR NO MORE TIRED THAN I USUALLY WAS
AT THE END OF A WORKING DAY . . . .
NO,
THE ONLY
TIRED I WAS,
WAS TIRED OF
GIVING
IN.

Rosa Parks

2 December ➤➤ Timnit Gebru

One of the biggest issues of current times is AI, ML and LLM – artificial intelligence, machine learning and large language models. AI is the theory and development of computer systems that can perform tasks normally requiring human intelligence. Machine learning is the use and development of computer systems that are able to learn, adapt and analyse data without following explicit instructions. LLM uses deep learning algorithms to perform natural language processing tasks. Trained on large amounts of text, they generate human-like text, as well as being able to summarize data and answer questions.

Chances are that you will have used LLM, such as ChatGPT, and there are many potential advantages – science and research, number-crunching, gathering information, medical diagnoses, etc. But there are also challenges, too, one of them being the protection of copyright. That's to say, LLM use a real human person's own creative work without permission or payment to train computers or imitate work. This is theft. In January 2025, the UK government published its AI Opportunities Action Plan. There were many excellent ideas contained within the paper, but sadly the threat to copyright in its current form was clear and that growth of AI companies would be at the expense of the growth of the creative industries, which bring more than £129 billion to the UK each year.

The other challenge is what we might call in-built bias or

discrimination. Because so many of the people involved in the creation of AI/ML/LLM come from similar backgrounds, there is a lack of diversity within the programming workforce. This, in turn, leads to a bias in the way AI operates, particularly in terms of ignoring the voices of women, people of different ethnicities, working-class people, people with disabilities or different genders. Also in January 2025, Mark Zuckerberg – the founder, chairman and CEO of Meta – announced that he was stopping all diversity, equality and inclusion programmes, days after announcing that he would be halting all human fact-checking on META's platforms, including Facebook and Instagram. He also talked about wanting to capture 'masculine energy' within his companies. At the time of writing, a wholesale dismantling of inclusivity programmes across all US institutions – led and financed by a small coterie of tech billionaires – is underway, from science to education, arts institutions to the military.

This desire to exclude women and others from the technological workspace is nothing new. On 2 December 2020, one of the relatively few senior women working in the field, Timnit Gebru, announced on Twitter (now X) that Google had forced her out. The circumstances surrounding her departure were murky, but Gebru was highly respected in the field and had been the co-leader of Google's ethical AI team.

Gebru, who was born and raised in Ethiopia, went on to found Black in AI, advocating for more Black roles in AI development and research. She is the founder of the Distributed Artificial Intelligence Research Institute (DAIR).

As for the rolling backwards of ambitions for a diverse and varied workforce, signs are that women in science and technology – in companies from META to AI start-ups – are forming networks to fight back against those who want to silence women's voices in this most crucial of areas.

3 December ➔ International Day of Persons with Disabilities

In 1992, the UN General Assembly designated 3 December as the International Day of Persons with Disabilities. The aim was to promote a better understanding of disability issues, support the rights of people with disabilities and change global perceptions. One of their most important goals is to extend the idea of what constitutes a disability and explaining how some disabilities may not be visible.

There are also many incredible women with disabilities whose success and visibility in their chosen field help to change perceptions of disability, including: comedienne and writer Francesca Martinez, who has cerebral palsy; performer and choreographer Claire Cunningham, a multi-disciplinary artist based in Glasgow who was born with osteoporosis and performs on crutches; Jenny Sealey, the Artistic Director of Graeae Theatre Company, who is profoundly D/deaf; British actress, broadcaster, comedienne and disability rights activist Liz Carr, who has used a wheelchair since the age of seven because she has arthrogryposis multiplex congenita; and Welsh television presenter and former wheelchair racer Tanni Grey-Thompson.

Of course, we should be mindful and celebratory of people with disabilities every day of the year. But having 3 December as a focus, when so many women like all of those mentioned above might talk about their experiences, is an excellent way to reinforce the point that everyone matters.

4 December ➤➤ Edith Cavell

Born in Norfolk on 4 December 1865, Edith Cavell was working as Matron in a teaching hospital for nurses in Belgium when the First World War broke out in 1914. She was known for treating both German and Allied soldiers equally. However, when the Germans took control of Belgium, she started to help smuggling Allied soldiers to safety through an underground tunnel in the hospital.

Cavell was arrested in 1915, tried at a court martial, found guilty and sentenced to death along with others involved in the network. Despite international outrage she was executed by firing squad on 12 October 1915.

She became a symbol of the Allied cause. When the war was over, her body was brought back to Britain and a service was held in Westminster Abbey before she was taken home to Norfolk to be buried in Norwich Cathedral. On the many monuments to Cavell, some of her much-quoted final words (opposite) are engraved . . .

Edith Cavell

5 December ➺ Phillis Wheatley

During the years of the American War of Independence, Phillis Wheatley became the first published African American poet.

An enslaved woman originally from West Africa, Wheatley was taken to America as a child on a slave ship in the mid-1700s, and bought by the Wheatley family in Boston. We do not know her original name. The Wheatleys recognized her talent – though, of course, any success she had would benefit them – and helped her writing to find an audience. Bigotry and racism in America obliged them to go to Britain, where the Methodist abolitionist Selina Hastings helped Wheatley's poetry to be published.

There were obstacles. Wheatley had to prove (questioned by eighteen men) that she was the author of the poems, but she triumphed. The first of her poems was published in 1767, and by 1771 her work was being circulated widely in London. Her most famous poem – 'On Being Brought from Africa to America' – is a searing protest against slavery. There are thirty-nine poems in her 1773 collection *Poems on Various Subjects, Religious and Moral*, and it's thought that as many as 145 other poems by her may have been lost.

Despite her success, Wheatley didn't really benefit from her amazing talent. She returned to America a free woman, and married, but died in poverty in Boston on 5 December 1784.

6 December ➤➤ Amelia Bloomer

We've already met American entrepreneur, businesswoman and women's rights campaigner Amelia Bloomer, who was part of the 19th-century 'free clothing' movement for women.

But did you know she was also the first woman to own, operate and edit a newspaper for women? *The Lily* first hit the news-stands in 1849 in Seneca Falls, New York, as a monthly news-sheet. Later, it became bi-weekly, publishing on the first and third Thursdays of the month. With an all-female writing team, the paper advocated for women's property and voting rights, for practical and comfortable clothing, and for women campaigning together to build a fairer society.

7 December ➤➤ Kateryna Bilokur

Because it is not certain exactly when she was born in 1900, 7 December was chosen as the official birthday of the Ukrainian folk artist Kateryna Bilokur.

Born into impoverished circumstances in Ukraine (then part of the Russian Empire), Bilokur left school at the age of six or seven, making it hard for her to get accepted for any kind of artistic training. But she always drew, in pencil, then watercolours and later in oils. Her reputation grew in the 1930s and 1940s as a leading figure in naive art – a form of painting that is elegantly simple and unpretentious, like folk art, often produced by artists who have had no formal training at art school.

Bilokur is particularly known for her beautiful, vibrant paintings of flowers. She was named People's Artist of Ukraine, an honorary title that recognizes outstanding contributors to art in the country.

Bilokur is honoured on Ukrainian stamps, 1988

8 December ⇒ Desdemona

On 8 December 1660, the first woman appeared on the English stage, playing Desdemona in Shakespeare's *Othello*. Before this, women's roles were played by young men and boys.

It is odd that for such a momentous occasion we are not quite sure who the actress was – there were several women in the late 17th century who were well-known for their Shakespearian roles, so the first female Desdemona might have been played by Margaret Hughes, Anne Marshall or Katherine Corey.

Times have changed. Now, the gender-swapping is mostly in the other direction, with dazzling female actors taking on traditional male Shakespearian roles. In 1899, Sarah Bernhardt was the first woman to play Hamlet (others include Maxine Peake and Cush Jumbo), and Kathryn Hunter was the first to play King Lear in 1997.

9 December →→ The Mothers of the Plaza de Mayo

The 'Mothers of the Plaza de Mayo' – *Las Madres* – were Argentinian mothers who dared to protest against the military dictatorship that ruled Argentina in the 1970s and 1980s. The organization was formed, in part, out of an attempt by mothers to find their 'disappeared' children during Argentina's 'Dirty War'. Babies and children were taken from their parents and given to families who were loyal to the dictatorship, the intention being to brainwash the children so they could not grow up to be political opponents of the government. A similar tactic is being used by Russia in its war against Ukraine, where it's estimated that as many as 20,000 Ukrainian children may have been abducted and given to Russian families.

Between 1976 and 1983, the Argentinian military regime abducted, tortured and killed thousands of political opponents. The first protest of *Las Madres* was held in the Plaza de Mayo in front of the presidential palace on 30 April 1977. They were ordered to disperse, but the courageous women continued to walk slowly, arm-in-arm, around the square. Every week more mothers joined the protests.

Las Madres attracted international attention with their emblematic white headscarves, holding photos and names of their disappeared children and their pleas for their safe return. The regime retaliated and murdered three of the founding members of the movement. Others were beaten and detained, but it did not stop their peaceful resistance. Even after the dictatorship was ended in 1983, *Las Madres* continued to march, demanding all the military personnel involved in the disappearances be put on trial.

10 December ➺ Selma Lagerlöf

The Swedish author Selma Lagerlöf was announced as the first female winner of the Nobel Prize in Literature on 10 December 1909.

Lagerlöf was born in November 1858. Her work was rooted in the folk tales, legends, and stories inspired by the countryside of her home. Her debut novel, *Gösta Berling's Saga*, was adapted into a silent film in 1924 that helped launch Greta Garbo's career. A Swedish-American actress, Garbo was one of the most glamorous and famous screen stars of the silent and Golden Age movie era in America.

As Lagerlöf celebrated her Nobel win at the Grand Hotel in Stockholm, 1,200 women also gathered at the hotel for a party to honour her achievement. As well as her fiction, her letters to her friend, lover and literary collaborator, the Jewish-Swedish writer Sophie Elkan, were published in the early 1900s.

11 December ➤➤ Eleanor Rykener

On 11 December 1394, a sex worker called Eleanor Rykener was arrested in London. She had agreed to have sex with a man on Soper's Lane off Cheapside and fixed a price. Medieval London's anti-prostitution laws made this risky and, unfortunately, Eleanor and her client were discovered by city officials while engaging in 'that detestable, unmentionable, and ignominious vice' (as the court documents later put it). They were both hauled up before the Mayor of London for questioning. While she was being questioned, it was revealed that Eleanor, still wearing the dress she had been arrested in, had been born a man – John Rykener. In modern terms, we might describe her as transgender.

Eleanor's remarkable story is preserved in one single document, the record of her questioning, which is held in the London Archives. Written on a parchment roll, the document went unnoticed for several centuries due, in part, to deliberate censorship and an attempt to hide Eleanor's gender non-conformity: the summary described the case as an 'examination of two men charged with immorality'.

The document was uncovered by researchers in 1995 and, since then, has generated a huge amount of scholarship and popular interest, asking questions such as what it means to describe a 14th-century person as 'trans'? Was Eleanor's 'crime' sodomy, sex work, gender non-conformity or something else entirely? And – perhaps the most conspicuous gap in the record – what happened to her after this one recorded moment of her questioning?

Eleanor's early life – when she was presumably still known as John – is unknown. We know that she lived in Oxford before coming to London, but have no idea when she started to pass as a woman. During her questioning, Rykener revealed she had been taught to have sex 'in the manner of a woman' by a fellow sex worker and describes herself being 'dressed in women's clothing'. It seems, too, that as well as working as a sex worker, she also worked as an embroideress and barmaid, suggesting that her feminine self-presentation was not confined to sexual role-playing. In other words, she lived her entire life as a woman. It also came out in her testimony that she had sex with women (mostly nuns), as well as with men, so might well have defined herself, in modern language, as bisexual or gender fluid.

We will never know Eleanor's real motivations – we don't even know if she was found guilty of the charge or faced punishment. What we can imagine, though, is that she must have been an exceptional, resourceful person making her way in the medieval world on her own terms.

12 December ➤➤ Henrietta Swan Leavitt

Another of the 'Harvard Computers' (see 13 April) was American astronomer Henrietta Swan Leavitt. Her discovery of how to measure vast distances between Earth and far distant galaxies accurately led to a shift in our understanding of the size and nature of the universe. Her discoveries became known as 'Leavitt's Law'.

Born in Massachusetts in 1868, Leavitt began working as a volunteer assistant at the Harvard College Observatory before being hired by the astronomer and physicist Edward Pickering in 1902 to measure and catalogue the brightness of stars. Because women were not allowed to operate telescopes at the time, she had to do this from the observatory's photographic plate collection. Like Annie Jump Cannon, whom she worked alongside, Leavitt suffered from progressive hearing loss and became totally D/deaf.

Leavitt died on 12 December 1921 and her death halted the process of her Nobel Prize nomination – as we've seen, only living people can be honoured. But the asteroid 5383 Leavitt and the crater Leavitt on the moon are named after her to honour D/deaf women and men who have worked as astronomers.

13 December ➻ Taylor Swift

Are you a Swiftie? Do you have 'Shake it Off', 'Bad Blood, 'Look What You Made Me Do', 'Cruel Summer' or any other song by the multi-talented, genre-busting American singer-songwriter superstar Taylor Swift in your liked songs?

Born in Pennsylvania on 13 December 1989, Swift signed her first record deal in 2005. She started as a country singer with albums *Taylor Swift* and *Fearless*, then experimented with rock, electronic and pop, and then released the hip-hop inspired album *Reputation* in 2017. Her autobiographical documentary *Miss Americana* explored indie folk music, and in 2024 she put out *The Tortured Poets Department.* She excels in an incredibly diverse range of musical genres, when most people can shine in only one.

Not surprisingly, Swift is one of the world's bestselling music artists, winning multiple awards – including (at the time of writing) fourteen Grammys, a Primetime Emmy and thirty MTV video music awards. The highest-earning female touring act, she has already racked up more than 200 million ticket sales worldwide. She's also the first music billionaire, the world's richest female musician and the only person from the world of the arts to be named *Time* Person of the Year.

Her sixth concert tour, the Eras Tour (and the concert film that went with it) are the highest-grossing tour and concert film of all time. Fans from all over the world – including the UK's Prince William, actresses Nicola Coughlan, Cate Blanchett and Phoebe Waller-Bridge, director Greta

Gerwig and British prime minister Keir Starmer – flocked to see her when she performed in London in 2024.

Articulate in her support for women's rights and for women and girls having control over their own lives and careers, Swift is a true global icon and role model.

14 December ➤➤ UK General Election, 1918

The first general election in the UK where women over the age of thirty – and with certain property qualifications – were allowed to vote took place on Sunday, 14 December 1918. About 8.5 million women were eligible to cast their ballots. Sixteen women exercised their right to stand as parliamentary candidates, including Christabel Pankhurst, Emmeline Pethick-Lawrence, Charlotte Despard and Constance Markievicz, who was the only one to be elected (though she, like all other members of the Irish Republican party Sinn Féin, did not take her seat). The first woman to take her seat was Nancy Astor, after winning a by-election in 1919.

It was not until the Equal Franchise Act was passed in 1928 that all women over the age of twenty-one were finally given voting rights on the same terms as men. The next general election was held on 30 May 1929 and became known, as a result, as the 'Flapper Election', because of the large numbers of young women who voted for the first time ('flappers' were a rebellious female subculture of the time). It was also the first general election contested by the new Welsh nationalist party, Plaid Cymru.

15 December ➤ **Sirimavo Bandaranaike**

As we come towards the end of our year, it's time to meet the world's first female prime minister, the Sri Lankan politician Sirimavo Bandaranaike. A controversial figure, she was first elected in July 1960 for a five-year term and went on to serve as prime minister on two further occasions.

Born in 1916, after her husband was assassinated in 1959 Bandaranaike took over as leader of the Sri Lanka Freedom Party (SLFP). She won a decisive victory in the elections the following year and became prime minister. To start with, Bandaranaike continued her husband's socialist economic policies and the active encouragement of Buddhism and the Sinhalese language and culture. But she introduced a law making Sinhalese the only official language, something that alienated the large Tamil minority in the country and which helped sow the seeds for the catastrophic civil war that would devastate Sri Lanka between 1983 and 2009.

In her second term as prime minister, from 1970 to 1977, Bandaranaike pursued more radical policies, including land reform, nationalizing industries and changing the name of the country from Ceylon to the Republic of Sri Lanka. Thanks to economic stagnation, charges of corruption and ethnic tensions, her party was trounced in the 1977 elections. She was appointed prime minister for a third time in 1994, after her daughter was elected president in a changed system. Her other children also became key figures in Sri Lanka's political landscape.

Bandaranaike died from a heart attack in 2000 and is remembered as a powerful, though highly controversial, figure.

16 December ⇒ Emily Hobhouse

On 16 December 1913, the National Women's Monument in Bloemfontein, South Africa, was unveiled. One of the women honoured was the British humanitarian, pacifist and aid worker, Emily Hobhouse.

Hobhouse was born in St Ive, near Liskeard in Cornwall, in 1860. When the Second Anglo-Boer War broke out in South Africa in 1899, she became involved with humanitarian organizations in the UK and sailed for the Cape Colony in December 1900. The Boer Wars were conflicts in the late 19th and early 20th centuries between the British and Dutch-Afrikaaner settlers, who had first settled in South Africa in the 17th century.

At that stage, Hobhouse didn't know that the British had built concentration camps to imprison Boer women and children. All she knew was that the majority of the victims of the British scorched-earth policy – where the dominant forces destroy everything in sight, whether hospitals, houses, schools or humanitarian aid organizations – were women and children.

Hobhouse was horrified by what she found: desperate, filthy and inhumane quarters, disease, lack of food or medical supplies, a high death rate. She worked tirelessly to improve conditions in the camps, she petitioned Parliament in London, and although her honesty and criticism of British policy did not make her popular with politicians or the newspapers, she did not give up.

Hobhouse was made an honorary citizen of South Africa, but she was never given the recognition she deserved in the UK, and her death in London in 1926 after a lifetime of service to peace and humanitarian work went largely unreported by the British media.

17 December »» Edith Smith

The First World War changed women's lives in so many different ways, not least of all by the fact that women were able to work in occupations previously reserved for men. Step forward, Edith Smith, the UK's first female warrant police officer with full powers of arrest.

Smith was sworn in as a police constable with official powers of arrest in Grantham, Lincolnshire, on 17 December 1915. During the First World War, about 4,000 women were part of voluntary patrols, aiming to ensure orderly behaviour in parks, railways stations and other public spaces. Others were employed by the Ministry of Munitions to supervise women workers in the munitions factories. But Smith's role was different because she had the same powers as a male police officer. Her appointment was seen as controversial – the idea of a woman having the power to arrest a man was challenging to some – and the Home Office itself even tried to say that women didn't count as 'proper persons' in the eyes of the law in order to block her appointment.

There's no doubt that Smith was a pioneer and a trailblazer, but her life wasn't easy. She left the police service after the end of the war and went into nursing, where she was employed as a Matron Nurse at a nursing home, but gave it up because of ill health.

Smith died by suicide on 26 June 1923, after taking an overdose, and her name was all but forgotten. Her grave at Halton Cemetery in Runcorn was unmarked until two modern-day policewomen launched a fundraising campaign to buy a headstone. In June 2018, a blue plaque was erected at her house in Oxton.

18 December ➤➤ Billie Eilish

The American singer-songwriter Billie Eilish is the youngest person to headline at Glastonbury.

Eilish – whose full name is Billie Eilish Pirate Baird O'Connell – was born in Los Angles on 18 December 2001. She burst onto the music scene in 2015 with 'Ocean Eyes'. Since then, hits like 'Bad Guy', 'Birds of a Feather' and 'Everything I Wanted' have followed. She performed the theme song for the James Bond film *No Time to Die* and wrote and performed the haunting 'What Was I Made For?' for *Barbie* in 2023, gaining a second Academy Award in the process.

Alongside all this, Eilish finds the time to campaign for climate change awareness, women's reproductive rights, gender equality and animal rights.

19 December ➤➤ Emily Brontë

Although she only wrote one incredible novel and two hundred poems (few of which were published in her lifetime), the English novelist Emily Brontë has had a huge influence on literature and attitudes towards women writers.

The fourth of six children (two older sisters died when they were children, her brother died in his twenties) Emily and her surviving sisters, Charlotte and Anne, transformed the opportunities for women writing. They first published their work under the pseudonyms of Currer, Ellis and Acton Bell.

Emily's only novel, *Wuthering Heights*, was published in

1847, a year before her death on 19 December 1848. A novel about obsession, about race, about domestic violence, about Victorian hypocrisy, about ghosts and, most of all, about the power of landscape, Brontë drew inspiration from the Yorkshire Moors above Haworth where the sisters lived with their vicar father. Although some Victorian critics attacked it for its so-called immorality and violence, *Wuthering Heights* is one of the biggest-selling novels of all time. It has never been out of print, and the tragic story of Catherine Earnshaw and Heathcliff is known all over the world.

It wasn't until September 2024 that the memorial in Poet's Corner at Westminster Abbey was changed to spell the sisters' surname correctly, from Bronte to Brontë.

20 December ➤ Mitsuko Uchida

The Japanese-British pianist Mitsuko Uchida is one of the great classical pianists and conductors of the 20th century.

Born on 20 December 1948 in a coastal town not far from Tokyo, her father became the Japanese ambassador to Austria when she was twelve years old, and the family moved to Vienna. Uchida enrolled at the Vienna Academy of Music and gave her first Viennese recital two years later.

Now a naturalized British citizen, Uchida has performed with the world's great orchestras and is particularly celebrated for her interpretations of Mozart and Schubert. She is also the joint Artistic Director of the Marlboro Music School and Festival in Vermont in the United States.

21 December ➡ Marie-Sophie Germain

Founded the previous year, the newly renamed École Polytechnique in Paris began to take students on 21 December 1795. It would go on to become one of the most important schools of mathematics, engineering and administration in the world.

The French mathematician Marie-Sophie Germain was brilliant. Born in Paris in 1776, she largely taught herself from books and from lecture notes begged, borrowed or stolen from students attending the École Polytechnique – as a woman, she was not allowed to attend.

Writing under the pseudonym of Monsieur LeBlanc, Germain engaged fellow mathematicians in dazzling, written mathematical debate, only later revealing her true identity. She worked on elasticity, number theory and went a long way to proving Fermat's Last Theorem. In 1816, she was the first woman to win a prize from the Paris Academy of Sciences for her essay on elasticity theory.

22 December ➳ Gertrude 'Ma' Rainey

The American classic blues singer and early recording artist, Ma Rainey, died on 22 December 1939 in Georgia.

She blended blues with minstrel and vaudeville traditions, and wrote love stories about bisexuality and lesbianism rather than sticking to the traditional 'girl meets boy/boy leaves girl' songs popular at the time. Ma Rainey owned and managed two theatres and was a huge influence on other Black American performers and writers, including Bessie Smith, Angela Y. Davis and Alice Walker.

23 December ➡ Teresa Carreño

This was the first full day on Earth of the Venezuelan virtuoso pianist, Teresa Carreño, who was born on 22 December 1953 in Caracas. Sometimes called the 'Valkyrie of the Piano', she was also a composer, a soprano and a conductor.

In a career spanning more than fifty years, Carreño was responsible for popularizing the works of other contemporary composers and was particularly celebrated for her interpretations of the work of Norwegian composer, Edvard Grieg. She herself composed more than seventy-five works for solo piano, voice, choral ensembles and orchestras.

24 December ➤➤ Helena Normanton

On Christmas Eve 1919, the day after the Sex Disqualification (Removal) Act was passed in the UK, Helena Normanton was the first woman to be admitted to the Middle Temple, one of the four so-called Inns of Court where barristers in England and Wales train.

This is far from the first 'first' to her name, so take a deep breath: Normanton was the first woman to get a divorce for her client, the first woman to be lead prosecutor in a murder trial, the first woman to conduct a trial in America; the first woman to appear at both the High Court and the Old Bailey. Together with Rose Heilbron, Normanton was one of the first two women appointed King's Counsel (KC) in 1949. Add to this, she was the first woman to keep her surname after marriage – radical – and keep working, and even the first married British woman to have a passport in the name she was born with rather than her husband's name.

An active feminist and campaigner for women's equality under the law, Normanton was also a supporter of the Campaign for Nuclear Disarmament (CND). She died in 1957.

In October 2021, a blue plaque was unveiled at her London home in Mecklenburgh Square by Brenda Hale, a judge who was the first female president of the Supreme Court in the UK.

25 December ➾ Jodie Whittaker

Doctor Who first hit British television screens in 1963. A Time Lord, the Doctor travels through time in the TARDIS (which looks like an old-fashioned police box), administering justice and fighting aliens, including the Daleks, the Cybermen and The Master.

The franchise was revitalized by writer and producer Russell T. Davies in 2005, and the storylines, and characters, became much more representative of modern times. But although the Doctor's companion was often a woman, *he* was always a man. Then, during the show's Christmas Special, 'Twice Upon a Time', on 25 December 2017, it was revealed that the new Doctor would be a woman – Jodie Whittaker. Ironically, she is the only Doctor to date not to have had her own Christmas Special.

Whittaker played the role from 2018 to 2022. In 2023, Ncuti Gatwa became the first Black actor to take control of the TARDIS.

In May 2025, it was revealed in the season finale that Ncuti Gatwa would not be returning as the Doctor in the next series and that Billie Piper would be coming back . . . as Rose, the Doctor's assistant, or as the Doctor herself? We'll all have to wait and see.

26 December ➡ Mary Somerville

The Scottish scientist, mathematician, astronomer and educational pioneer Mary Somerville was born in Jedburgh on 26 December 1780. She was taught to read by her mother, and attended a girls' school for a year when she was ten, but otherwise she taught herself from the family library. Her studies included Latin and mathematics, botany and geology.

In 1816 she moved to London with her second husband and became friends with fellow scientists and mathematicians such as Caroline Herschel, William Herschel and Charles Babbage. It was then that Somerville began to write. Among her books were works explaining astronomy to a general reader, and her book *Physical Geography* is considered the first ever geography textbook in the English language.

Along with Caroline Herschel, Somerville was the first female honorary member of the Royal Society. Somerville College, one of the first two women's colleges at Oxford University, is named after her. It's also said that the word 'scientist' was actually invented to describe Mary Somerville – before her, the phrase was always 'man of science'.

27 December » Benazir Bhutto

The Pakistani politician Benazir Bhutto was the first woman elected to head a democratic government in a Muslim-majority country. Together with Jacinda Ardern, Bhutto is the only other world leader to have given birth in office.

Born in Karachi in 1953, she was Prime Minister of Pakistan from 1988 for two years, then was re-elected from 1993 to 1996. Bhutto was assassinated on 27 December 2007 in Rawalpindi, where she was campaigning ahead of elections scheduled for the New Year. Shots were fired after a political rally and a suicide bomb detonated, killing twenty-three other people. Bhutto was rushed to hospital but could not be saved.

28 December ➳ Maggie Smith

Minerva McGonagall, Lady Violet Crawley, Miss Jean Brodie, chances are that you will have seen the indomitable actress Maggie Smith on the big screen or the small.

Maggie Smith was born in Ilford on 28 December 1934. A brilliant comic and serious actor, who did not suffer fools, she lit up the stage and the screen in a dazzling career that lasted more than seven decades. From the National Theatre to the Royal Shakespeare Company, the West End to Broadway, *The Best Exotic Marigold Hotel* to *Gosford Park*, her roles ranged from Desdemona in *Othello* to Alan Bennett's unwanted house guest in *The Lady in the Van* and everything in between.

Among the many trophies and awards jostling for space on her mantelpiece were two Oscars, three Golden Globes and a Tony. A *grande dame* of the acting world, she died in September 2024 at the age of eighty-nine.

Piertotum Locomotor.

29 December ➤ Christina Rossetti

Since we are still in the Christmas period, it seems only right to remember the author of one of the UK's most popular and enduring English carols, 'In the Bleak Midwinter'.

The English poet and children's author Christina Rossetti was born in London in 1830 into a family of writers – her father was an Italian poet in exile. Her siblings were all writers, and her eldest brother was the acclaimed Pre-Raphaelite artist Dante Gabriel Rossetti. Christina was the model for many of his paintings, including *The Girlhood of Mary Virgin*.

Their house in Charlotte Street was full of books and artists of all kinds were regular guests. But bad times were around the corner. Rossetti's father became ill and could not work, and her mother and sister were obliged to become governesses. Rossetti became increasingly lonely and began to suffer from the depression that would haunt her for the rest of her life. Her religious faith was both a comfort to her and sometimes also a burden. She wrote devotional poetry and also poems for children, including the collection *Goblin Market and Other Poems*, published in 1862.

Rossetti died on 29 December 1894.

30 December ➤➤ Sarah Gilbert

On 30 December 2020, the Covid-19 vaccine developed by Sarah Gilbert for Oxford-AstraZeneca was approved for use in the UK.

A Professor of Vaccinology at the University of Oxford, Gilbert was leading a team of scientists – and there were others in laboratories all over the world – working desperately against the clock to find a vaccine to protect people against Covid-19. The World Health Organization (WHO) had been informed on New Year's Eve the previous year that there were a cluster of cases of what looked like pneumonia in Wuhan in China, and that people were dying. From these early warnings, it became clear that the world was about to suffer a pandemic that would leave no community, no country, untouched.

It is estimated that nearly eight million people have died worldwide from the virus or complications following the virus, though exact figures are hard to pin down. In the UK, more than 270,000 are thought to have died during the pandemic, a figure that surely would have been much higher were it not for the work of the brilliant Sarah Gilbert, among others.

31 December ➵ The Spice Girls

If you're a singer or in a band, there's nothing better than having the Christmas or the New Year's No. 1 single in the UK.

In 1998, the pop phenomenon The Spice Girls became the first band since The Beatles in the 1960s to have three Christmas/New Year's No. 1 hits in a row: '2 Become 1' (1996), 'Too Much' (1997) and 'Goodbye' (1998).

The Spice Girls – aka Ginger (Geri Halliwell), Posh (Victoria Beckham), Baby (Emma Bunton), Sporty (Mel C) and Scary (Mel B) – sold more than 100 million records worldwide, making them the bestselling girl group of all time.

Happy New Year to five fabulous women.

Razzle-Dazzle

Whether you're a performer or a creative, it can be precarious trying to make a living as an artist. You have no job security or regular salary, you're reliant on people employing or commissioning you, you have to hope that people will buy your work. You might be in favour one day and out of fashion the next.

But the flip side of this is that you are your own boss. If you are a writer and have pen and paper (or a laptop), you can write. If you are an artist and have paints or clay, you can create. If you are a composer and have a computer or piano to work on, you can let the music come to you and note it down. If you are a singer or an actress, you can find ways to perform.

Of course, materials are expensive, art studios are difficult to find, a composer needs an orchestra or a band to bring her work to life. It takes courage to stand up on stage and entertain people. But the act of creation, of invention, of using your talent, is still within your power.

We've seen women having to fight hard to be lawyers and doctors, pilots and scientists, teachers and politicians. And it's the case that women and girls have often been prevented from studying art or being allowed to publish or compose or create. But many of us are attracted to the creative life all the same. So, as we come to the end of our journey, here are a few more feminist heroines with a little razzle-dazzle who've created joyous, surprising and wondrous things. Because every act of creation, of performance, of invention, expands our horizons, helps us to see things from a different point of view, and connects us with the past. Art matters. Music matters. Books matter.

Imagination matters.

The Flemish painter Caterina van Hemessen was born in Antwerp in 1528. She is considered to be the first woman to paint a self-portrait, a kind of 16th-century selfie. She is sitting at her easel wearing a black over-partlet with red velvet undersleeves, her hair covered by a white hood.

In Limousin in central France in the early 19th century, Jeanne Villepreux-Power was the daughter of a shoemaker and a seamstress. She originally worked as a dressmaker creating beautiful wedding gowns for society ladies. But, in time, she became fascinated by marine biology. Her research and eye for detail led her to invent . . . the aquarium!

Lizzie Magie was a 19th-century American feminist writer – and games designer – from Illinois. She supported the economic theory proposing all government taxes should be done away with and replaced by a single tax based on land.

Caterina van Hemessen, Public Art Collection, Kunstmuseum Basel

Does this sound familiar? As a way of explaining her ideas, Magie created *The Landlord's Game*, a sort of unknown older sister to the world-famous board game *Monopoly*.

The 20th-century Cuban artist Ana Mendieta used her own body as both inspiration and canvas, drawing on her feelings of exile from Cuba and feminist interpretations of violence, identity and belonging. In 1973, she performed *Rape Scene*, which was created out of the rape and murder of a fellow student at the University of Iowa.

Equally radical, Adong Judith is the co-founder of the all-female theatre company Silent Voices Uganda. In Tunisia, Jaila Baccar she co-founded the New Theatre in 1976 to create work outside the mainstream.

The 20th-century magician Ellen E. Armstrong was the only African American woman to have her own touring magic show. A true entertainer, her tour poster promised '250 laughs in 50 minutes Magic Show'. Adopting the stage name of 'Mistress of Modern Magic', with sleight-of-hand tricks including 'Hippity-Hop Rabbits', she travelled all over America for more than thirty years.

Last but not least, the meeting of The Magic Circle on 9 October 1991 was historic. Founded as an organization for magicians in London in 1905, the council voted to admit the first women, including Debbie McGee and Fay Presto. But it was also remarkable for another reason – at the same meeting, the council voted to expel a member called Raymond Lloyd. He was in fact a she – Sophie Lloyd had joined eighteen months earlier, having rehearsed speaking and behaving as a man. The meeting notes state Lloyd was expelled for 'deliberate deception'.

In 2024, the Magic Circle announced they were trying to track Lloyd down to say sorry and admit her back into the society. After tricking the world's most famous society of magicians, perhaps unsurprisingly she managed to disappear! Laura London, the first female chair of the Magic Circle, put it like this: 'It's almost as if they just made her vanish from thin air, tried to brush it under the carpet, but obviously now the story has come out and we're so desperate to right this wrong.'

The organization issued an apology and launched a public appeal to find her. Finally, after years of searching, Sophie Lloyd was tracked down. In April 2025, in a special ceremony, she was finally welcomed back into the Magic Circle . . . as herself.

Razzle-dazzle indeed . . .

Last Words

We've come to the end of our feminist year, spending time with hundreds of amazing women, girls, trans and non-binary people on the way. Each one is unique, each one is their own person. At the same time, they have certain things in common.

First, everyone we've met lived life on her own terms. They didn't give in to pressure, or allow themselves to be persuaded to be someone they weren't. They held firm to their beliefs, even if everyone around them thought differently.

Second, we've seen how attitudes change over time and can differ in other parts of the world. Some of the ideas of fifty years ago already seem out of date or short-sighted. This will be the same in another fifty years' time, when some of the ways we see things today will seem painfully out of touch or old fashioned. That's OK. Each new generation discovers its own truths – but it's why we should take care to consider people's words and actions in the context of their time and place.

Third, each of the women and girls believed in their own instincts and shared a desire to change things, often to make things fairer and more equal, in order to build more successful, more caring, more dynamic societies.

They have other characteristics in common too, human qualities that underpin everything: courage, fortitude, curiosity, determination, honesty, self-confidence, a belief in fairness, ambition, strength. They also knew – and we understand this even in 2025 – that not everything is within our control. We live in an imperfect world and don't always have the power to stop terrible things from happening, or being said or done, particularly now when technology is putting unparalleled power in the hands of a very few individuals. But all of us, like our feminist heroines, can choose to live our lives well.

The question is, what does that mean?

For me, it means trying to achieve change through hope rather than through criticism or attack. It means being honest, not deceitful. It means prioritizing love and kindness over hate and self-interest. It means trying one's best and not being afraid to fail. It means thinking about – and listening to – other people rather than seeing everything through a selfish lens. It means supporting other women and girls and speaking up for those who cannot speak for themselves.

Finally, remember this. We all make mistakes, we all do things we regret, we're a mass of contradictions. Every day, we learn a little more, grow a little more. Like the women and girls in this book, all we can do is to not waste a minute and try to leave a positive footprint on the world as we pass through.

Above all, be yourself and make your one precious life count.

Glossary and Abbreviations

ANC – African National Congress. A South African political party that began life as an anti-apartheid liberation movement.

CND – founded in 1957, the Campaign for Nuclear Disarmament is a non-violent organization campaigning to abolish nuclear weapons and other weapons of mass destruction.

coalition government – a government made up of politicians from different, sometimes opposing, political parties when no one party has won a majority in a general election. Some electoral systems are designed to produce coalitions, as they can mean a wider diversity of views are represented in government policies.

Dame – the title used by women awarded a GBE or DBE (see **Order of the British Empire**). The male equivalent is 'Knight'.

DSAuk – Dwarf Sports Association UK. Founded in 1993, it is a sporting charity aiming to make sporting opportunities accessible and enjoyable to anyone and everyone of restricted growth in the UK.

English Heritage – a charity that looks after hundreds of historic sites in every corner of England. Some are internationally famous buildings or estates, others are local treasures. Since 1986, it has also run the blue plaques scheme.

ERA – Equal Rights Amendment. A proposed amendment to the US constitution to ban sex discrimination.

FA – the Football Association is the governing body of men's and women's football in England. The Scottish FA, the FA of Wales and the Irish FA govern the game in Scotland, Wales and Northern Ireland respectively.

FIFA – the *Fédération Internationale de Football Association* is the governing body of world football.

FLOTUS – First Lady of the United States is a title given to the wife (the 'First Lady') of the American President.

freedom rider – a person who challenged the racial segregation of Black and white people on public transportation in the US.

Fondation pour la Mémoire de la Shoah – a French organization dedicated to financing, researching and remembering the millions of Jewish people who died in the Holocaust (the 'Shoah') during the Second World War.

general strike – a term used when workers from many different industries coordinate withdrawing their labour at the same time in order to achieve political or social change.

Gestapo – the Gestapo was the secret police force of Nazi Germany and, later, Nazi-occupied Europe. It played a central role in numerous atrocities, including the Holocaust.

ghetto – an area of a city where people are forced to live, always poorer and overcrowded and kept apart from the rest of the population. The word is particularly used to describe areas where Jewish people were segregated from other people. During the Holocaust of the Second World War, more than 1,000 Nazi ghettos were established to imprison European Jews.

ghostwriter – someone who writes a book on behalf of another person, but is usually not credited.

glass ceiling – a phrase invented by American management consultant Marilyn Loden in 1978 to refer to an invisible barrier that prevents women from advancing their careers. It's now used to describe the invisible barriers to anyone from an under-represented group. The barrier is 'invisible' because while, technically, there is no hard-and-fast rule stopping women or others from being promoted, sexism and conscious or unconscious bias from those above the ceiling keep others below it. The first women in a particular field to achieve something or reach a certain position of seniority are often said to have 'shattered the glass ceiling'.

Great Famine – a seven-year period of mass starvation in Ireland from 1845 until 1852. It was triggered by a blight that destroyed the potato crop – the primary food source for a third of Ireland's population – and was compounded by the policies of the landowning class and the British government. Nearly a million died and another million Irish people emigrated.

HMD – Holocaust Memorial Day was established in 2005 to commemorate the six million Jewish people and all others who were murdered in the Holocaust, under Nazi persecution. It takes place on 27 January each year.

IBA – International Bar Association. Set up in 1947 shortly after the creation of the United Nations, the IBA is the global organization for international legal practitioners, bar associations and law societies.

IRA – the Irish Republican Army was a paramilitary organization fighting to reunite Northern Ireland with the Republic of Ireland. Over the course of the 20th century, it split into several separate groups, including the Provisional IRA, which was designated a terrorist organization by the British government.

IVF – in vitro fertilization is a technique where an egg is removed from the ovaries and fertilized with sperm in a laboratory when a couple is having trouble conceiving. The fertilized egg, called an embryo, is then returned to the woman's womb to grow and develop as in any other pregnancy.

IWD – International Women's Day.

Jim Crow laws – these were local and state laws introduced in the southern United States in the late 19th and early 20th centuries. They enforced racial segregation in education, public spaces, public transportation, places of work and worship. The laws remained in force until 1965.

KC – a King's Counsel (or QC, Queen's Counsel, when the monarch is a woman) is a senior lawyer appointed by the Crown. Members wear silk gowns of a particular design – being appointed as King's Counsel is known informally as 'taking silk' – and KCs are often colloquially called 'silks'.

MBE – Member of the British Empire. See **Order of the British Empire** for more information.

MEP – Member of the European Parliament.

MI5 – Military Intelligence, Section 5 (to give it its full title) is the UK's domestic counter-intelligence and security agency.

MOW – the Movement for the Ordination of Women was an organization set up in 1979 to campaign for the right of women to be ordained as priests in the Anglican Church.

MP – Member of Parliament in Great Britain and Northern Ireland.

NAACP – National Association for the Advancement of Colored People. An American civil rights organization formed in 1909 to fight for equality and justice for African Americans.

NASA – National Aeronautics and Space Administration. The agency that oversees the US space programme.

NAWSA – National American Women Suffrage Association.

Nazi – a member of the National Socialist German Workers' Party, a German fascist political party that controlled Germany from 1933 to 1945 under Adolf Hitler. The four main features of Nazism are racial purity – believing that White Europeans are superior to other races, especially Jews – territorial expansion, power and militarism.

Nineteenth Amendment – the legislation ratified in the United States in 1920 after years of campaigning that gave women the right to vote. However, discriminatory and racist laws in some states meant that many African American and other minority women were still not able to vote until much later.

NWPC – National Women's Political Caucus. An American organization dedicated to increasing women's participation in all political and public-life roles.

Order of the British Empire awards are given to individuals for their contributions to arts and sciences, their work with charitable and welfare organizations, and for public service outside the civil service. They are:

GBE – Knight or Dame Grand Cross

KBE/DBE – Knight or Dame

CBE – Commander

OBE – Officer

MBE – Member

BEM – British Empire Medal

Panthéon – an 18th-century building in the Latin Quarter of Paris. Originally intended as a church dedicated to the patron saint of Paris, in 1791 it became the burial place for France's most celebrated citizens.

patriarchy – a social system where men control a disproportionately large share of social, economic, political, legal and religious power, usually to the detriment of women and girls.

PEN International – a worldwide association of writers,

founded in London in 1921 to promote friendship, intellectual cooperation among writers everywhere, and free speech.

PhD – Doctor of Philosophy. This is the highest level of academic qualification in many fields of study. The research involved usually takes several years to complete, and has to be an 'original contribution to knowledge'. Those who are successful, can then use the title 'Doctor'.

Proms – the short name for the prestigious series of promenade classical music concerts that began in 1895 in London and are now held every year at the Royal Albert Hall. The name 'promenade' comes from the fact that there are no seats in certain sections of the hall, so audience members stand up or sit on the floor during performances.

Quakers – a Christian religious group, also known as the Religious Society of Friends, that originated in 17th-century England.

Righteous Among the Nations – a title given by the State of Israel to non-Jews (Gentiles) who helped Jewish people during the Second World War. The country with the most people honoured is Poland, where 90 per cent of the Jewish population were murdered by the Nazis.

SCLC – Southern Christian Leadership Conference. An African American civil rights organization founded in 1957. Its first president was Martin Luther King Jr.

SNCC – Student Nonviolent Coordinating Committee. An African American organization founded in 1960 by young people during the civil rights movement. It was dedicated to nonviolent, direct action.

SOE – the Special Operations Executive was an organization set up by Prime Minister Winston Churchill in 1940 to conduct espionage, sabotage and secret reconnaissance activities in Nazi-occupied Europe and to help local Resistance movements.

Spanish Civil War – a conflict fought in Spain between 1936 and 1939 between Republican (left-wing) and Nationalist (right-wing) forces, the latter under the leadership of General Franco. Because of the international political climate at the time, many people see it as a rehearsal for the battles between fascists and communists during the Second World War. The Nationalists won in early 1939, and ruled Spain until Franco's death in 1975.

SS – the *Schutzstaffel* was a paramilitary organization working for Adolf Hitler and the Nazi Party in Nazi Germany, and German-occupied Europe during the Second World War. It was responsible for many of the war's worst atrocities.

STEM – the abbreviation for people studying or working in fields of Science, Technology, Engineering and Mathematics.

trimester – human pregnancy is divided into three time periods called trimesters: the first is from conception to twelve weeks; the second is from thirteen to twenty-seven weeks; the third is from twenty-eight to forty weeks. Since 2002, the term 'fourth trimester' has been used to refer to the first twelve weeks after birth.

UN – United Nations. A diplomatic and political organization of many countries dedicated to maintaining international peace and global security. Established in 1945, it aims to develop international cooperation and act as a centre for coordinating the actions of member states. Its headquarters are in New York.

VAD – Voluntary Aid Detachment. A group of volunteers serving as nurses and orderlies during the First World War.

WEF – the World Economic Forum is held in January every year at Davos in Switzerland. Delegates from global business, government, civil society, media, climate activism and universities attend discussions about the most pressing issues of the time.

WHO – World Health Organization. The United Nations agency responsible for global public health.

WSPU – Women's Social and Political Union. The leading movement campaigning for women's suffrage in the UK from 1903 to 1918.

Zionism – a movement advocating for a Jewish national state in Israel and a safe, self-governing homeland for the Jewish people.

ŻOB – *Żydowska Organizacja Bojowa*, which translates as the Jewish Fighting Organization or Jewish Combat Organization, was a Polish resistance group particularly significant in the Warsaw Ghetto Uprising.

Acknowledgements

In 2022, I published a feminist history book called *Warrior Queens & Quiet Revolutionaries: How Women (Also) Built the World.* It was inspired by two things. First, I discovered how my own great-grandmother, Lily Watson, had disappeared entirely from the history books despite being a famous novelist in her day, and I wanted to know how that had happened. Second, I had launched a social media campaign – #womaninhistory – during the Covid-19 lockdown. In January 2021, I'd put out a message on Twitter (now X) asking people anywhere in the world to nominate a woman from history they wanted to celebrate or thought should be better known. Within days, thousands of people – many of them young people – had shared their suggestions and the idea for that book was born.

The following year, I took a one-woman show inspired by *Warrior Queens* on a theatre tour of the UK and Wales. Every night after the show, young women and their mothers, girls, boys and their fathers, teachers and educators, would come up to say how they wished there was a history book aimed at inspiring younger readers. So, when Macmillan Children's Books asked if I'd be interested in writing such a book for young adults, I jumped at the chance.

A book like this is complicated and there are many people who have helped along the way. A huge thank you to everyone at MCB, especially my wonderful editor Cate Augustin, assistant editor Tanny Hossain, illustrator Sophie

Bass, desk editor Amy Boxshall, designers Rachel Vale, Sue Mason and Tracey Ridgewell, copy-editor Fraser Crichton, proofreader Nick de Somogyi, head of publicity Clare Hall-Craggs, the amazing Pan Mac sales and reps and executive team. A special shout-out to my publicist Christian Lewis (who juggles all my projects – and my diary – so brilliantly and with such good grace). Thanks, too, to everyone at the Soho Agency, in particular Philippa Milnes-Smith.

As always, love and gratitude to family and friends for their continuing love and support, in particular my indomitable mother-in-law Granny Rosie (aka Rosie Turner), my sisters Beth Huxley and Caroline Matthews, my brother-in-law Benjamin Graham and my nieces and nephews – especially Ellen Huxley for her Scrabble skills and shared passion for the Lionesses!

Finally, as always, to my first love and first reader, Greg Mosse, our inspirational children Martha Mosse and Felix Mosse, their fabulous partners Ollie Halladay and Fabienne Zigrit and now our grandchildren, the glorious Finn and newest addition Lily. Without you, none of this would matter.

Picture Credits

pxiv Pretoria Women's March of 1956 © South African History Online

pxv Ticket to WSPU procession on Sunday 21 June 1908 © Wikimedia Commons

p8 Runner Kathrine Switzer attacked by race official Jock Semple while running in the 1967 Boston Marathon © Harry Trask / Wikimedia Commons

p34 Dorothée Pullinger pictured with a Galloway car © Daily Record

p37 Amrita Sher-Gil, Self-portrait (1931) © Wikimedia Commons

p41 Painting of Sappho by Julius Johann Kronberg 1913 © Julius Kronberg / Wikimedia Commons

p42 Murasaki Shikibu © Wikimedia Commons

p69 Doria Shafik © AFP/Getty Images

p70 Mary Barbour statue in Govan Cross, Glasgow, by Sculptor Andrew Brown © Lesley Mitchell / Wikimedia Commons

p72 A stamp printed in Germany shows Sophie Scholl, circa 1991 – part of the 'Women in German History' series © neftali / Shutterstock.com

p74 Boudica statue on Westminster Bridge in London © maziarz / Shutterstock.com

p80 Stamp of Hattie McDaniel – part of the US's Black Heritage commemorative series © spatuletail / Shutterstock.com

p83 Dick, Kerr Ladies Team, 1923 © Wikimedia Commons

p85 Fara Williams in 2014 © James Boyes / Wikimedia Commons

p110 Photo of 'The Dinner Party' by Judy Chicago © Gabriel Fernandes / Wikimedia Commons

p128 Hilda Clark wearing the Quaker star, armband, circa 1915 © Library of the Society of Friends © Quakers in Britain

p138 Just Stop Oil supporters protesting in Whitehall, London, in 2023 © Alisdare Hickson / Wikimedia Commons

p148 Gladys Thomas, Mary Ellis, Annie Hughes-Griffiths and Elined Prys hold the women's peace petition outside the White House in 1924 © WCIA (Welsh Centre for International Affairs)

p162 Emily Williamson sculpture created by Eve Shepherd MRSS SPS © Eve Shepherd

p171 Millicent Garrett Fawcett statue in London © Ben Gingell / Shutterstock.com

p182 An illustration of Amelia Bloomer in *The Illustrated London News*, 1851 © T. W. Brown / Wikimedia Commons

p190 Anne Frank © Anne Frank Fonds Basel / Getty Images

p193 Nellie Bly in *The World* newspaper in 1890 © Bettmann/Getty Images

p200 Oil painting of Bouboulina © Wikimedia Commons

p207 Junko Tabei climbing in 1985 © Jaan Künnap / Wikimedia Commons

p209 Mary McLeod Bethune with her students, circa 1905 © Wikimedia Commons

p217 Dorothea Lange's 'Migrant Mother' © Rawpixel.com / Shutterstock.com

p226 French feminist Hubertine Auclert, holding a banner saying 'Women's Suffrage' © Charles Gallot / Wikimedia Commons

p243 'I Wait' – a photograph of Rachel Gurney taken by Julia Margaret Cameron in 1872 © The J. Paul Getty Museum, Los Angeles / Wikimedia Commons.

p255 Emmeline Pankhurst and Elizabeth Wolstenholme-Elmy at the head of the

Women's March in Hyde Park, London, Sunday 21 June 1908 © Wikimedia Commons

p264 Ninette de Valois performing in *Les Biches* © Bibliothèque nationale de France / Wikimedia Commons

p277 El Saadawi protesting on her 80th birthday in 2011, as part of the Egyptian Revolution © Jenny Matthews / Getty Images

p282 Portrait of Sarah Siddons playing Euphrasia in *The Grecian Daughter* at the British Theatre, 1771 © Wikimedia Commons

p281 Photograph of Frida Kahlo © marhus / Shutterstock.com

p297 Photograph of Ida B. Wells, circa 1890s © Wikimedia Commons

p301 Copy of the signature page of the Declaration of Sentiments, U.S. Library of Congress © Library of Congress Wikimedia Commons

p318 Gisèle Pelicot © Obatala-photography / Shutterstock.com

p326 Gerda Taro, 1937 © Wikimedia Commons

p333 Fanny Blankers-Koen competing in the hurdles © IISG (International Institute of Social History) / Wikimedia Commons

p336 Lillian Ngoyi © Azola Dayile / Wikimedia Commons

p338 Edith Wharton with her dogs Miza and Mimi © E. F. Cooper. Source: Beinecke Rare Book & Manuscript Library, Yale University. / Wikimedia Commons

p342 Schulman with three other soldiers in the Molotov Brigade in Naliboki Forest, Belarus, December 1944 © Cassowary Colorizations / Wikimedia Commons

p347 Hutchins' seaweed illustrations © Wiki Commons

p353 Greta Thunberg outside the Swedish parliament, 10 January 2020. © Liv Oeian / Shutterstock.com

p369 Women's March 1956 in Pretoria, South Africa © ANC Archives/african.pictures/Bridgeman Images

p374 Greatest Woman Swimmer in the World advert in 1885 © Tom Merry / Wikimedia Commons

p391 Whina Cooper at Māori March, 1975 © Christian Heinegg / Wikimedia Commons

p395 Ginsburg in the US Supreme Court, Washington, DC, USA in 1993 © Rob Crandall / Shutterstock.com

p424 Aloha Wanderwell and husband, Walter, next to her Ford Model T motorcar © Wikimedia Commons

p433 Ursula von der Leyen speaking during a media conference after a meeting of the College of Commissioners at EU headquarters in Brussels, Belgium in 2023 © Alexandros Michailidis / Shutterstock.com

p440 Salsa Soul Sisters Harriet Alston and Shirley Carvin at Gay Pride March, 1978 © Pat R. Chin / Lesbian Herstory Archives. Archival materials from Salsa Soul Sisters Special Collection and Exhibition

p448 Forever Free by Edmonia Lewis, 1867 © Wikimedia Commons

p449 Inez Milholland leading the women's suffrage procession, Washington, March, 1913 © Everett Collection / Shutterstock.com

p461 Mary Robinson © photowalking / Shutterstock.com

p461 Vigdís Finnbogadóttir © Rob C. Croes (ANEFO) / Wikimedia Commons p462 Elisabeth Domitien © Wikimedia Commons

p462 Maria de Lourdes Pintasilgo © Roland Gerrits (ANEFO) / Wikimedia Commons

p473 Ruth Handler, Mattel Inc. Co-Founder and Barbie Doll Inventor, 1994 © Vicky Kasala Productions / Getty Images

p490 The first Scottish women to graduate from The University of Edinburgh © The Picture Art Collection / Alamy

p496 Higuchi Ichiyō © Wikimedia Commons

p499 Mural of The Mirabal Sisters in Paris © Laurent Seignobos / Wikimedia Commons

p508 Henrietta Lacks by Helen Wilson-Roe © Mareks Perkons / Shutterstock.com

p510 Nakano Takeko, Jinan, Japan © Torstein Barnhardt / Wikimedia Commons

p526 Bilokur is honoured on Ukrainian stamps, 1988 © Post of Ukraine / Wikimedia Commons

p559 Caterina van Hemessen, Public Art Collection, Kunstmuseum Basel © Wikimedia Commons

Permissions for Quotes

The author and publisher would like to thank the following for permission to use their copyrighted material:

Atwood, Margaret: quote on page 261 © *Guardian* News & Media Ltd 2025; **Carson, Rachel:** quote on page 134 from *Lost Woods: The Discovered Writing of Rachel Carson* (Beacon Press, 1998); **El Saadawi, Nawal:** quote on page 279 from an interview with Joseph Mayton in *The Progressive*, Vol. 75, No. 12 (December 2011/January 2012) © *The Progressive*; **Fox, Martha Lane:** quote on page 376; **Gillard, Julia:** quote on page 408 from speech speech against a motion by Tony Abbot (2012); **Ginsburg, Ruth Bader:** quote on page VII from 'Justice Ginsburg ready to welcome Sotomayor' by Bill Mears (2009) © CNN; **Goodall, Jane:** quote on page 306; **Harris, Kamala:** quote on page 447; **Khan, Irene:** quote on page 220; **Levi-Montalcini, Rita:** quote on page 73 from *Congressional Record* (Bound Edition), Volume 159 (2013), Part 1, [Extensions of Remarks] pages 103–104. From the U.S. Government Publishing Office, www.gpo.gov; **O'Connor, Sandra Day:** quote on page 287; **Parks, Rosa:** quote on page 517 from *Rosa Parks: My Story* (Puffin, 1999); **Rich, Adrienne:** quote on page 164 from 1974 National Book Awards (National Book Foundation Archives); **Shepherd, Nan:** quote on page 78 from *The Living Mountain: A Celebration of the Cairngorm Mountains of Scotland* (Canongate Books, 2011); **Schulman, Faye:** quote on page 344; **West, Rebecca:** quote on page VII, from *The Clarion*, 14 November 1913; **Yousafzai, Malala:** quote on page 435 from a speech given at the United Nations Youth Assembly in New York (July 12th 2013)

Every effort has been made to trace and contact the copyright holders, but if any have been inadvertently overlooked the publisher will be pleased to make the necessary arrangement at the first opportunity.